Black Sailors
in the Civil War

USS *Lehigh* was assigned 23 Black sailors during the war. Several of them are seen here. Most of them mustered aboard between 1863 and 1864. John Maxmore was a 17-year-old New Yorker who enlisted almost immediately after the New York Draft Riots in July 1863. Moses S. Gardner was also from New York City. He signed on as a first-class boy, as did Maxmore. In addition to *Lehigh*, between 1862 and 1867, Gardner, an 18-year-old who enlisted for three years, served aboard USS *Unadilla, Montauk, Nipsic* and *Estrella*, during his naval career. The third New Yorker on the crew, 23-year-old landsman John H. Bowman, also joined the Navy right after the New York riots. All three were short—each averaged about five feet in height. This information came from the National Park Service's database of Black sailors during the Civil War. (Naval History and Heritage Command)

Black Sailors in the Civil War

A History of Fugitives, Freemen and Freedmen Aboard Union Vessels

JAMES H. BRUNS

McFarland & Company, Inc., Publishers
Jefferson, North Carolina

Also by James H. Bruns: *Razzle Dazzle: United States Navy Ship Camouflage in World War I* (McFarland, 2022)

LIBRARY OF CONGRESS CATALOGUING-IN-PUBLICATION DATA

Names: Bruns, James H., author.
Title: Black sailors in the Civil War : a history of fugitives, freemen and freedmen aboard Union vessels / James H. Bruns.
Other titles: History of fugitives, freemen and freedmen aboard Union vessels
Description: Jefferson, North Carolina : McFarland & Company, Inc., Publishers, 2023 | Includes bibliographical references and index.
Identifiers: LCCN 2023002378 | ISBN 9781476690544 (paperback : acid free paper) ∞
ISBN 9781476648392 (ebook)
Subjects: LCSH: United States. Navy—African Americans—History—Civil War, 1861–1865. | United States—History—Civil War, 1861–1865—Participation, African American. | United States—History—Civil War, 1861–1865—Naval operations. | African American merchant mariners—History—19th century. | Fugitive slaves—United States—History—19th century. | BISAC: HISTORY / United States / Civil War Period (1850–1877) | HISTORY / Military / United States
Classification: LCC E591 .B78 2023 | DDC 973.7/58—dc23/eng/20230118
LC record available at https://lccn.loc.gov/2023002378

BRITISH LIBRARY CATALOGUING DATA ARE AVAILABLE

ISBN (print) 978-1-4766-9054-4
ISBN (ebook) 978-1-4766-4839-2

© 2023 James H. Bruns. All rights reserved

No part of this book may be reproduced or transmitted in any form or by any means, electronic or mechanical, including photocopying or recording, or by any information storage and retrieval system, without permission in writing from the publisher.

Front cover image: Interracial gun crew on the deck of USS *Miami* on the James River. *Miami* was a double-ender, which meant it had bows on either end and could go in either direction without turning around. This made it easier to escape from tight situations. Over time *Miami* was manned by 86 Black sailors. Most of these fugitives and freemen proudly enlisted in the fall of 1863 as Black bluejackets.
(Library of Congress)

McFarland & Company, Inc., Publishers
Box 611, Jefferson, North Carolina 28640
www.mcfarlandpub.com

For Chris, Donald, Samantha, Daniel,
Amanda, James, and Joe

Acknowledgments

I am indebted to people I've never met. I owe a great deal of gratitude to the interviewers and editors of the Federal government's Slave Narrative Project of 1937–1938 and the countless Americans that were interviewed regarding their experiences as slaves. Most of the interviewees were in their 80s when they were interviewed, but the pain of bondage was still fresh in many of their minds. Every American should read these recollections to better understand the inhumanity of slavery and its legacy today. I also wish to thank those involved with compiling the National Park Service's database of Black sailors during the Civil War. This is an extremely important initiative, one that pays tribute to America's Black seamen and their essential service in winning the war.

I wish to thank Seth Kaller for furnishing many of the rare and historic manufacts that appear in this work.

I'm also extremely grateful to the various institutions and agencies that have furnished historic documents and photographs of the artifacts and rarities highlighted in this book, including the National Museum of the United States Navy, the Library of Congress, the Minnesota Historical Society, the New Hampshire Historical Society, the National Archives and Record Administration, the National Park Service, and the Smithsonian Institution.

Table of Contents

Acknowledgments	vi
Preface	1
Introduction	3
1. "That will do": Towards Freedom	5
2. Runaways	19
3. Robert Smalls	40
4. Northern Black Mariners	44
5. Recruiting in Major Cities	47
6. Welcome to the Navy	57
7. The Need for Army Contrabands and Its Fleet	66
8. From Overseers to Boatswains Mates	76
9. Blue-Water Black Bluejackets	80
10. Brown-Water Black Bluejackets	88
11. The Great Exodus in 1862 and 1863	91
12. Seizing the Lower Mississippi: David Farragut, the Minority Flag Officer	104
13. Capturing the Upper Mississippi: Andrew Hull Foote, the Union's Pious Sailor	118
14. Vicksburg: The Gibraltar of the Confederacy	133
15. Prizes and Problems Along the Red River	147
16. Coffee	174
17. The Safest Service	176
18. Marked Passing	183

Table of Contents

19. Black Bluejacket Valor	186
20. The Union Navy's War on Salt	193
21. Mobile Bay	199
22. The Union's Starships	209
23. The Aftermath	215
Chapter Notes	221
Bibliography	227
Index	229

Preface

In 1937, James Southall, a former slave from Tennessee, was interviewed in Oklahoma as part of the Federal Writers' Project, a unit of the Works Progress Administration. In all, more than 2,300 former slaves were interviewed as part of this New Deal project. In a thoughtful moment during his interview, Southall reflected on the Black journey in America. "God created us all free and equal," he said. "Somewhere along the road we lost out." This book focuses on how Black sailors helped African Americans find their way to freedom.

Most of the slave narratives recorded in the 1930s vividly recall the moments of liberation. For most, it followed a pattern in the memories for those held in bondage: The Yankee soldiers or sailors arrived, and shortly thereafter, the masters informed the slaves that they were free. The progress and outcome of the war brought with it such freedom. Equality, however, was a different matter. It could not be equally bestowed by force of will or fairness of thought, and as a result, every mechanism was used to negate it, including fear, bigotry, Jim Crow laws and voter suppression, which continues today. Unfortunately, the road to equality and justice that James Southall envisioned has yet

Runaway children, such as this unidentified youth, found a haven as young sailors. (Library of Congress)

Preface

to be achieved. However, for the time, the level of equality enjoyed by Black sailors aboard Federal warships was far beyond anything comparable in civilian life. That equality, such as it was, was cemented in combat, deadly trials where every man relied on every other man to do his duty to protect their ship and the lives of their crewmates.

What all sailors share, then as now, is the knowledge that in the heat of battle color doesn't matter!

This book draws heavily upon the diaries of Gideon Welles, the Navy's Secretary during the Civil War. Welles was the architect of the utilization of Black sailors to win the war. He made that happen. He was a true believer in their capabilities. He also believed in their full emancipation, and anxiously awaited that to come true. Following the Battle of Antietam on 17 September 1862, Welles got his wish, saying: "God had decided the question in favor of the slaves."

A note on terminology: Throughout this book, I've used the words of the times, some of which may be offensive to the modern reader, such as "contrabands" to describe self-emancipated southern slaves. The terms "contrabands" and "contraband slaves" commonly appeared in newspapers, government reports, and correspondence, beginning in the summer of 1861, because southern slaveholders insisted their slaves were their personal property and demanded their runaways be returned. As property, war-related contraband of any type used to support the South's rebellion were subject to destruction, dispersion, or utilization by Federal forces. Because slave labor was exploited throughout the South to sustain the war, slaves were characterized as invaluable southern possessions subject to seizure. The word "contraband" did not apply to slaves held in slave-holding border states that remained loyal to the Union, such as Maryland and Delaware. Those runaways were subject to being returned to their owners because those states were not in rebellion. Additionally, the word "mulatto" has been used here to describe light-skinned Black sailors, or those of mixed racial heritage, because it was the official term used to describe the race of Black sailors in Union naval records during the 1860s, and it is used in the National Park Service's / Howard University's African American Civil War Sailors Project's database. As further clarification, the naval rating of "Boy" was not a racial reference. Male youths were permitted to serve in the Union Navy as young as 13 years of age, with parental permission.

Introduction

After lifetimes in bondage, the Civil War gave Black Americans the ability to fight back against oppression on a national scale. Within the Navy, fugitives and freemen alike got the chance for a fair fight, doing their parts with like-hearted White sailors to win the war to abolish slavery. In the Navy, unlike in the Army, these Black bluejackets weren't considered second-class sailors. They were first-class war fighters. They earned their anchors. Unfortunately, because of their lack of access to literacy, few contraband sailors left written records of their service. But despite this omission, their meritorious service and personal valor were no less important or inspirational. All of them believed that they could effect positive change in the lives of Black Americans. They also believed that they had roles to play in the preservation of the Union, since they believed that the United States held the rightful path to freedom and equality. The war was the first step on that seemingly

For Black sailors, having their photographs taken created rare and cherished keepsakes. (Library of Congress)

Introduction

Southern planters, circa 1855. (Library of Congress)

ageless journey. Perhaps the readers of this book will finally complete that odyssey.

This book pieces together stories and narratives that highlight the little-known roles played by Black sailors. It is illustrated with photographs and manufacts from government and private collections, as well as some of the few photographs of Black sailors who served in Federal service. Welcome aboard!

1

"That will do": Towards Freedom

On inauguration day, 4 March 1861, Abraham Lincoln had no idea what to do about the issue of slavery. His mind was in a purgatory between freedom and the status quo. He disliked slavery. The thought of it made him miserable. He told his friend Joshua F. Speed in 1855 that the sight of slaves being hunted down and carried back to their unrewarded toils "was a continual torment to me."[1]

In addressing his well-wishers and detractors on that March day he said he prayed for and promised a peaceful solution to the slavery question short of war. "I have no purpose, directly or indirectly, to interfere with the institution of slavery in the States where it exists," he insisted, adding, "the property, peace and security of no section are to be in anywise endangered by the new incoming Administration."[2]

Yet even before those olive branches were uttered, one by one the southern states had begun seceding from the Union and Lincoln's hopes for a peaceful resolution to slavery became less likely. All it would take for hostilities to erupt was a thoughtless spark. That flashpoint came in Charleston Harbor. And the war came.

At the start of the war, the Federal Navy could count on approximately 7,600 sailors and 1,200 officers. Roughly one quarter of these officers resigned their naval commissions, or were dismissed, when the southern states began leaving the Union. Manpower was a major problem. A shortage of ships was also an issue. The Federal Navy in April 1861 consisted of a total of 49 suitable ships, roughly half of which were laid up or on foreign station. In the spring of 1861, both the North and the South structured naval strategies for fighting the war. Their approaches were totally different.

The Union's approach for executing a naval war was never formally adopted, but it made sense, so it was implemented. It was called the "Anaconda Plan." Like a giant constricting snake, it envisioned first strangling

PRIME GANG

OF

235 NEGROES,

BELONGING TO THE

Estate of the late Gen. Jas. Gadsden,

WILL BE SOLD AT

THE MART, IN CHALMERS STREET,

BY

SHINGLER BROTHERS,

ON

Monday, 9th of January, 1860.

TERMS:

One-half, Cash; balance payable in twelve months, secured by a Bond and Mortgage of the property, and approved personal security, with interest from day of sale. Purchasers to pay **SHINGLER BROTHERS** for papers.

'The' Pioneer Steam Presses of James & Williams, 16 State, opposite Chalmers Street.

Broadside concerning the sale of 235 slaves at Charleston, South Carolina, just prior to the war. (Library of Congress)

the South into submission by blockading its principal ports and inlets, thus barring it from exporting its principal cash crop—which was cotton—and from importing essential war materiel. Simultaneously, Union naval forces would begin to seize as many of the South's major ports as

1. "That will do": Towards Freedom

possible, capturing them one at a time. Simultaneously, inland Federal water flotillas would strangle the South by way of the Mississippi River and its tributaries by seizing all Confederate strong points along the rivers, thereby blocking the South's inland water routes. Gideon Welles wasn't keen on the Anaconda Plan, initially believing it too audacious for a country with such a small navy.

Maintaining the blockade would be difficult. The southern coastline stretched over 3,500 miles, from the Chesapeake Bay to the Rio Grande River. Along that length were roughly 190 harbors and inlets that could furnish sanctuary for blockade-runners and privateers, but luckily, less than a dozen ports had sufficient infrastructure for moving cotton to the coast and war materiel inland. Those suitable ports were the Union Navy's chief targets to close or capture at all costs and the South's principal sites to defend at any price. Hundreds of ships were needed to mount an enforceable blockade. This prompted the Navy to buy any available merchant ships suitable for commissioned service and to convert them into makeshift warships. The Navy also contracted for a new class of warships that could be constructed in just 90 days based upon a standard set of plans.

Additionally, Secretary Welles doubted the plan would be internationally enforceable. The plan was to be a test not only in the United States and Confederate conflict, but for any nation, to determine if a blockade would be accepted by other nations. At issue was the fact that a "blockade" was recognized between independent nations, but in this case, the blockade was intended to close off America's own ports. The only way that this made sense was if the North and the South were independent belligerent nations. The Federal government never accepted that status. Welles told the President that he wasn't certain what to tell his naval officers. "I am embarrassed as to the instructions I am to give our naval officers in relation to the interdiction of commerce with the ports in the insurgent states if the interdiction is to be by blockade, then the rules and principles of international law must govern—the Confederate States must be considered and treated as a distinct nationality—their collectors, revenue officers, clearances, registries &c are to be recognized as legitimate."[3] This didn't sit well with Welles. He had already resolved this in his mind, telling the President on 5 August 1861: "Our right as a nation to close our own ports will not, I take it for granted, be questioned, or be permitted to be questioned. They are within our jurisdiction and control and the right cannot be surrendered to foreign dictation without a surrender of our nationality." Instead of thinking of this as a traditional blockade, Welles opted to see it as the

United States exercising its own authority over its own ports. Welles told Lincoln that under this way of thinking, "those who disregard our authority and laws, do so at their own peril."[4]

Foreign governments weren't certain how to handle this quandary either. England had already issued a Proclamation of Neutrality on 13 May 1861, and France followed suit in June. The Netherlands did the same in June, as did Spain, and Brazil issued its Proclamation of Neutrality in August. Neutrality posed questions regarding the taking on of cargo by foreign-flagged vessels in southern ports. This was resolved by a decision by the judge of the Southern District of New York that Secretary of State William Seward sent to Lord Richard Lyons, the British minister to the United States, in October, advising him that "to take on board cargo after the commencement of the blockade, with a view to avoid any future misunderstanding upon the subject you are informed that the law, as thus interpreted by the judge, will be expected to be strictly observed by all vessels in ports of insurgent states during their blockade by the naval forces of the United States."[5]

After more than a year into his first term, Lincoln's quandary regarding emancipation remained. Lincoln first broached the idea of emancipation to Navy Secretary Gideon Welles and Secretary of State Seward on 13 July 1862, while the three were riding in a carriage to the funeral of Secretary Stanton's infant son. Lincoln told the men that this was the first opportunity he had had to mention the subject to anyone, but he wanted their frank views of the proposition. After hearing the men out, Lincoln continued to revisit the subject several times during their ride. Later that night Welles confided in his diary: "It was a new departure for the President, for until this time, in all our previous interviews, whenever the question of emancipation or the mitigation of slavery had been in any way alluded to, he had been prompt and emphatic in denouncing any interference by the General Government with the subject."[6]

Welles wanted emancipation all along. He viewed slavery as a root cause of the rebellion and its elimination as integral to the preservation of the Union. "Were slavery out of the way, there would seem to be no serious obstacle to the reestablishment of the Union," Welles argued.[7] Lincoln gradually came around to Welles' way of thinking, but that realization took time. In 1861 slavery wasn't the issue and Welles accepted that, writing: "The President's policy ... is to preserve the Union. Slavery or anti-slavery is secondary to that. If the Union can be preserved in no other way than by letting slavery remain as it is or was, he would say let it remain. If it can be preserved in no way but by abolishing, why then

1. "That will do": Towards Freedom

abolish."[8] To this Welles added, "Some make slavery the first great question,—others make abolition. He does neither." For Lincoln, emancipation was foremost a military necessity, one that he believed was a key to preserving the nation. "We must free the slaves or be ourselves subdued. The slaves were undeniably an element of strength to those who had their service, and we must decide whether that element should be with us or against us," he said. This decision made unification and emancipation the Union's principal war aims. When warned that emancipation might be seen as unconstitutional, Lincoln discounted that notion, saying the South could not have it both ways. "The rebels ... could not at the same time throw off the Constitution and invoke its aid," he reasoned.[9] Lincoln also withheld issuing the Emancipation Proclamation until he had a major military victory in hand, lest the North appear weak and incapable of subduing the South. With the issuance of the Proclamation of Emancipation on 1 January 1863, Welles believed that slavery in *all* the states was ended, not just in those states in rebellion at that time. But Welles wouldn't wait for that.

On 25 September 1861 Secretary Welles issued orders to Flag Officer Louis M. Goldsborough, commander of the Atlantic Blockading Squadron, to begin enlisting contrabands into naval service. Welles insisted that Blacks be considered as equals aboard ship, telling Goldsborough, "These can neither be expelled from the service to which they have resorted, nor can they be maintained unemployed, and it is not proper that they should be compelled to render necessary and regular service without a stated compensation. You are therefore authorized, when their service can be made useful, to enlist them for the naval service, under the same forms and regulations as apply to other enlistments." That same day, Welles pushed Goldsborough to begin sealing the inlets along the North Carolina coast, except Hatteras Inlet, using stone ships. Because of a gale at the time, Goldsborough could not begin the process until after 27 September, but with his new-found Black manpower he began the process of blockading North Carolina by sinking bulkheads. For countless new Black "bluejackets" this was their first assignment as Union naval warfighters.

The manpower shortage continued throughout the war. On 24 May 1863 the crew of USS *South Carolina* spotted a piece of white cloth flying on Bull's Island, South Carolina. Upon investigation, the ship's landing party discovered 13 runaways from various plantations in the vicinity of Christ Church Parish, sheltering on the island awaiting rescue. *South Carolina* picked up the contrabands and the ship's commander, James Almy, and convinced five of them to join the Navy. All five enlisted for a single year's

Black Sailors in the Civil War

tour of duty, which was a typical term for most Black recruits uncertain of a naval career. Judging from muster records, Almy's five recruits are thought to be Philip Mosque, Bob Lowndes, Cuffee Judd, Fortune Johnson and Ben Johnson. All mustered into the Navy on 1 July 1863, serving together aboard USS *Vermont*, which was stationed at about that time off Port Royal Harbor, South Carolina. Records show that these five sailors served for one year and all five listed their places of birth as South Santee, South Carolina.

At the same time, the Flag Officer in command of the South Atlantic Blockading Squadron complained to Gideon Welles that he was about to lose too many Black sailors because their terms were about to expire. The loss of so many now-experienced hands would cripple his fleet. By the spring of 1863 Black sailors had become essential to naval operations.

Outwardly, Lincoln continued to promote his hesitant view on emancipation, but in his heart his position was changing. An editorial by Horace Greeley, publisher of the *New York Tribune*, called for Lincoln to abolish slavery. In response to what Greeley called "The Prayer of Twenty Million," on 22 August 1862 the President wrote in part: "If I could save the Union without freeing *any* slave I would do it, and if I could save it by freeing *all* the slaves I would do it, and if I could save it by freeing some and leaving others alone I would also do that. What I do about slavery and the colored race, I do because I believe it helps to save the Union, and what I forbear, I forbear because I do *not* believe it would help to save the Union." Lincoln knew the troubles any moves toward abolition would cause, especially for the border states. He had used this explanation often enough during his various stump speeches to know the numbers by heart. In a speech focused on the failings of the Kansas-Nebraska Act of 1854, for example, he highlighted that in just the five key border states—Delaware, Maryland, Virginia, Kentucky, Missouri, and the District of Columbia—there were over 867,000 slaves. That was one quarter of the country's entire slave population. Freeing those slaves would be highly problematic. Lincoln knew that if he took such a radical step as full emancipation in any of the border states so early in the war, he risked further dissolving the Union.

It is said that while the President prayed diligently for God's support on the issue, he needed the support of the citizens of Kentucky and Missouri even more. That support included slaveholders, which in Kentucky outnumbered those in Mississippi. Anything he might do had to exclude these border states. As a result, slaves in those states had a tougher road to freedom than those held in bondage within the Confederacy.

Major General Henry Halleck, commanding all Union forces in

1. "That will do": Towards Freedom

Missouri in 1861, grasped the President's predicament. He had hastily replaced John C. Frémont, who had announced that, as military commander of Missouri, he was emancipating the state's slaves. Lincoln couldn't allow that to happen and still expect to keep Missouri within the Union. Within days of replacing Fremont in Missouri, Halleck issued *General Order Number 3*. Issued on 20 November 1861, this order demanded that Union commanders in Missouri become neither "slave stealers nor slave catchers." To Halleck's way of thinking, this was to be accomplished by not allowing any civilians, including fugitive slaves, sanctuary or visitation rights in any Federal camps or forts. He characterized *General Order Number 3* as a security measure, saying that such slaves—and White civilians, particularly newsmen and newspaper artists—might serve as Rebel spies, reporting on troop strengths, plans, and conditions within areas under Federal control. (In the case of slaves, this was a highly specious claim, but it was what Halleck put forth as justification in banning "hangers on" like meddlesome members of the press corps.)

At the same time, Halleck made clear that dealing with runaway slaves was a civilian matter, except if *General Order Number 3* were ignored. Then, violations became a military matter. It didn't take long for that to happen. When the commanding officer of one camp returned a female slave belonging to the father-in-law of the Missouri-born commanding officer of another unit, Halleck called foul. He ordered the slave released for a violation of his order, charging that both officers were guilty of "slave catching." In another instance, when 16 runaway slaves from a pro–Rebel group were detained at a federal camp prior to being turned over to the local sheriff for resale after 30 days if not claimed by their owners in accordance with Missouri law, Halleck ruled that the 16 were not to be resold but instead returned to the army to work off the cost of the clothing they received from his quartermaster. While this contradicted his own *General Order Number 3*, Halleck amended his ruling regarding the 16 runaways, saying, "This order will in no way debar any one from enforcing his legal rights to the services of these negroes. Such rights, if any exist, can be enforced through the legal tribunals of this state, whose mandates will always be duly respected by the military authorities of this department, so far as may be."

Because of the threat of insurrection within the State of Missouri, on 2 December 1861 President Lincoln placed Missouri under martial law, suspending the writ of habeas corpus and authorizing Halleck to exercise the law "as he found necessary." While empowered to use martial law, Halleck continued to tiptoe around the state's laws governing slavery, thus keeping Missouri safely within the Union and its slaves securely in bondage.

Halleck was considered a competent military administrator, but a miserably timid field commander. His lack of skill on the battlefield hampered his subordinate commanders, including exceptional officers such as William T. Sherman, John Pope, and Ulysses S. Grant. To keep him from meddling with such good officers—men who would fight—Lincoln moved Halleck to Washington, D.C., where he became the Army's "General-in-Chief," basically the army's head bureaucrat.

Despite Lincoln's outward reservations concerning slavery, particularly in the border states, for free men of color, such as Frederick Douglass, and abolitionists, such as Gideon Welles and Montgomery Blair, Lincoln's first Postmaster General, this was a war to abolish slavery, and its end couldn't come fast enough. Blair was fully committed to the cause. A lawyer, he had helped to argue the Dred Scott Case and assisted in the legal defense of John Brown.

Between July and mid–September Lincoln had spoken privately with each of his Cabinet members on the issue of emancipation. He knew each one's perspective on the subject. However, William Russell, a visiting war correspondent from the *London Times,* couldn't come to grips with the mindset of slave holders and their slave bosses. He was perplexed by their hypocrisy. In his diary in 1863 he wrote, "The first place I visited with the overseer was a new sugarhouse, which Negro carpenters and masons were engaged in erecting. It would have been amusing, had not the subject been so grave, to hear the overseer's praise of the intelligence and skill of these workmen, and his boast that they did all the work of skilled laborers on the estate, and then to listen to him, in a few minutes, expatiating on the utter helplessness and ignorance of the black race, their incapacity to do any good, or even to take care of themselves...."[10] Russell also calculated those slaveholders would have done better financially if they had freed their slaves and treated them as a paid workforce, but alas, he wrote, "Not one planter of the many I have asked has ever given an estimate of the annual cost of a slave's maintenance, the idea of calculating it never comes into their heads...."[11]

The misfortunes of the Army were constantly in President Lincoln's head. They weighed on his mind constantly, especially early in the war, when the Army was losing battle after battle. The Navy on the other hand, was experiencing success after success. This led to a growing belief within the Navy that "the Navy must end the war! The Army cannot do it!"[12] At one point, Gideon Welles, commented on this general situation in his

1. "That will do": Towards Freedom

diary, noting: "There is very little from the Army that is decisive or satisfactory. Constant fighting is going on, killing without any battle. The bodies of our brave men, slain or mutilated are brought daily to Washington by hundreds.... But our army holds on with firmness, and persistency, and courage,—being constantly reinforced."[13] In a letter to his wife at roughly the same time he lamented, "Our army is back where it was last winter,—in larger numbers, but with pretty much the same efficient generals, who have had a year's experience that has cost the nation more than a hundred millions. If the tuition has been instructive the nation may stand the cost. I trust no time will be lost in reviews and showy parades, but that early and rapid blows will be struck." "Our army operations have been a succession of disappointments," wrote Welles.

In taking over from outgoing Secretary of War Simon Cameron in January 1862, Edwin M. Stanton inherited a department that was aptly described as a "great lunatic asylum." By micromanaging the War Department, Stanton brought order out of chaos, but Army victories remained elusive, so much so that by the fall of 1862, Assistant Secretary of the Navy Gustavus V. Fox wrote to Rear Admiral David Farragut, "It is a dark time for us just now, and the country asks for another naval victory."

Luckily, on 17 September 1862, Lincoln got the Union land victory he so desperately needed at Antietam Creek in Maryland. This victory afforded him the opportunity to announce the preliminary Emancipation Proclamation. At a special Cabinet session on 22 September 1862, Lincoln made his final decision. He read the document to the group, which contributed a few subtle revisions. After that, Lincoln handed the proclamation to the Secretary of State for general publication the next day. The declaration proclaimed that if the states then in rebellion did not end the war and rejoin the Union by 1 January 1863, all the slaves in those rebellious states would become free.

The issuance of this first step towards full emancipation relieved Lincoln of the great flaw to that time in his argument for not freeing the slaves. By then many Blacks were already serving in the Union's Army and Navy, and could not be expected to return to their prior condition after victory, or armistice; nor could they return to the Union. They were owed more than that. Now slaves had a major reason to run. Black males also had a major reason to join the Union Navy, where they were treated more as equals than in the segregated Army. The Army initially only accepted Blacks in menial positions such as civilian teamsters, laborers, waiters, and cooks. The Navy accepted them from the start as warfighters on an equal footing to White sailors, but at a limit of 5 percent of the naval force.

Black Sailors in the Civil War

That limit was rescinded and, as a result, enlistments among Black sailors began to rise steadily.

For the first time, self-emancipated slaves could keep whatever they earned. Prior to freedom, if a slave were rented out to do an odd job, his wages went to his owner. Some masters might give the worker a pittance, but that was purely optional. Now, freed Black sailors could keep everything they earned from the U.S. For many, this was the first real money that they had ever earned that was truly theirs.

From a variety of standpoints, Lincoln believed that he had the executive power to resolve the issues of full emancipation. For one, it was a timeless practice that war-related enemy property could be seized during wartime. Prize courts resolved questions of ownership of the seized property and declared a prize value to be distributed in accordance with a well-established formula used to adjudicate such property as enemy ships and cargos. Some of the proceeds from the sale of the seized naval property

An integrated crew. On deck everyone had to work well together and lived in relative harmony. Unlike the segregated Army, it was not uncommon for ships to be manned by Black, Hispanic, Asian-Pacific Island, and White sailors. (Library of Congress)

1. "That will do": Towards Freedom

were distributed to the crew or crews that captured the prize. Black sailors shared in the distribution of prize money equally with Whites.

One early step in the right direction came with the passage of the Compensated Emancipation Act, which paid Washington's slaveholders to free their 3,185 slaves. This wasn't signed into law by Lincoln until 16 April 1862 and didn't take effect until July of that year, but it was applauded as a model of what could be done by the government. In the nation's capital the Compensated Emancipation Act was wildly successful. Another step forward was the passage of a pair of Confiscation Acts, one in 1861 and another in 1862, which allowed for Union military forces to free slaves that came within their lines on a case-by-case basis. These were bolstered on 17 July 1862 when Congress passed extensive legislation declaring slaves "free of servitude," including "all slaves of persons hereafter in any way giving aid and comfort to the rebellion ... and escaping from such persons ... and taking refuge within the lines of the [Union]." This Act covered all runaways aiding the Federal military. The Act also extended to a slave's entire family. A further *General Order*, issued on 14 November 1863 declared slaves "free on enlisting" in Federal service.

While Lincoln officially demurred on full nationwide freedom, slaves everywhere simply began emancipating themselves. The President planned to issue an initial announcement of the intention of emancipation but couldn't risk doing so until there was a clear-cut northern victory.

While letters, petitions and resolutions of support flooded into the Executive Mansion, the preliminary Emancipation Proclamation was greeted on Capitol Hill by Judicial and Legislative silence. This lack of pushback was gladly accepted as Constitutional concurrence. The wisdom for and Constitutionality of the Proclamation was therefore officially unquestioned, except for a few state leaders, such as Louisiana, that asked that it not pertain to specific parishes because of their level of Federal subjugation.

The final Emancipation Proclamation was signed late on New Year's Day, 1863. After greeting guests to the Executive Mansion for much of the day, the President's hand was painful and trembling. Afraid that people might believe that he had trepidations about signing the Proclamation if his signature appeared shaky, he waited. The unanticipated suspense alarmed folks—like Frederick Douglass—who was anxiously awaiting news of the signing. There were fears that Lincoln might be having second thoughts. According to the *Rochester* (New York) *Express*, Lincoln explained to his honored guests, "If my hand trembles when I sign the Proclamation, all who examine the document hereafter will say, 'He

MEN OF COLOR!
TO ARMS! TO ARMS!
NOW OR NEVER

This is our Golden Moment. The Government of the United States calls for every Able-Bodied Colored Man to enter the Army

For Three Years' Service

And join in Fighting the Battles of Liberty and Union.

A MASS MEETING

Of Colored Men, will be held on

FRIDAY, JULY 17,

AT 8 O'CLOCK, P. M., AT

WASHINGTON HALL

SOUTH CAMDEN, N. J.,

To Promote Recruiting Colored Troops for Three Years or the War.

FREDERICK DOUGLASS

And other Distinguished Speakers, will Address the Meeting.

U. S. Steam-power Job Printing Establishment, N. W. Corner of Third and Chestnut Streets. Philada.

Frederick Douglass 1863. Broadside proclaiming: "ARE FREEMEN LESS BRAVE THAN SLAVES." More than a Million White Men Have Left Comfortable Homes and joined the Armies of the Union to save their Country. Cannot we leave ours, and swell the Hosts of the Union, to save our liberties, vindicate our manhood, and deserve well of our Country. MEN OF COLOR! the Englishman, the Irishman, the Frenchman, the German, the American, have been called to assert their claim to freedom and a manly character, by an appeal to the sword. The day that has seen an enslaved race in arms has, in all history, seen their last trial.... By all your concern for yourselves and your liberties, by all your regard for God and humanity, by all your desire for Citizenship and Equality before the law, by all your love for the Country, to stop at no subterfuge, listen to nothing that shall deter you from rallying for the Army. Come Forward, and at once Enroll your Names for the Three Years' Service. (Seth Kaller, Inc.)

1. "That will do": Towards Freedom

hesitated'"[14] At last, Lincoln picked up the gold pen intended for that purpose and signed the Proclamation. Looking up with a smile, the President announced, "That will do."[15] What was done ensured that "all persons held as slaves within any State or designated part of a State, the people whereof shall then be in rebellion against the United States, shall be then, thenceforward, and forever free...."

In an 1864 letter to the editor of the *Frankfort* (Tennessee) *Commonwealth*, Albert G. Hodges, President Lincoln made his feeling regarding slavery crystal clear: "If slavery is not wrong, nothing is wrong. I can not [sic] remember when I did not so think, and feel." At the same time, the President addressed his course of action concerning the importance of using African-American men in the war effort, telling Hodges: "When, in March, and May, and July 1862 I made earnest, and successive appeals to the border states to favor compensated emancipation, I believed the indispensable necessity for military emancipation, and arming the blacks would come, unless averted by that measure. They declined the proposition; and I was, in my best judgment, driven to the alternative of either surrendering the Union, and with it, the *Constitution*, or of laying strong hand upon the colored element. I chose the latter. In choosing it, I hoped for greater gain than loss; but of this, I was not entirely confident. More than a year of trial now shows no loss by it in our foreign relations, none

A runaway before joining military service. (Library of Congress)

in our home popular sentiment, none in our white military force,—no loss by it any how [sic] or any where [sic]. On the contrary, it shows a gain of quite a hundred and thirty thousand soldiers, seamen, and laborers. These are palpable facts, about which, as facts, there can be no caviling. We have the men; and we could not have had them without the measure."

2

Runaways

Prior to 1860, Federal warships finding runaways returned them to the nearest magistrates. When a runaway was picked up on a beach near Pensacola by the crew of USS *Boston* in 1838 after he escaped from a slave dealer transporting him from Norfolk to Alabama, he was turned over to officials at Pensacola so he could be returned to his rightful owner. "Plenty of slaves run away," remembered former slave Elizabeth Sparks. "If they catch them they beat them near to death."[1]

Now the shoe was on the other foot. Beginning on 6 August 1861, fugitive slaves were declared to be "contraband of war." After that Union warships became places of refuge for runaways.

USS *Mount Vernon* began taking on fugitive slaves in July 1861 while operating in the Rappahannock River. Six were picked up on 15 July from the Stingray lighthouse where they had taken refuge. According to the runaways, they fled because of talk by their masters of using them as suicide squads, sending them in waves to attack Union soldiers. The commander of the *Mount Vernon*, Oliver S. Glisson, reported, "[By the slaveholders] taking this course has caused much excitement amongst the negro population, who are deserting in every direction." Two more boatloads were taken aboard the following night. Of those picked up by *Mount Vernon* that week, four slaves owned by Joseph Moore appear to have ultimately enlisted in the Navy. These include John, Samuel, Miles, and Peter Hunter. They mustered in July 1862, serving aboard USS *Roman*. The immediate opinion of Navy Secretary Gideon Welles, expressed to Silas Stringham, the Flag Officer in charge of the Atlantic Blockading Squadron at the time, was "It is not the policy of the Government to invite or encourage this class of desertion, and yet, under the circumstances, no other course than that pursued by Commander Glissen could be adopted without violating every principle of humanity. To return them would be impolitic as well as cruel, and, as you remark, 'they may be made serviceable on board our storeships,' you will do well to employ them."

Black Sailors in the Civil War

The exodus on the Rappahannock River continued, growing from a trickle to a torrent. *Mount Vernon* continued rescuing runaways throughout the summer and into the fall. Among the rescued were George Gilmore, Newman Webster, Robert Wilson, Balinar Robinson, Crusoe Henderson, Atwell Taylor, Paul Hudley and Wednesday James. All were put to work aboard *Mount Vernon* and other ships in exchange for food and clothing. *Mount Vernon* would ultimately be manned by 48 Black sailors during the war, and she was far from alone. In one day, USS *Stars and Stripes* received 44 runaways while patrolling on the Rappahannock. She would ultimately be manned by 52 Black bluejackets.

Later in 1862, *Mount Vernon's* temporary hands were taken to Hampton Roads, where the flag officer in charge of the Atlantic Blockading Squadron ordered that they be parceled out among ships fitting out for blockade duty. Because of this, several of *Mount Vernon's* 1861 fugitives appear to have ultimately mustered aboard various ships as the war progressed. Along with the order to disperse *Mount Vernon's* contrabands, all commanders of the receiving vessels were tasked with ensuring that none of the fugitive slaves from *Mount Vernon* were from the Union's slave-holding states, as those had to be returned to their masters.

Runaways aboard USS *Vermont* at Port Royal, South Carolina, in 1861. (Library of Congress)

2. Runaways

Southerners were shocked by the scale of the exodus. In July 1862 Confederate Brigadier General Gideon Johnson Pillow complained to Jefferson Davis, "The Federals are sweeping this country of its negroes. They have, with bodies of armed men, driven off nearly all the negroes in Arkansas." The general believed his slaves were being driven off against their will. "They shoot the negroes attempting to escape, and handcuff and chain those refusing to go." All of this was untrue. No one was holding back, but still Pillow insisted, "They have driven off all I had—men, women, and children—nearly 400 in number. Can no retaliatory measures be adopted?" The rhetorical answer was "no!" Freedom could no longer be delayed or denied if the chances arose.

Unless a commander made a stupid mistake, which a few did, there would be no more handing runaways back. In May 1862, a slaveholder from Elizabeth, North Carolina, demanded that Commodore S.C. Rowan, commanding the naval flotilla in the North Carolina sounds, allow him to retrieve his favorite servant who had fled to Roanoke Island and the protection of the Union Navy. On 8 June 1862, Welles said no, advising Rowan: "As similar applications may frequently be made, it is proper to remind you that persons who have enlisted in the naval service cannot be discharged without the consent of the Department, and that no one should be 'given up' against his wishes."[2] Welles' order covered both those fugitive slaves who enlisted and those who simply sought freedom within the protective arms of the United States Navy.

Not all commanders understood, or willfully ignored, Welles' instructions and the law that was passed to prohibit the return of runaways. On 26 July 1862 Welles had to reprimand Captain Thomas Tingey Craven for sending a midshipman and sailors to search for roughly 40 fugitives that had sought naval refuge. A few of the runaways had even enlisted in the naval service. Craven ordered the former slaves to be returned to their former owner, including those who had enlisted. Once they were handed over, and within sight of the crews of USS *Brooklyn*, Craven's ship, they were stripped and whipped. Acting Lieutenant Selim Woodworth was stunned by Craven's actions. He had given the runaways refuge. To him, it was unthinkable that any captain would knowingly surrender United States sailors into slavery. Woodworth complained of Craven's actions to the squadron's commanding officer, David Dixon Porter, who notified Navy Secretary Gideon Welles of the outrage. Craven was immediately summoned to Washington to explain himself. Once at Navy Department headquarters, Craven fully admitted that he had indeed dispatched a midshipman and sailors with orders that if they should find any of the runaways in question they should be turned over to their lawful owners. In his defense, Craven insisted that any orders contrary from Welles hadn't obviously been adequately transmitted throughout the fleet, because he was unaware of any such directives. As a result, he claimed, he wasn't insubordinate, nor could he be charged with acting contrary to orders that he never received.

Welles was still furious and chastised Craven, saying, "The act itself, as stated and admitted by you, is not warranted by instructions, by usage or by law, but is in derogation of each."[3] The law of 13 March 1862 was crystal clear in this case. It declared that "all persons in the military or naval service of the United States are prohibited from employing any of the forces under their respective commands for the purpose of returning fugitives from service or labor who may have escaped from any persons to whom such service or labor is claimed to be due, and any officers who shall be found guilty by a court martial of violating this article shall be dismissed from Service." Craven was court martialed and was suspended for his transgression.

Ex-slave Ellen Cragin's mother had a serious transgression too. "She didn't work in the field," Ms. Cragin told an interviewer with the slave narrative project. "She worked at a loom. She worked so long and so often that once she went to sleep at the loom." The master's son, Tom Pike, caught her napping and began beating her. In an instant Cragin's mother took a pole out of the loom and began beating the boy in turn. She "beat him nearly to death with it," said Ms. Cragin. Realizing what she had done, her mother took off. "She went out and got on an old cow that she used to milk—Dolly, she called it. She rode away from the plantation because she knew they would kill her if she stayed. She got plumb away and stayed away." That was the last time that Ms. Cragin saw her mother until after freedom.[4]

When the first Federal gunboat appeared near the Polk plantation, the Polk family fled. Cragin and the other hands didn't run. They stayed right there. Her father met the sailors when they came to search the plantation. The sailors were generous. They gave the slaves coffee, sugar and a whole lot of other things. "Anything they wanted, they would get," said Ellen Cragin. Her memory was a bit foggy after all the years, but she knew it was a Union gunboat. It "ran under the water," she remembered, which was typical of the partially submerged appearance of river monitors.[5]

"The White people said, 'That boat's going to carry some of [the slaves] away from here one of these days.' And sure enough, it did carry one away." The lone escapee was a slave named Charles who had helped old

2. Runaways

A highly lethal double-turreted river monitor on the James River. (Library of Congress)

man Polk bury a barrel full of money so the Union sailors wouldn't find it. "He was the first one spotted the boat that morning—Charles was. And he went away on it," taking the barrel.[6]

USS *Young Rover* carried away many. It was like a runaway magnet. While she was operating on the Rappahannock River during the summer of 1862, dozens flocked to her. Many of their owners in Lancaster County, Virginia, petitioned to get their property back. B.B. McKenney lost seven. George Lee lost five slaves. Griffin Williams also lost five, as did A.M. Sanders. All the former slaveholders claimed they were loyal Unionists who never took up arms against the government. James Gresham's petition summed up the sentiments of the others. "I think it but just and right that these servants should be returned, and have every reason to believe that the Government at Washington has no intention of depriving me of my property," he wrote. The slave owners were wrong. That is precisely what the Navy did. All the runaways were transported to Fort Monroe to begin lives of freedom.

Slave owners seemed to consider their slaves to be physically nonexistent, as if they were invisible. This failure allowed one of the North's greatest spy masters—Elizabeth Van Lew—to plant a servant in the Confederate White House in Richmond. This obscure and insubstantial agent conveyed overheard conversations, which, when written, were placed inside blown out eggshells that within hours were in Union hands.

Black Sailors in the Civil War

That same shadowy existence applied to a Georgia slave, Mrs. Celestia Avery's oldest brother, Percy. She recalled that her brother saw where their master buried his money to keep it from falling into the hands of the Federals. She was somewhat pleased to tell her interviewer that "when the Yanks came looking for the money, he carried them straight to the swamp and showed them where the money was hidden."[7]

Judge Kimball's slaves didn't rat their master out at Mobile. He had a huge hole dug in the yard so he could bury several bales of cotton. According to Nannie Bradfield, the pit was covered, and an immense woodpile was placed over its top. Much later, when the Yankee soldiers were heard in the distance, their drums beating as they marched, the judge ordered his male house slave to go get an old white sheet and hang it out in the front of the house. The man was in such a panic he grabbed his mistress's best tablecloth and hung it instead. The judge was hospitable. He asked the officers to join him for a simple breakfast of fried potatoes. With the officers out of the way, the first thing the soldiers wanted to know was where the master had hidden his valuables. No one said anything because they knew that the sale of that cotton would help tide them over, feeding them all when the war ended.[8]

The same sort of thing applied at Cornella Robinson's plantation. She was another Alabama slave child who remembered that her mistress hid her jewelry in the slave cabins, where it remained safe when not much else did. "The Yankees was a hurricane," the about 80-year-old woman recounted. The bluecoats, she said, cleaned out everything, especially the smokehouse. "They even left the lard bucket as clean as your hand. They tore up everything they couldn't take with them."[9] Temple Herndon was amazed at the Yankee's appetites. "They was all the time hungry. There was things they ask for when they come was something to put in their stomach. And chicken! I aint never seen even a preacher eat chicken like them Yankees. I believe to my soul they aint never seen no chicken till they come down here. And hot biscuits too. Them soldiers didn't turn down no hams neither."

It happened almost everywhere else outside Mobile. One former slave remembered that the Yankees rode their horses into the front yard of her plantation house and tore up everything looking for money and jewelry. "They asked me where it was hid, and I told them I didn't know and they said I was lying, and iffen I didn't tell them they would kill me." She was lying. Her master had told her to hide his gold pocket watch in her apron, and the soldiers saw her do it and could hear it ticking. The watch, and everything else of value was taken, including every crumb of food and fodder.[10]

2. Runaways

Shepherd Rhone's opinion was "The only reason the Yankees whipped the South was they starved em."[11] The Yankees not only took everything from Charlie Rigger's plantation, they also set fire to his master's great house. They tried twice to burn it down. "It went out every time," noted Rigger. Frustrated, the soldier left with the house standing, but "they left it clean and bare."[12] In Phillips County, Arkansas, one resident complained that the Yankees robbed and plundered everything, taking or destroying all the corn, livestock, and cured meat, leaving the populace with nothing but empty plates. Henrietta Ralls said that her "White folks made me hide things." Anything the soldiers wanted they took. "They wouldn't talk to old mistress—Drunetta Ralls—just talk to me and ask where things was," the 88-year-old woman remembered of her last time on the Ralls plantation in Arkansas.[13]

Slave silence depended largely upon their masters. Those who were charitable and humane to their hands had their kindnesses reciprocated. Mean masters were more often as not outed. As one former slave recalled, her mistress inflicted so many tears on her people that it was good for her to cry for a change.

Many of the slaves around Mobile went to the city after Emancipation, including Ella Dilliard and her mother. Ella didn't remember much about her father. His name was Green Childress because he was owned by people by that name, but the Childresses took him to Texas and she never saw him again. What she did vividly recall was seeing her first steamboat. "Look at that house sitting on water," she remembered saying to her mother.[14]

A punitive slave bell rack, without the bell. Some runaways were strapped with such contraptions so their masters could always find them. Many of the punished had to wear such devices for months or even years. (Library of Congress)

Black Sailors in the Civil War

Texas was seen as a slaveholder's haven. To Patsy Moore, held by the Armstrong family, "Old master sold his plantation [in Tennessee] and come to Texas just before freedom, because nobody think they'd have to free the slaves in Texas."

Beatings were an everyday occurrence. "They whipped for most any little trifle," recalled eighty-six-year-old Jacob Manson, who was one of 50 slaves belonging to Colonel Ben Eden.[15] The reasons pretty much didn't matter, but there were some things that slave masters didn't tolerate. For ninety-five-year-old Albert Jones it was reading. "You better never let master catch you with a book or paper, and you couldn't praise God so he could hear you. If you done them things, he sure would beat you," he told an interviewer with the slave narrative project in 1937.[16] Eighty-year-old Jane Lassiter agreed. She was held on Dr. Kit Council's plantation in the lower edge of Chatham County, North Carolina. "There was no books or learning of any kind allowed. You better not be catched [sic] with a book in your hands. That was something they would get you for."[17] Former South Carolina slave Victoria Adams said she knew precisely why slaves weren't allowed to read or write. "The reason they wouldn't teach us to read or write was 'cause they was afraid the slaves would write their own pass and go over to a free county. One old [man] did learn to write his pass and got 'way wid it and went up North."[18] According to Georgia Baker, who was raised on Confederate Vice President Alexander Stephens' plantation, slaves were more afraid of newspapers than they were of snakes. Just having a newspaper in your hands was enough to condemn you.[19] For slaves the safest way of passing along news was "you tell me, I tell you, but be careful" said James V. Deane, a former slave from Charles County, Maryland.

For William Moore, held on the Weller plantation in Texas, the Weller children would read to the slaves without their parents' permission. "Some of them children," he told an interviewer in the 1930s, "used to read us little things out of papers and books. We'd look at them papers and books like they something mighty curious, but we better not let Marse Tom, or his wife know it!" Moore said his master beat slaves with a bullwhip, and when he was feeling overly vengeful, he'd whip them with a handsaw, "the teeth going crosswise." The saw was used for major infractions, and he knew that being read to would bring out the worst in old man Weller.

Humane Tom Warren held the opposite point of view. He taught his slaves at Helena, Arkansas, to read. The best reader was his man servant, Tom. When the local newspaper arrived with news of a pending Yankee attack, Tom took to reading it to a whole group of field hands. Passersby

2. Runaways

noticed the gathering and the sight of Tom reading a newspaper. Certain that it was going to create a slave uprising among the slave populations in advance of the Union's arrival, the local community demanded that Tom be jailed and punished. Worse, a lynching party quickly gathered. The mob of about 40 broke into the jailhouse to beat and hang Tom, but instead, the first man into his cell was immediately knocked out cold. No one dared to be next, but that didn't stop Tom. In Cora Gillem's telling, "[Tom] almost tore that jailhouse down." Luckily, the Union Army occupied Helena, and Tom quickly enlisted to get away from there. Cora, who belonged to Tom Warren's father, claimed to be eighty-six when she talked about the incident, but admitted, "I have never been entirely sure of my age." The worsening war news always upset her master, Cora recounted. It made him so sick, that he often had to take to his bed in misery. "It always made him sick to hear that freedom was coming closer and closer. He couldn't stand to hear about that. I always remember the day he died. It was the fall of Vicksburg. When he took a spell, I had to stand by the bed and scratch his head for him, and fan him with the other hand. He said the scratching pacified him."[20] Nothing pacified some folks when they heard a slave praying. "Any one heard praying was given a good whipping; for most masters thought their prayers no good since freedom was uppermost in every one's head," recounted Celestia Avery, who was born into slavery in Troupe County, LaGrange, Georgia. Her master was particularly mean and universally hated. "He whipped unmercifully and, in most cases, unnecessarily," she said. Her grandmother prayed every day and on one occasion her prayers were overhead by the master. In a fit of rage, he tied her to a tree and beat her till her body was raw all over. She was left hanging there all day, until, in the darkness, her husband cut her down.[21]

Whenever Will Glass' grandparents prayed, they did it under a washpot. "Uncle Anderson said that they would sometimes go off and get under the washpot and sing and pray they best they could." This required them to dig a small pit, just big enough for them to sit in with the pot overtop of them. Dora Richard's mother would "hide behind a tree so the boss man couldn't see 'em when they was prayin'."[22]

Wilson Norcross' mistress had a different view. She taught every one of her plantation's children to say the Lord's prayer and read some passages from the Bible. She knew it was against the law to do so, but she didn't care, because she believed it was their right to be brought to godliness. She insisted that every child attend Sunday school and she taught from an old-fashioned Catechism. Nearly fifty years after the fact he could still recite one:

Black Sailors in the Civil War

> Jesus keep me near the cross,
> There's a precious fountain,
> Free to all, a healing stream,
> Flows from Calvary's mountain.

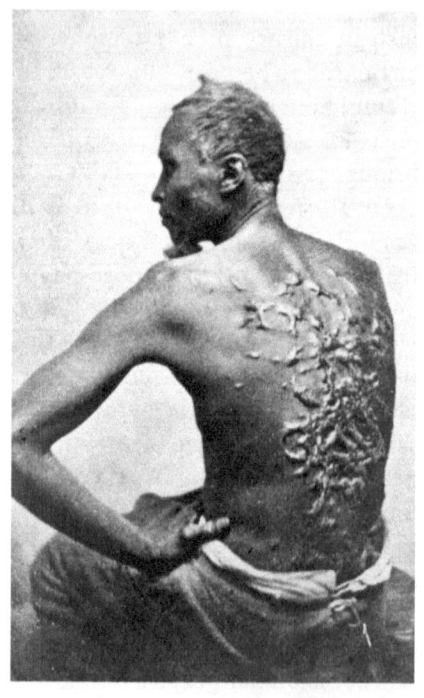

If she was caught, Norcross' mistress planned to defend her actions by saying that she only wanted her slaves to know how to pray, how to tell the truth, and to always do the right things in the sight of God, such as not to steal. How could she be punished for doing God's work? She never faced charges, but her efforts did have an abiding impact upon Wilson Norcross, who became a pastor when freedom came. Norcross didn't have an easy life. "My mother and father were carried from me when I was only nine years old, but as soon as chance presented itself, I ran away and went to them. My White people brought me back, and as they were not cruel to their slaves they did not 'buck' me."[23]

An escaped slave named Gordon, also known as "Whipped Peter," reveals the ravages to his back at Baton Rouge caused by repeated beatings. This photograph includes a notation on the reverse from Assistant Surgeon J.W. Mercer with the 47th Massachusetts Volunteers saying that Gordon's scarred back looks like what he saw when he examined over 400 ex-slaves on 4 August 1863 at Camp Parapet, Louisiana. Within months of the fall of New Orleans, former slaves began making their way into that city. By the fall of 1862 there reportedly were more than 10,000 fugitives sheltering there. Benjamin Butler was the first to refer to these self-emancipated persons as "Contrabands of war." They were formerly property of the South, which was in rebellion against the United States, and therefore as confiscated property they were entitled to the seizure, liberty, protection, and use of the Union military. Many of the freedmen seeking work at Camp Parapet, just north of New Orleans, were organized by General Benjamin Butler into three regiments of Louisiana Native Guards. These were the nation's first all-colored military units. These regiments participated in the battle of East Pascagoula, Mississippi, and the siege of Port Hudson. (Library of Congress)

2. Runaways

Norcross was lucky, many slaves were severely disfigured by beatings. Some were literally beaten to death.

In 1937, Jordon Smith, a former slave from Georgia, told interviewers about how bad beating could be: "A [man] run off and stayed in the woods six month. When he come back he's hairy as a cow, 'cause he lived in a cave and come out at night and [illegible] round. They put the dogs on him but couldn't cotch him. Fin'ly he come home and master say he won't whip him and Tom was crazy 'nough to 'lieve it. Master say to the cook, 'Fix Tom a big dinner,' and while Tom's eatin', master stand in the door with a whip and say, 'Tom, I's change my mind; you have no business runnin' off and I's [going to] take you out jus' like you come into the world.' Master gits a bottle whiskey and a box cigars and have Tom tied up out in the yard. He takes a chair and say to the driver, 'Boy, take him down, 250 licks this time.' Then he'd count the licks. When they's 150 licks it didn't look like they is any place left to hit, but master say, 'Finish him up.' Then he and the driver sat down, smoke cigars and drink whiskey, and master tell Tom how he must mind he master. Then he lock Tom up in a log house and master tell all the [slaves] if they give him anything to eat he'll skin 'em alive. The old folks slips Tom bread and meat. When he gits out, he's gone to the woods 'gain. They's plenty [runaways] what stayed in the woods till surrender."²⁴

Wesley Graves' father took to the woods in 1861. "His master wanted

A pair of runaway youths at Baton Rouge in their tatters. (Library of Congress)

to carry him to the army with him and he run off and stayed in the woods three years." At that time the plantation's mistress sent him a message that she'd free him if he'd come home. "He stayed out till the War closed," said Graves. "He wouldn't take no chances on it."[25]

In addition to beating, collaring, crippling, and branding, bloodhounds were another thing that slaves greatly feared. Alice Dixon, an ex-Arkansas slave, recalled the terror of her master's dogs, all ten of them. "Them dogs would get you," she recounted. When her Uncle Henry Jones ran off and was gone for much of the day, Dr. Newton, her master, unleased his hounds. The dogs sniffed out Henry, who climbed a tree for safety. The dogs wouldn't let him down until they were leashed. Henry was lucky he was up a tree. If the dogs had caught him on the ground, they would have mauled him. Slave hunters with dogs encouraged such vicious attacks, even telling cornered slaves that if they ever touched a dog, they'd be shot, even if the snarling dogs did attack. Dogs could turn a runaway into raw beef, recalled another former slave. As for Henry, he still had to endure Dr. Newton's wrath. "Them Newton's whipped the skin right off Uncle Henry's back," recounted Ms. Dixon.[26]

According to hand-me-down wisdom from runaways the best way to throw off the dogs was to place pepper in

THE LASH.

One of a series of full-color album cards produced by William A. Stephens depicting the horrors of slavery in 1863, "The Lash" shows a brutal and bloody flogging in progress. In addition to whipping posts, slaves were lashed to fence rails and fence posts for beatings. Others were tied to trees or were simply held down on the ground. The next card in this series shows the same slave beating the overseer to death with a large tree limb. (Library of Congress)

2. Runaways

your socks and run without shoes. "It make de hounds sneeze," recounted Walter Rimm, a former slave from Texas, during his interview in 1937.[27]

Joe Clinton was a former slave on the Clover Hill Plantation. He recalled worse. His mind reflected to the plantation's overseer, Harvey Brown, who he characterized as "About the cruelest man that I is ever seen."[28]

Brown was a terror. He beat on the slaves all the time. The offense didn't matter. When a slave named Henry came in from the fields with a partially filled cotton bag, Brown berated him for his meager pickings and gave him a whipping. Henry was so mad about the beating that he set fire to his cotton bag and ran away. Henry hid out in the delta cane breaks all the following day. Rather than chase him down, Harvey Brown

The bondage of Wilson Chinn included leg shackles and braces to keep him from running. The bells on his slave collar have been removed. (Library of Congress)

sent a slave into the bayou to find Henry and tell him to come back or Brown would unleash the hounds to come and eat him. Henry returned because he was rightfully fearful of the dogs, but he came back without his bag. That set Brown off. "With that Mr. Harvey lit into him like a bear, lashing him right and left," said Joe Clinton. Henry took off running again but was quickly cornered at the cook house. This time Brown took a piece of firewood to Henry. He beat him so badly that he thought he likely killed Henry. According to Joe Clinton, the overseer ordered one of those nearby to "go get some boards and make a coffin for [this man] what I done killed." Henry didn't die but it took him days to recover from Brown's beating.[29]

It wasn't all that uncommon for slaves to die at the hands of cruel masters or overseers.

To keep their slaves from becoming fugitives, some masters resorted to using outlandish scare tactics, concocting wild stories about the Bluecoats. Such fear mongering included tales of how the northern devils only wanted to sell runaway slaves into bondage at Haiti or Cuba, where they'd be worked to death. Another tale was that the Yankee jacklegs only wanted slave bodies to use as fertilizer on their otherwise barren

Left: Union seaman George W. Commodore was a freeman from Baltimore. He enlisted as a landsman there on 5 July 1864 for a three-year term. In October 1864 he mustered aboard USS *Adolph Hugel*. He was one of 55 Black sailors to serve aboard that vessel during the war. At any given time roughly one-third of *Hugel's* 31-member crew was comprised of Black sailors, particularly fugitives from Maryland, Virginia and Washington, D.C. Baltimore contributed 1,110 African-American sailors during the war. Maryland's Eastern Shore contributed 61 and Washington, D.C., provided 458. (National Archives and Records Administration)
Right: Like White sailors, Black seamen embellished their uniforms with embroidery. If you'll look closely, you'll see that the cuffs of this sailor's uniform are highly decorated. (Gettysburg College Special Collections and College Archives; used with permission of Angelo Scarlato)

2. Runaways

fields. Another fear tactic was to assure their slaves that the Yankees would shoot them on the spot or that the Bluecoats would cut off their feet. Caroline Richardson was told that by her mistress. "One day Miss Betsy [Ransome] comes out in the yard and says to the children 'you has got the habit of running to the gate to see who can say howdy first to our company, well the Yankees will be here today or tomorrow and they ain't our company. In fact iffen you runs to the gate to meet them they will shoot you dead." Her mistress assured them all that the Yankees would kill every one of them, men, women, and children. Fearing that Miss Betsy's warning might be true, as soon as the Bluecoats were heard coming, "the whole hundred of us runs an hides." Most would-be runaways knew better, and for those with doubts, the appearance of a Black soldiers and bluejacket on the roads and along a coastline and on inland waterways was an instant curative.[30]

Runaways close enough to Federal camps, fortifications or naval bases sought refuge there from masters and slave-hunters.

Others fled to the various hidden slave enclaves along the coastal marshlands where an array of entrepreneurial runaways often operated homegrown enterprises, selling produce, fish and handmade treats

The fancy needle work on this white summer sailor's flat hat was done by an unknown seaman on board USS *Hartford*. (National Park Service)

to Union sailors. For a time, Richard Slaughter survived off selling little snakes and terrapins to the sailors to eat. From such settlements hideaways could hitch a ride on a seller's bumboat to sanctuary aboard a Federal warship.[31] Others on waterways left the moment they saw a Federal vessel in the distance.

Others signaled for help from the shoreline. As it was for so many slaves, the shoreline was Richard Slaughter's ticket to freedom. His escape as a teenager was made easy by the fact that his master, Dr. Richard Epps, moved his family and slaves from his farm on an island in the James River down around Norfolk in June 1862. "Where I was born, there is a lot of water," Slaughter told an interviewer with the slave narrative project. "Why there used to be as high as ten or twelve Dutch three masters in the harbor all the time. In those days a good captain would hide a slave way up in the top mast and carry him out of Virginia to New York and Boston."[32]

Slaughter also vividly recalled the burning of the Gosport Navy Yard at Portsmouth, Virginia. The United States Navy had already burned the Gosport [Norfolk] Navy Yard in April 1861, including ships awaiting crews and repairs there. Among the capital ship's that were burned to the waterlines were USS *Germantown*, USS *Raritan*, USS *Columbia*, USS *Dolphin*,

For many held in bondage, deliverance came by water aboard a Union warship, seen in the distance, in this woodcut illustration from an issue of *Harper's Weekly*. (Library of Congress)

2. Runaways

USS *Delaware,* USS *Columbus,* USS *Plymouth,* and USS *Merrimack.* Because of its age and condition, USS *United States* was simply abandoned. *Merrimack* would be refloated and rebuilt, transforming the hulk into the Confederate iron-clad CSS *Virginia.*

For a time, the Confederates operated the Gosport Navy Yard. Shortly after that the Rebels abandoned the yard, too, and the Union Navy moved back in.

That is when ex-slave Mary Jane Wilson's father went to work there as a teamster. From his Navy pay "He began right away buying us a home."[33]

By June 1862 the Union Navy was again operating on the James, York, and Elizabeth Rivers in support of General McClellan's agonizingly slow Peninsular Campaign to capture Richmond. Union gunboats shelled the towns along the rivers and bombard the nearby plantations, forcing White families into basements. Under cover of the bombardments, the ships would go along picking up obvious runaways signaling from the shoreline.

Richard's father was among those who signaled a gunboat to stop. The obliging ship—USS *Miami*—took Richard and his entire family, including all his cousins, to City Point. Instead of joining the Navy Richard signed on as a water boy in the Union Army.[34]

The arrival of gunboats on 14 July 1863 prompted 10 slaves to run off in broad daylight from Charles Hill Carter's plantation (better known as Shirley Plantation in Virginia between Richmond and Williamsburg). Five more left two days later from the same plantation on the bank of the James River. By then Carter had lost 33 of his slaves. By the summer of 1864, Carter, whose family established the plantation in 1613, making it the oldest plantation in Virginia, had lost 72.

Reports of refugee recoveries became commonplace on every waterway. USS *Forest Rose,* operating on the Mississippi River on 15 September 1864, picked up 70 refugees.

There were also occasions when fleeing slaves were used as bait. USS *Ozark,* operating around Tunica Bend, Mississippi, in 1865 reported sending an armed boat ashore to bring off some contrabands who had hailed the vessel. After they were taken aboard the boat a group of concealed guerrillas opened fire on the landing party, killing one sailor and wounding two other seamen. Everyone else got away safely when the *Ozark* opened fire on the woods where the guerrillas were hiding.

If runaways didn't seek out Union protection, frequently Union sailors sought them out. Ship commanders learned to be lenient whenever a

Black Sailors in the Civil War

Sketch of a guerrilla attack on a Union sailor on the James River by Alfred R. Waud, an illustrator for *Frank Leslie's Illustrated Newspaper*, done in 1862. (Library of Congress)

landing party included one or more Black bluejackets. In reconnoitering the countryside Black sailors were often late in returning to the gathering point. They were sometimes late by as much as hours. But rather than charging them with desertion or reporting them for being absent without leave, the commanders tended to simply watch and wait. Before long, the truant sailors would reemerge with a group of runaways in tow from a nearby farm or plantation. Typically, the wait was worth it. The slaves, who most southern Whites considered to be invisible, saw and overheard everything. Such contrabands furnished valuable intelligence on the location of salt works, stores of hidden cotton, Rebel camps, troop concentrations and the location of Confederate mine fields in the rivers. One slave picked up on the James River confirmed the important fact that the upper reaches of the river were heavily mined, saving countless sailors' lives. Others overhead conversations from officers returning home on leave on conditions at the front and planned operations. Fugitive slaves constituted the Union's greatest unorganized spy network because there were so many of them and they came from every part of the South. Unfortunately, the gathering of information was hit and miss. The Union never had an organized way of debriefing the contrabands on what they knew about

2. Runaways

the enemy. Had they done so it might have considerably shortened the war.

The report of the commander of USS *Ethan Allen*, Acting Master J.A. Pennell, illustrates the value of such slave intelligence when he reported on 23 December 1864 off St. Simon's Sound, Georgia:

> "Having learned from a contraband that there was a picket station at Troop's plantation, twenty miles up the Altamaha river, I fitted out an expedition and left the ship at dark on the evening of the 20th instant, with launch and howitzer, and other boats, with three officers and forty men, arriving at the plantation at 2 a.m.; sent my guide for an old negro, who, I had been informed, could lead me to the camp. He soon came down to the boats and informed me that they were encamped at a house about two miles inland, and offered to lead me to them, which duty he performed faithfully. We arrived at the house at 3 a.m. and surrounded it; captured seven of the picket men with seven horses and their arms, consisting of five rifles and one old flint-lock musket; a corporal and one man that was on guard duty escaped."

In addition to a group of Rebel prisoners, Pennell's raiding party came away with seven contrabands, one serving as his guide back to his boats. Such tidbits were never well coordinated but were acted upon piecemeal. Those had consequences. As example, later that night Pennell's force was unexpectedly attacked by a group of about 60 Confederate riders. After hastily recovering from the initial shock of the attack luckily a discharge from his Dahlgren landing howitzer convinced the Rebels to flee into the woods. Had Pennell coordinated with any other vessels in the area he might have had an overwhelming reception for his nighttime attackers, possibly killing or capturing most of the band.

Acting Master J.G. Wells, commanding USS *Midnight*, repeatedly relied on colored refugees as his landing party's guides to a salt works at St. Andrew's Bay, Florida. On 4 December 1864 he reported that he "had reason to believe, by what I could glean from refugees, that there was considerable salt-making on the bays above here that he dispatched ... an expedition." This netted 16 salt-makers and three contrabands. One of the freed slaves immediately enlisted. The others declined because they had left their families and wanted to go back for them. On 16 January 1865 *Midnight's* crew destroyed another salt work. This time Well's crew came away with over 30 slaves seeking freedom.

For some in the south the only way to get salt was to boil the dirt from an old smokehouse. That was what former slave Adora Rienshaw's family was forced to do.

Black Sailors in the Civil War

Other slave-holding families were forced to trade for it, including trading their slaves.

Almost everywhere there was a naval shore engagement groups of fleeing slaves materialized. At Bayou Teche, Louisiana, as example, a skirmish with a landing party from USS *Carrabassett* and 30 Rebels led to a full-scale attack on the ship itself. This ended with the discharge of several rounds of shrapnel from the ship's guns. The shelling convinced the Rebel force to flee but even before the smoke had cleared, the ship's commander, Acting Volunteer Lieutenant Ezra Leonard, discovered nine colored refugees at the shoreline waiting to be taken aboard.

Even if there were no runaways brimming with valuable intelligence to be found, such landing parties typically returned with a bounty of poultry and produce from nearby farms to supplement the cook's pots.

Some slaves refused naval help. Commander F. Stanley, in charge of a ship at Bull's Bluff, South Carolina, in February 1865, was amazed to discover that the region had "large numbers of slaves, but every one of them refused our offers to accompany us or the army."

Others couldn't or wouldn't help. In another case, USS *Potomska's* frustrated commander, F.M. Montell, attempted to locate the Singleton plantation around Magnolia Bend on the Cooper River in South Carolina, where many slaves were said to have been herded together to march them

This *Harper's Weekly* illustration from July 1862 depicts contrabands fleeing to USS *Kingfisher* off the coast of Florida. (Library of Congress)

2. Runaways

to "safety" at Georgetown, South Carolina. The few slaves that did seek his help were fearful of furnishing any information about the plantation's whereabouts for fear of reprisals against their families. Montell's reconnaissance proved futile, but his frustration was short-lived. Within days the Federal Navy captured Georgetown. In surrendering the town on 25 February 1865, the city's wardens accepted Rear Admiral John A. Dahlgren's version of the emancipation proclamation, which declared that in accordance with Federal law, slavery was immediately abolished. Dahlgren's declaration went a bit further by requiring former slaveholders to provide each of their former slaves at Georgetown with 60 days' worth of food.

3

Robert Smalls

Robert Smalls wasn't waiting for help from the northern Navy. In 1862 Smalls was the pilot of the Confederate Army steamer *Planter*, an armed dispatch boat built in 1860 at Charleston, South Carolina. When he learned that the *Planter* was to move four cannons outside the harbor,

Robert Smalls, the "captor" of the transport steamer *Planter*, as illustrated in the 14 June 1862 issue of *Harper's Weekly*. Smalls was born at Beaufort, South Carolina, on 5 April 1839. He was hired out at age 12 for $16 a week, of which he was allowed to keep $1. The remainder went to his White master, Henry McKee, who was also his father. (Library of Congress)

3. Robert Smalls

including a large seven-inch rifle, Smalls realized that it was time to go. As anticipated, the cannons were placed aboard, and the boat was made ready for its run the following morning.

When the captain of the boat, C.J. Relyea, went ashore against orders on the evening of 12 May 1862, Smalls put his escape plan into motion. Smalls hastily gathered up his family, along with his brothers, and ushered them all aboard *Planter* under the noses of 20 guards protecting Brigadier General Roswell Ripley's command headquarters only a few feet from the wharf. Smalls dressed in attire that from a distance and in the darkness looked precisely like he was the boat's rightful captain. He did this by

Robert Smalls successfully pirated *Planter*, depicted here leaving Charleston harbor under cover of darkness on 13 May 1862. The Union Navy turned *Planter* into a Federal gunboat. (Library of Congress)

wearing what the boat's captain typically wore, including a large brimmed straw hat. His attire, and his gestures and posture, were highly convincing. The others in the group acted like the typical civilian sailors, who made up *Planter's* usual crew.

While the boat usually had eight crew members, no one questioned the appearance of 15 "sailors." The charade worked. At about 2:00 a.m., they quietly began building up steam sufficient to steer *Planter* away from the wharf. By 3:30 in the morning on 13 May, they cast off. Because Smalls was the boat's pilot, he knew all the necessary recognition signals needed to run safely past Charleston's bristling fortifications.

With Confederate and South Carolina flags flying, and the two long and one short bursts from the boat's steam whistle as a signal to the harbor's forts for safe passage, at 4:30 a.m. *Planter* slipped past the forts towards the open ocean. With no one in pursuit, and once safely beyond the range of the forts' guns, Smalls hauled down the Rebel flags and hoisted a white bed sheet. His plan was to surrender to the first Federal warship in the naval blockading force he could find, which was USS *Onward*. Flag Officer Samuel Francis Du Pont boasted to a United States Senator that "the steamer is quite a valuable acquisition to the [blockading] squadron,"[1] but that wasn't all that was of value. *Planter* was indeed a real prize, but more valuable still was what was in Smalls' head. Not only did the ship have secret Confederate signal flag codes aboard that would prove invaluable to the Federal fleet, but Smalls knew all about recent Confederate troop withdrawals around Charleston and the placement of Rebel mines that the Navy exploited.

For his initiative, Smalls and his 15-member

An unidentified sailor. (Library of Congress)

3. Robert Smalls

"crew" were awarded half of the value of *Planter* and her cargo as prize money. Smalls also was allowed to continue as USS *Planter's* pilot, and subsequently became her captain. As such, he was the first African-American commander of a U.S. naval vessel.

Smalls became a one-man recruiting office for the Navy. During the remainder of the war, he enticed thousands of liberated slaves to become bluejackets.

In October 1862 the Black citizens of New York honored him with a gold medal. The inscription on the medal, which was on display at the National Museum of the United States Navy in Washington, D.C., reads: "Presented to Robert Smalls by the colored citizens of New York, October 2, 1862, as a token of their regard for his heroism, his love of liberty and his patriotism."[2]

4

Northern Black Mariners

Among the earliest northern Black sailors to enlist in the Union Navy was Zachariah Caldwell, a lobsterman from New Bedford, Massachusetts. He enlisted on 7 December 1861 and was mustered aboard USS *Paul Jones* as an ordinary seaman. (After the war Caldwell returned to New Bedford and his lobster pots.) With an ancient maritime tradition, New Bedford contributed 57 of her sons as Black mariners to the Union Navy, including John F. Carter and Timothy T. Brown. (Carter also returned to New Bedford, where he died in February 1888.)

New Bedford also had the lingering legacy of the earlier presence of Frederick Douglass, a one-time counterfeit sailor. Black mariners were highly respected, and Douglass used that esteemed status as his disguise when he ran away from his Maryland owner.

Originally named Frederick Bailey, on 3 September 1838, Douglass fled from bondage dressed as a sailor. His costume was the handiwork of his betrothed, Anna

Anna Murray Douglass remained married to Frederick for 44 years until her death. Because he was constantly on the road giving speeches or on the run, the family's five children insisted that he was always their mother's favorite guest. Anna's house in Rochester also hosted hundreds on their journey on the Underground Railroad. (Library of Congress)

4. Northern Black Mariners

Murray, a free Black woman whom he had met in Baltimore. By selling her feather bed, she also provided him with the money he needed to make good his escape.

To further his charade as a sailor, Douglass had actual seaman's papers that weren't his own but described him well enough to pass in case he was stopped. The sham wasn't so far-fetched that it couldn't work. When Douglass was in his late teens he was hired out as a hull caulker to a Fells Point shipyard in Baltimore. He used a "devil" and a caulking mallet to drive tarred hemp into the seams of hull planks to seal them from leaks. There he became acquainted enough with nautical terms, at least sufficient in discussions to sound convincing if questioned. Now, at about 20, he was ready to run.

Writing in his memoirs in 1882, Douglass wrote: "My knowledge of ships and sailor's talk came much to my assistance, for I knew a ship from stem to stern, and from keelson to cross-trees, and could talk sailor like an old salt."[1] Douglass left Baltimore, making it as far as Havre de Grace, Maryland, before boarding a train for New York City. Once in New York, he was hidden in a safe house provided by David Ruggles. There he changed his name to Douglass. Anna Murray quickly traveled to New York City. The couple was married at the home of David Ruggles on 15 September 1838. From there, Douglass and Anna moved to New Bedford. Eventually the family relocated to Rochester, New York. For years, the future author and orator was a fugitive; Douglass' freedom was purchased in 1847. That year he also published the weekly *The North Star*, his anti-slavery newspaper that went into circulation on 3 December 1847. The influential paper survived until 1851, when, for financial reasons, it was merged with the *Liberty Party Paper*.

A majority of the of the Black watermen who

Young Frederick Douglass (Wikimedia Commons)

enlisted in the Navy were born into maritime communities in the northern and mid–Atlantic coastal states. Some communities were particular birthplace recruitment hot spots, including Norfolk, Virginia; Baltimore, Maryland; New York City; Camden, New Jersey; and Delaware City, Delaware. Isaiah Burton, Francis Butler, Robert Carr and William E. Carle were among the professional Black sailors born at New York City who enlisted. Henry Brown, John Brown and Robert Brown were experienced mariners from Delaware City, a tiny port hamlet near Fort Delaware, located on what was known as Pea Patch Island. Charles Brown and James E. Brown were among those born at Camden, New Jersey.

While it came as a shock for some urban White recruits, the Navy's insistence on strict discipline was not alien to runaways and professional Black watermen who understood that mistakes at sea could be lethal. True to the nature of seasoned seamen they were willing to extend a helping hand as role models to raw Black recruits and willing White city boys.

Carte-de-Visite of an unidentified New Orleans contraband. (Library of Congress)

5

Recruiting in Major Cities

At the start of the war, the South's eight major ports capable of conducting a significant amount of foreign trade included Norfolk, Wilmington, Charleston and Savannah on the Atlantic coast: and Pensacola, Mobile, New Orleans and Galveston on the Gulf coast. Norfolk and Pensacola were neutralized by the Federal garrisons holding the forts at the entrance to their harbors at the outbreak of hostilities. Fort Monroe, at the entrance to Norfolk, remained a major Union bastion throughout the war. In the case of Pensacola, under an agreement negotiated in January 1861 with officials from the State of Florida, Fort Pickens on Santa Rosa Island was to be held by the Union, while Forts Barrancas and McRae were to be held by units of the Alabama and Florida militias. Florida also took control of the Pensacola Navy Yard, which was never a major shipbuilding facility. To hold Fort Pickens, and neutralize the value of the Pensacola Navy Yard as a center for making even minor ship repairs, in February 1861 the Navy positioned the vessels USS *Brooklyn, Sabine, Macedonia* and *St. Louis* off Pensacola's harbor. Five days after Fort Sumter was fired on, Fort Pickens was reinforced in compliance with President Lincoln's orders, by his saying, "I want that fort saved at all hazards."[1] While the remaining southern ports became the North's chief naval targets, every southern haven was subject to attack. Beginning with the capture of the Confederate forts guarding the strategic inlet at Cape Hatteras in late August 1861, port after port gradually felt the effects of the Anaconda's squeeze.

With or without Army assistance, naval forces began seizing or neutralizing key towns along the coast. Port Royal, South Carolina, was captured on 7 November 1861; Ship Island, Mississippi, was seized on 3 December 1861, thus neutralizing Biloxi, Pascagoula and Gulf Port; Fernandina, Florida, was seized on 3 March 1862; Brunswick, Georgia, was seized on 9 March 1862; New Bern, North Carolina, was captured on 14 March 1862; Norfolk and Pensacola were evacuated by the Rebels on 10

Black Sailors in the Civil War

May 1862; and Brownsville, Texas, was evacuated on 2–4 November 1863. Black bluejackets participated in each of these actions, operations made easier by the South's realization in February 1862 that it lacked the manpower to defend adequately its seacoast and offshore islands, except at strategic points that protected major ports.

The remaining ports along the Atlantic—Charleston, Savannah, and Wilmington—were heavily defended, and proved harder to capture. Underwater obstacles, shoreline fortifications with large caliber cannons, chain barriers and submerged mines were used to impede access to harbors. Rear Admiral John Dahlgren's attempt to force his fleet's way into Charleston's harbor was blocked by obstacles that forced his ships to perform an awkward about-face in the narrow shipping channel under constant enemy fire. Among the underwater obstacles used by the South were giant picket-fence-like devices constructed of large timbers, some as long as 30 feet. Each picket measured 12 inches by 14 inches, and the tops of each picket were shaped into points which were capped by iron spear tips which could pierce a ship's hulls. To clear away such obstacles, Dahlgren tried an experimental device known as the "Devil," which was an offspring of the creative genius of John Ericsson. The Devil, which was chained to the bow of an attacking monitor, acted like a waterborne bulldozer blade to clear away obstacles. It was fitted out with grappling irons and could also be fitted with a spar torpedo for blowing up impediments to the fleet's progress. Unfortunately, the Devil proved difficult to manage. It tended to ride up onto the deck of its mother ship, or under her hull's overhang, threatening to damage what she was intended to protect. There were also fears that if the lead monitor with the Devil attached had ever to perform any maneuvers in a narrow shipping channel, she might inadvertently bump up against another Union vessel, and cause the bow-mounted torpedo to explode.

Unable to break through the barriers barring access to inner harbors of these key remaining Confederate ports, the Union opted instead to blockade them.

Then there was the Mississippi River. President Lincoln thought that controlling it was essential. He advised Army and Navy commanders that he wanted the river secured as soon as possible. That was a tall order. The Mississippi River is a massive watershed, flowing 2,340 miles, with tributaries draining from 31 states Union control of the river was a paramount military priority.

Inland water bastions began falling one-by-one too, including Memphis, Tennessee, on 6 June 1862; Grand Gulf, Mississippi, on 3 May 1863; Port Hudson, Louisiana, on 9 July 1863; Vicksburg, Mississippi, on 4

5. Recruiting in Major Cities

July 1863; and Yazoo City, Mississippi, on 13 July 1863. Again, Black sailors saw action in all these riverine operations.

On the Mississippi, New Orleans was the true prize. It was the southern gateway to the great river. Flag Officer David Farragut received his sailing orders on 20 January 1862. His instructions were, when ready, to proceed up the Mississippi River and reduce the defenses that guarded the approaches to New Orleans. If Farragut could accomplish that objective, he was to create as much panic as possible along the lower Mississippi and take as many towns as might fall under his guns, holding them until the Army could occupy them. But first and foremost, nothing, he was told, was to distract him from the fall of New Orleans, the South's largest and wealthiest city. While Farragut was coming up-river, Flag Officer Andrew Hull Foote was moving downstream and seizing point after point. Under the cover of smoke and darkness on the night of 23 and 24 April, the Union fleet sailed north towards New Orleans; Farragut commanded from USS *Hartford*. As the first vessels passed through a chain obstruction that had been broken two nights before, the Confederate Forts Jackson and Saint Philip began firing at the Federal ships. Dodging fire rafts and fighting an intense engagement with the Confederate River Defense Fleet, Union gunboats passed the enemy forts and anchored on the New Orleans levee. Realizing the futility of resistance against the awesome firepower of Farragut's ships, Confederate militia abandoned the city, prompting the unruly surrender of the South's most prosperous port on 25 April 1862.

News of the seizure of New Orleans served as a clear and decisive demonstration of the lengths to which the North was prepared to go in forcibly holding on to the Union and in freeing the slaves, town-by-town, and city-by-city, if necessary. Additionally, the growing sense within the Navy was that if the Army was unable to win the war, the Navy must do it! This sentiment began to permeate the Navy's mindset.

The fall of New Orleans freed hundreds of slaves, but some of those gaining freedom shocked northern sensibilities to the core.

Although Cora Gillam had some telltale White features, she was treated as Black and kept in slavery, although her brother and sister weren't. According to Miss Gillam, her father wasn't a slave. "My father was Mr. McCarroll from Ohio. He came to Mississippi to be the overseer on the plantation of the Warren family where my mother lived. My brother and sister were free folks because their White father claimed them. Brother was in college in Cincinnati and sister was in Oberlin college." The double standard was merely skin deep.

In captured southern towns, as in the North, the Union Navy

Black Sailors in the Civil War

Wrapped in an American flag as a symbol of their new-found protection and freedom, these three children were among those rescued at the thriving slave market at New Orleans. The boy is Charles Taylor, an eight-year-old who was sold in Virginia by his White father, Alexander Wethers, and taken to New Orleans by a slave-trader for resale. The boy's mother was a mulatto also owned by Wethers. The girls—Rosina Downs and Rebecca Huger—had similar situations. Cards such as this were sold throughout the North with the net proceeds going to support the education of freed people of color in New Orleans. While appearances in this case clearly created a double standard, northerners were generally outraged over the sale of such seemingly "White" children as slaves by their White parents. The travesty was that children possessing Black features that were fathered by their White masters were being sold all the time with no similar outcry. (Library of Congress)

5. Recruiting in Major Cities

established recruitment centers. In some big cities there were more than one. Each of these was called a "U.S. Naval Rendezvous." They were places where potential recruits could gather and consider the advantages of naval service and, if suitable, where they were given a cursory physical examination and judged on their mental acuity before being admitted to the ranks. Those considered to be "idiots" were rejected on the spot.

As a further inducement for men to enlist, in 1864 Congress authorized signing bonuses for those willing to serve for two- or three-year terms.

Many slaves fled to northern big cities, such as Boston, Philadelphia and New York. As penniless newcomers, they quickly encountered the darker side of city life. Most food shops in the slums were operated as combination grocery and liquor shops by selling "rotgut" gin to anyone with a penny or two in their pocket. Suitable places to sleep were hard to find.

Initially founded by the Ladies Home Missionary Society and overseen by a Methodist Episcopal minister, a large mission house in the slums of New York originally included a school for children, and a workroom for ladies to manufacture cheap clothing. It began as a place of refuge. Unfortunately, within a year, the minister was run off and the five-story mission building became a dwelling for the most desperate sorts: people with no place else to go and nothing but the clothes on their backs. Without the reverend's oversight, many of the building's nightly tenants were beggars, pickpockets, harlots, thieves and murderers. At times the loathsome flophouse housed as many as 1,000 wretched Black and White souls. All were forced to sleep on its hard floors. Space on the floor was a premium. No one dared to bring in bedding, because it took too much space. If anyone tried it, someone else would set the occupied mattress on fire to claim the space. Each night people had to fight to find and then to hold onto their meager space on the floor. Murders were common occurrences; the average was at least one a night. Most of the knifings were over space; however, one of those killed was a young girl who begged a penny on the street, only to be murdered for it on the mission's third floor later that night. Her body lay there for nearly a week before someone hauled it off to occupy her bloodstained place on the floor. Some other lodging places took White renters, but few accepted Black tenants.

The summer of 1863 was a particularly hard time for contrabands in many northern cities, especially those in the poorer parts of lower New York City.

In March 1863 President Lincoln announced the implementation of the Conscription Act, and, in July of that year, the carnage of the Battle of Gettysburg was reported. This combination caused New York City to erupt in violence. Rioting, lynching, looting and killing, especially aimed at Blacks, were practiced. Rioting also broke out in Boston, Philadelphia and Brooklyn as well as lesser populated northern communities. Massachusetts's governor, John Andrews, relied upon troops from the forts protecting Boston harbor to help quell the unrest. Demonstrations in Philadelphia were also quickly dealt with.

In New York a delegation of prominent citizens hastily wired President Lincoln on the evening of 13 July to say: "Our City having given her militia at your call is at the mercy of a mob which assembled this morning to resist the Draft & are now spreading fire & outrage—several buildings in different wards are in flames & the 'Times' & 'Tribune' offices are at this moment threatened. New York looks to you for instant help in troops & officers to command them and to declare martial law." The delegation included John Jay and George Templeton Strong, who was on the executive committee of the U.S. Sanitary Commission. They advised Lincoln that, "Telegraph wires cut in all directions."

Lincoln immediately ordered troops still at Gettysburg dispatched to deal with the rampaging mob, but these would take several days to be deployed. Until they arrived local police and militia units had to contend with a city in rebellion.

Hiram Paulding, the commandant of the Brooklyn Navy Yard, did his part by ordering a pair of warships from the Yard to take up positions off lower Manhattan as a show of force in protecting the Treasury depository. He also ordered small gunboats to patrol the harbor and monitor principal streets along the waterfront with orders to fire upon any disruptive groups. Additionally, he organized a detachment of sailors and marines to assist the police in containing the violence in the city until the Army arrived. Much of 13 and 14 July were punctuated by the deafening sounds of fire bells, gunshots, breaking glass and murderous screams from the lower east side of the city. Churches and houses that belonged to Black people were looted and burned.

A Black orphanage also was set on fire. Many of the facility's 230 children trapped inside the multi-story inferno were screaming for help, but none of the rioters in the streets lent a hand to help the terrified children after the adults had looted the structure. A policeman tried to shepherd some of the horrified children out the back of the orphan asylum, but he was caught by the street toughs and beaten to death in front of the petrified kids. By then the orphanage was a mass of flames. A few of its children stood in the street in utter shock. Soon after, no more screams were heard

5. Recruiting in Major Cities

from the engulfed shell of the building. Finally, the surviving children were gathered, along with a number of Black refugees, by 40 police officers and 100 Zouaves. As the mob pressed in on the group, the Zouaves fixed their bayonets, and the police ordered the crowd to stand back. Fearing the worst, the mob gave way, and the children and others were safely escorted to Blackwell's Island (now Roosevelt's Island), which housed a prison, and the City's lunatic asylum that opened in 1839.

In the chaos, two of the orphanage's charges were inadvertently left behind. These included a six-year-old boy and a young girl who thankfully were given temporary asylum by kindly neighbors until the children could be ushered safely to Blackwell's Island.

Believing the Island to be an unsuitable place to settle the children until permanent accommodations could be found, several influential New Yorkers approached a hotel in the city about temporarily accepting the children, but that establishment refused because of the orphans' color. A second hotel was asked to shelter the children, and that establishment willingly agreed to give them temporary refuge in a safe part of town. Many in the city believed that New York's Democratic governor, Horatio Seymour, was among those who should shoulder much of the blame for allowing the rioting to continue for as long as it did. At the height of the crisis, Seymour went through the city to promise New Yorkers that he'd end the draft if they'd stop the rioting. The hard-core roundabouts realized that Seymour's promise was nonsense. They continued their rampage.

Others blamed the regular Army's weak reaction to the riot as far too timid for their tastes. They thought that Major General John Ellis Wool, who was tasked with putting down the rowdies, was too old and meek for the job. Instead, many would have preferred someone like Major General Benjamin Butler to deal with the disorderly, predominantly Irish elements of the city. Although leading New Yorkers personally detested Butler, they appreciated the fact that he was a vicious pit-bull who would suppress civic unrest. However, Butler wasn't called upon.

By 1:00 p.m. on 14 July 1863, the wealthy New Yorker George Templeton Strong recorded in his private journal, "Hurray, there goes a strong squad of police marching eastward down this street—followed by a company of infantry with gleaming bayonets." The troops from Gettysburg, many of them New York Regiments, had finally begun arriving. Order was fully restored on 16 July. With the restoration of calm, a Federal commission was called to investigate the causes behind the New York draft riots, one of which was simmering racial animosity towards the city's Black population.

Black Sailors in the Civil War

The death toll among Blacks was officially 11, but at least 70 more were listed as missing. That number was highly suspect as under representative of those who were dead or missing. Some of the lynched were cut down and strung up again. Many of the bodies left in the streets were mutilated beyond recognition. An unknown number of Blacks were forced into the East River, where they drowned. And an uncertain number were unrecognizably burned in their looted homes. Others simply packed up and fled, taking their injured and dying with them.

A committee of New York's merchants was established to raise funds to assist the many Black families made homeless and jobless because of the violence. For runaways arriving in several northern cities that summer it was the worst possible timing. There were few places to find safe shelter and there was festering animosity in the streets.

The previous November, Mrs. Lincoln had been so moved by the wretched appearance of fugitives fleeing to New York that she pledged money to get them proper clothing and bed coverings. She wrote to her husband for money to cover her pledge, since the weather was growing colder and the need, greater. She told the President that she knew

In addition to being merciless, if called upon, the "Beast," a nickname General Benjamin Butler earned in New Orleans as its military governor when he authorized ladies who disrespected Union soldiers and sailors to be treated as common street walkers, may likely have used Colored troops to suppress the rioters in New York City. Butler had commanded Irish troops and the mob in New York were mostly Irish. He also claimed to be Irish, but really wasn't. As a Boston politician, he helped to promote himself by claiming that he was Irish to get Irish votes. This cartoon Carte-de-Visite depicts Benjamin Butler as the "Bluebeard of New Orleans" for his edict on the treatment of the city's women during his military occupation. His decree on the treatment of women greatly offended southerners and alarmed John Bull (symbolizing the British). (Library of Congress)

5. Recruiting in Major Cities

he wouldn't mind her request, but she needed the funds by that afternoon. She directed him, "Please answer by return mail & send f[unds]," since she had given her word that she and the President would help, and her word simply had to be kept. Her thought was that he could easily take the money from a $1,000 military relief fund he had just received as a donation from a generous citizen. Mrs. Lincoln reasoned that the soldiers already had sufficient support, and the refugees, next to nothing. Covering her $200 pledge proved harder to accomplish, but her commitment was met.

In the summer of 1863, conditions were even worse. Blacks had been attacked and killed by street rioters. Joining the military was clearly a safer alternative then living in fear and squalled urban surroundings. In the Army, 14 Black regiments had been formed by August 1863 and 24 others were being created. Enlistments in the Navy also were increasing. Among the naval enlistees at New York City right after the riots were Francis Langdon (1 August), Frederick Clark (3 August), John H. Thomas (5 August)

The North had the advantage of exploiting access to runaway slaves seeking Union naval protection. Many of these were subsequently employed as Black sailors. (Library of Congress)

and Joseph Pierce (6 August). Pierce, Thomas and Clark were mariners before the war. All three were rated as Seamen and two served aboard USS *Quaker City*. No ship assignment is listed for John Thomas. It was a lucky assignment for Pierce and Clark. *Quaker City* was one of the Navy's greatest prize takers. During the war, her 163-man crew seized 17 vessels and all shared in the distribution of the prize money resulting from the sale of the seizures. Both men went home with substantial war wealth.

The draft riots also caused a spike in enlistments of Black sailors in other major northern cities during the latter half of 1863.

6

Welcome to the Navy

The degree of welcome varied by service and situation. While the Army maintained a segregated structure and was initially hesitant to consider Black service, the Navy was not. Lincoln's Secretary of the Navy, Gideon Welles, embraced contrabands with open arms. He accepted their employment early on to alleviate the critical manpower shortages within his rapidly expanding blue and brown water operations, which had been brought about by the creation of the Anaconda Plan. As early as September 1861, Welles planned to take advantage of freed slaves. He instructed Flag Officer Samuel Francis Du Pont, who commanded the South Atlantic Blockading Squadron, on 25 September, that "the Department finds it necessary to adopt a regulation with respect to the large and increasing number of persons of color, commonly known as 'Contrabands,' now subsisted at the navy yards and on-board ships-of-war. These can neither be expelled from the service, to which they have resorted, nor can they be maintained unemployed, and it is not proper that they should be compelled to render necessary and regular services without compensation. You are therefore authorized, when their service can be made useful, to enlist them for the naval service, under the same forms and regulations as apply to other enlistments. They will be allowed, however, no higher rating than 'boys' at a compensation of ten dollars per month and one ration per day."[1]

The rank of "boy," largely assigned to Black sailors, helped to placate those who required an artificial distinction between White and Black sailors, since to do otherwise might assuage the myth of White superiority. Such pacification was acceptable to Gideon Welles if it meant getting men to man warships. Welles revised this guidance to Du Pont on 2 July 1862, saying, "Amongst the persons known as contrabands who have sought the protection of the United States, please ascertain if there are any men physically competent who are willing to enlist in the Navy for service in the Pacific at landmen's wages. If so, a vessel will be sent to take 150 of them to the Isthmus. About the same number could be used advantageously in the vessels now fitting for sea, as shipping does not keep pace with the Naval wants."[2]

The presence of Black seamen among ships' companies was nothing new. They had been represented on American merchantmen and commissioned warships since the founding of the Republic.

Well before the war, there were limits on Black enlistments in the Navy. The threshold was 5 percent of common bluejackets, but this was hard to monitor and maintain. Many of the Navy's senior sailors in 1861 began as midshipmen who oversaw integrated crews. Their acceptance within the naval service came as no significant culture shock, as opposed to within Army commands. The Army had another problem. It was plagued by the operational chaos that, until the arrival of Edwin Stanton as Secretary of War, prevailed with the War Department. Such disarray thwarted the Army's effectiveness and its potential use of Blacks within its ranks.

By 1865, roughly 20 percent of all Union enlisted sailors would be African-Americans. Freed Black sailors fought in every major naval engagement of the war, serving as equals to White sailors, receiving equal pay within their ranks, enlisted promotion opportunities and legal treatment, but most important, "contrabands" represented a significant manpower advantage.

Segregation was impossible on a ship where sailors had to function and fight as a crew. Aboard ship all hands had specific tasks to perform based on proficiencies, and the color of those hands was inconsequential to the given duties assigned. There was equality in battle.

The consensus among officers was that freed Blacks made good sailors. Admiral Andrew Hull Foote, who initially commanded the upper Mississippi fleet until his death, fully embraced emancipation. Foote was the Navy's most pious officer. He believed abolition to be a religious imperative. Flag Officer David Dixon Porter, who later commanded the Navy's Mississippi River Squadron, was highly complimentary of Black bluejackets. He considered them first-rate war fighters. He was particularly impressed with their endurance as coal-heavers and their coolness under fire. Flag Officer Samuel Du Pont, commanding the blockading forces along the South Atlantic coast, agreed. He also thought them, as a group, to be fearless under fire. There were several key reasons why the Navy took the lead in enlisting Black fugitives, and in incorporating them within integrated naval crews, doing so about a year ahead of the Army. Even then, the Army refused ever to integrate "colored" troops with White soldiers. One reason for such reservations was the fact that Army generals tended to be political

6. Welcome to the Navy

animals. They were not professional fighting men. They didn't believe that their constituents would accept their state militias being made up of mixed-race regiments. Initially they believed that contrabands were useful only as teamsters and laborers. The Navy had no such organizational structure or poor perception. Its officer corps was composed of career sailors. Most began their naval service as young boys. David Farragut, as example, went to sea at age nine as a midshipman and commanded his first vessel, a prize ship taken by his adopted father's crew, at age 13.

The reasons why the Navy's leadership exploited Black manpower as quickly as it did, reflected its longstanding tradition of treating Blacks as equals to White crew members; the receptivity of so many of its Navy's senior officers to accepting Blacks for their seamanship based upon past experiences; and the centralized leadership structure within the Navy, in which the Secretary of the Navy called the shots. This allowed Gideon Welles, a visionary abolitionist who realized the need for good men to man the armada of ships, to amass Black manpower to strangle the South into submission. Welles was glad to exploit the availability of self-emancipated men. All these factors contributed to the Navy's use of African-Americans at a far greater rate than the Army, especially given the proportional size of the Army versus the Navy.

Two ways in which Blacks were treated differently within the Navy were in the reporting of casualties, and in their consideration for prisoner exchange if captured. White seamen who were killed, wounded, or missing in action were reported by their names and ranks. Black sailors had the added notations "(Black)" or "(Colored)" behind their names and ranks. These notations reveal to historians today that Black sailors sustained casualties proportionate to White crewmembers, given their proportional numbers aboard ship.

Black sailors were at a disadvantage when it came to being prisoners of war. Although the number of Black sailors held as prisoners by the South was never very large, nevertheless the Confederacy wouldn't consider exchanging them. A prime example of this involved three Black sailors from USS *Isaac Smith*, which was captured off South Carolina. The White crewmembers were all quickly paroled, but the ship's three Blacks were put in Charleston's jail awaiting their potential sale into slavery. The three, all apparently free New Yorkers, received very little food and no care. The imprisoned trio included Orin H. Brown, William H. Johnson, and William Wilson. The men were allowed to send out a single plea for help. Their letter stressed, "We belong to the United States Navy and we ask for aid and protection." Those overseeing prisoner exchanges in the South were deaf to any humane entreaties on behalf of the three captives. Such callous disregard for the care of the three Navy prisoners caused Secretary of War Edwin Stanton to order on 3 August 1863 that three Rebel captives from South Carolina units be selected and held as hostages in close confinement. They were to be treated exactly as the three sailors were being abused in Charleston's jail, fed the same scant amounts, given the same small rations of water, and cared for in a like cruel manner. Series II, Volume VI of *The War of the Rebellion: A Compilation of the Official Records of the Union and Confederate Armies and Navies*, published in multiple volumes in the 1890s and 1900s, makes little further mention of the outcome for either threesome. There is no additional service information shown for Brown, Johnson and Wilson in the National Park Service's / Howard University's African American Civil War Sailors Project's database, so it is unclear how they fared, but by 1863 cruelty and disregard towards captives was becoming commonplace on both sides.

After 14 months of no Black *or* White naval prisoner exchanges, in October 1864 Navy Secretary Gideon Welles pressed the issue with his Confederate counterpart, Stephen Mallory. One of the hang-ups was the Rebel refusal to exchange Black seamen. For the Confederacy, captured Black sailors had to be returned to their prior owners. This condition was totally unacceptable to Welles. In his private diary entry for 5 October 1864, he penned: "It was a question of property, and of local and legal right with them which we could not prevent. It was a complicated and embarrassing question, but [Mallory] must not suppose, nor would the country permit our countrymen to suffer in captivity on such a question. To absolutely stop exchanges because owners held on to their slaves when they got them was an atrocious wrong, one that I would not be a party to."[3]

Despite the risk of capture, the ability to count on faithful Black bluejackets to fill its ranks was among Uncle Sam's great naval advantages in this first modern naval war, a conflict where both sides were fighting with technologies that were on the cutting edge. Uncle Sam's Navy had men that were quick to grasp and capable to fight with these deadly new innovations.

Black sailors were well suited for naval service. They were, as a rule, obedient to commands. They were steady seamen. They possessed exceptional endurance, having previously been forced to toil from sun-up to sunset. They accepted the inflexible discipline demanded aboard ship. They were self-reliant and could be counted on in a fight. They also took well to shipboard routines, including caulking, scrubbing decks, standing watch, washing clothes and hammocks, and darning socks. President

6. Welcome to the Navy

Lincoln loved being aboard naval vessels because his socks were washed and mended often on a nightly basis, and his slippers were always perfectly darned when mending was needed. Lincoln also loved hearing negro spirituals, which were frequently sung at night aboard ships with larger Black crews. He would join in whenever the song was something he knew.

Black sailors were skilled with their hands. They were extremely brave and proved to be exceptional warfighters. They were fighting for their and their families' freedom! They also understood that surrender was not a tenable option. They learned that in many ways, not the least of which was the news that a squad of Black Federal soldiers had been separated from their fellow White Union prisoners of war at Jacksonville, Louisiana, on 3 August 1863, marched off to a prison camp in the wrong direction, and when far enough away from hearing, were all murdered. The Confederates responsible for the killings claimed that while being marched in the wrong direction four of the Black prisoners attempted to escape and were shot while fleeing. Those responsible then claimed that the foursome's dash for freedom prompted a mass stampede among the remainder of the prisoners, which were all also shot down. The stark reality, however, was that the Black prisoners were all marched far enough away from their White comrades to be massacred. If captured within the Confederacy, Blacks clearly could expect no mercy. Humanity in the South was afforded Black sailors and soldiers only aboard Federal warships or within Union lines.

Naval compassion was not unusual. The three most common reasons for punishments aboard ship—profanity, insubordination, and drunkenness—were seldom Black bluejacket offenses. The most common offense among all sailors was desertion. Desertion was a serious offense, punishable by death by a firing squad. When court-martialed, Black sailors tended to receive more lenient sentences. This was largely due to the council of judging officers listening sympathetically to the passionate reasons for the transgression and reacting with feeling because of the heart-wrenching stories of separation and loss. The presiding officers were obviously affected by thoughts of being faced with similar dilemmas. What if they had been forced to search for family members ripped from them over time, as had Matthew Harris, a landsman serving aboard USS *Cuyler*. Harris went missing in April 1863 and was gone for several days. When he returned, he was accompanied by his wife and children, whom he had singlehandedly retrieved from a plantation in Mobile. Harris was willing to accept whatever punishment was rendered for his actions, because he had safely reunited his family. In hearing his story, and the circumstances behind Harris' rescue, the court dismissed the charges.

Black Sailors in the Civil War

Such searches for scattered family members were common in the lives of most freed African Americans during the war ... and well after it. The situations appear for many to have continued as a great lifelong frustration. James Bolton, who was interviewed in Athens, Georgia, in the 1930s, spoke for many when he said: "To tell the truth, I don't rightly know how many grandchildren I've got.... My children is off from here and I wouldn't know to save my life where they is or what they does. My sister and brothers they is done died out what ain't gone off, I don't know for sure where none of them is now."[4]

Ank Bishop, who was born in 1849, never knew her grandparents. She said her mother, Amy Larkin, "was 'bidded off' from South Carolina to Lady Liza Larkin, whose husband owned a plantation at Tard, near Coke's Chapel, Alabama." Her mother was the only one of her family that was sold in a spectator's drive making its way around the South. As a result, "She left her mammy and daddy back there in South Carolina and never did see them no more in this life."[5] Charlie Aarons was owned by J.N. White, a shopkeeper in Mobile, who sold him when Aarons was ten years old. He told an interviewer in 1937 that after he was separated from them, he never saw or heard of his parents, brother, or sister again and never knew what became of them.[6] Advertisements in many local newspapers up through the 1900s sought information on the whereabouts of slave family members. Often such searches ended without resolutions.

President Lincoln was keenly interested in the integration of naval ship crews and humanizing shipboard punishments. When he once visited USS *Hartford*, he observed a small box-like structure on deck that was padlocked. When he asked what it was for, he was advised that it was the ship's "Sweat-box" that was used to punish insubordinate sailors and those guilty of other offenses. He was told that the ship's steam pipes ran through the box, creating a sauna-like atmosphere that caused sailors to think twice about further transgressions. Lincoln said that he wished to have the experience of being inside the "Sweat box," which was roughly three-feet square. As a safeguard, the President devised a hand-signal that he'd use when he wished to come out of the box. Removing his hat and coat, the President squeezed into the box and the door was sealed behind him. Immediately Lincoln had trouble breathing through all the steam. Within minutes the President's hand could been seen at the vents frantically giving the "help signal." He needed to come out. Lincoln emerged soaked with sweat and breathing heavily. He advised Navy Secretary Welles, who was with him at the time, that the use of sweat boxes aboard any United States flagged warship was hereafter forbidden by order of the

6. Welcome to the Navy

Commander-in-Chief of the Navy.[7] Sailors throughout the Navy were thankful. Punishments were prescribed by naval regulations for specific offenses. On paper at least, this was a safeguard to any overzealous officer who might bear a grudge against any of his sailors. It also ensured that Black sailors received the same degree of discipline as their Caucasian colleagues. This, of course, didn't eliminate an officer from going out of his way to find fault with a specific sailor and leveling a stream of charges against him for actual or trumped-up offenses; however, such practices defied the Navy's official policy.

Then there was the ship's "Jonah," who was hazed by the entire crew. Every ship seemed to have one.

Black bluejackets typically were good seamen. Because of their fighting capabilities, on some ships, such as USS *Minnesota*, entire gun crews were comprised of Black sailors. Other vessels, like USS *Wabash*, commonly used Black sailors as rammers because of their exceptional endurance and strength.

Many officers, such as David Dixon Porter and Samuel Francis Du Pont, went out of their ways to recruit Black sailors. Other Flag Officers, such as David Farragut, went further by recognizing and rewarding them for their meritorious conduct. What Farragut couldn't do was promote as many of his Black sailors as he liked to Petty Officer positions. This was a common problem throughout the naval service. In 1863, as example, the entire Navy had only 13 Black Petty Officers of the line.[8] That wasn't because of a lack of opportunity. There were ample Petty Officer of the line positions available, including boatswain's mate, gunner's mate, captain of the forecastle, quartermaster, quarter gunner, captain of the maintop, captain of the foretop, captain of the mizzenmast, captain of the hold, coxswain, and captain of the afterguard.[9] The small number of Blacks in any of these positions was due predominantly to the fact that White sailors chafed at taking orders from Black superiors. Emancipated sailors had indeed won their freedom and gained a bit of parity with White sailors, however, they had not ... and would not ... achieve equity in all things. This lack of upward mobility within Navy ranks prompted George E. Smith to do something unwise. Smith thought that since he couldn't find advancement as a Black warfighter within the Navy, he'd find it in the Army, where entire regiments were comprised of Black soldiers. Unfortunately, Smith deserted to make the switch in services. When his action was discovered, he was charged by the Navy with desertion. Despite strong Army intercession, and Smith's valid defense that the Navy's general treatment of men of color was biased, he was found guilty by a Navy court-martial and sentenced to five years in prison. The irony of this case was that Smith had the experience and ability to have been a fine Petty Officer. He hailed from the port of Sackets Harbor, New York, where he had been a sailor before the war. He had enlisted at Boston for a three-year term and received a rank of ordinary seaman. He was assigned to USS *William G. Putnam*, a wooden-hulled armed tugboat built in 1857, that had a crew of 62 sailors. Initially the Navy preferred three-year enlistment, but as the war ground on and sailors got harder to find, shorter terms became acceptable. The Navy's age restrictions on sailors were also relaxed as older fugitives signed on to serve.

As passed by Congress and signed into law by the President, the Conscription Act had a flaw. It allowed for the drafting of Petty Officers and non-commissioned sailors even in the situations in which they were already serving in another branch of the military. In April 1863 Navy Secretary Gideon Welles wrote to Secretary of War Stanton about this mistake, saying, "These men are now on duty, some on blockade service, some abroad, and the law which

This Carte-de-Visite bears the hand-written name "Charles Batties," but the National Park Service's database of Black sailors during war lists no such seaman. There is a James Bettes listed in the Civil War database. He was a 24-year-old from New Orleans who enlisted at New York City on 17 August 1863, a month after the New York draft riots. There also is a Charles W. Biddle in the database. He was from Philadelphia and enlisted in 1864, but neither man may be depicted here. (Library of Congress)

6. Welcome to the Navy

subjects these men to the draft is monstrous...."[10] Stanton said he was powerless to help unless Congress amended the law. This came at a time when the Navy was hard-pressed to man its ships at full capacity, and was contemplating asking for soldiers to become sailors, not the other way around.

7

The Need for Army Contrabands and Its Fleet

Random runaways weren't enough to fill the Navy's needs for sailors. What really helped to fill uniforms was the capture of major population centers in the South, and the Navy had proven to be good at that. As the naval service grew, so did the demand for sailors; so much so that on 5 August 1862, Navy Secretary Gideon Welles instructed Commodore Charles Wilkes, commanding the Union's James River Flotilla, "You will fill up the crews with contrabands obtained from Major General Dix, as there is not an available sailor North."[1] Two days later, Wilkes advised Welles that Dix had no contrabands to spare. This prompted the Navy Department to send a similar urgent request to Brigadier General James Wadsworth in Washington, D.C., for 100 of "the most strong and healthy contrabands."[2] These were to be shipped aboard USS *Powhattan* and *New Ironsides* to Philadelphia for immediate deployment. The Navy's manpower shortage was serious and constant. At times, the Navy became so desperate that it asked the Army to transfer soldiers to fill vacancies aboard ships. The Navy's requests were for men who had previous service aboard ships, such as merchant seamen, whalers, or fishermen. Instead, what little help the Navy received was often the dregs of the Army, including invalids and shirkers. The Navy also attempted to recruit sailors from Europe, but that failed.

These facts forced the Navy to rely on contrabands to function as quickly-trained seamen. No ship was truly immune from the manpower shortage.

Unable to get much help from the Army, the Navy went in search of whole communities of contrabands to entice.

In May 1862 Flag Officer Louis M. Goldsborough, commanding the North Atlantic Blockading Squadron, instructed his officers to rely upon runaways. "The large number of persons known as contrabands flocking to the protection of the United States flag affords an opportunity to provide

7. The Need for Army Contrabands and Its Fleet

in every department of a ship, especially for boats' crews, acclimated labor. The commanding officers under my command are required to obtain the services of these persons for the country by enlisting them freely in the Navy, with their consent...."[3]

On 15 August 1862 USS *Cimarron* hit pay dirt. "The contrabands are getting very numerous on [Jamestown] Island. They are crossing almost every day from the opposite shore," reported Commander M. Woodhull to his superior, Commodore Wilkes.[4]

By December 1862, the overall number of Union naval personnel increased to about 28,000 seamen and officers, some of whom came from the Army. Getting men from the Army to fill vacancies wasn't always a panacea. In February 1863, flag officer David Dixon Porter asked General Grant for soldiers to help crew the ships of the Mississippi Squadron. Grant obliged, furnishing 600 soldiers. After receiving these new hands, Porter issued instructions to his naval commanders to "treat them kindly, but let them feel that they must conform to naval laws." To Porter's way of thinking, "Great discretion will be required in the management of these men, who have hitherto led an irregular life and had but few examples of well-disciplined people before their eyes." That was an understatement. For starters, Porter had to convince some of the Army officers assigned to accompany the troops to leave their horses behind as there was no need for them aboard ships.

Rather than the sailors serving as role models of strict naval discipline, the soldiers assigned to USS *Benton* proved to be far from disciplined sailor-type material. The soldiers assigned to *Benton* had brought aboard a half barrel of whiskey that was used to fill their canteens. Within a matter of hours, the soldiers aboard *Benton* were all rip-roaringly drunk and refusing to do anything. Porter considered this to be mutiny and clapped them all in irons. Porter promptly sent the soldiers back to General Grant, saying, "They are pretty drunk now and insensible to reason, and I thought the shortest way was to put them out of sight." Porter did admit that his sailors proved to be less virtuous than he had hoped, saying, "the crew of the *Benton* ... are somewhat in a like condition, but more tractable."

Such Army antics left the Navy far short of what was needed to man it. Many successful recruits were young boys anxious to serve, or get away from home. This number of sailors was small compared to the needs of the Army, but some in Congress were concerned that too many potential recruits were ducking the Army and joining the Navy instead because it was seen as a safer service, which was true. Instead of grasping the logic of this and recognizing the need for an Army-oriented draft act, on 3 March 1863, Congress enacted the Enrollment Act—a military draft act. Passage of this Act only compounded the problem by not considering the manpower needs of the naval services.

In addition to its being one-sided, the adoption of the Enrollment Act was seen as directed to urban and particularly immigrant populations, which caused riots to erupt in several cities, the worst of which occurred in New York City in July 1863. Welles was deeply alarmed by the riots, recording in his diary for 15 July, "The papers are filled with accounts of mobs, riots, burnings, and murders in New York. There have been outbreaks to resist the draft in several other places. This is anarchy.... Unless speedy and decisive measures are taken, the government and country will be imperiled."[5] The riots were put down and peace restored, and the draft continued.

The lack of sailors for sea service was made harder by the occasional requirement to man shore batteries. On 2 June 1863, Navy Secretary Gideon Welles asked the Army for 100 soldiers to man the fort protecting the Navy Yard at Portsmouth, New Hampshire. The fort had just received 11 eight-inch guns and needed guards and gun crews. Welles furnished Secretary of War Edwin Stanton with an alternative. "If this cannot be done, this Department will man the guns with 100 contrabands, if you cannot furnish it with that number."[6] The Army confirmed that it would indeed furnish the needed liberated slaves. For its part, the Navy assigned Acting Master W.H. Smith to command the gun battery and lead the contrabands. Welles insisted that the Army furnish "Physically sound men—regularly enlisted are wanted, no others."[7] The contrabands came from Hampton Roads by naval steamer and were assigned to the Navy for at least a year.

Still desperate for sailors, in March 1864, Welles unsuccessfully asked the President to transfer 12,000 soldiers to the Navy.

Such Army transfers are one reason why we may never know the exact number of freed Blacks that served under naval command. Many of the soldiers transferred from time to time to the Navy were likely contrabands, but no one seems to have been keeping precise counts. Many have placed the overall average of Blacks in naval service from 1861 to 1865 as between 17 to 20 percent. The percentage is probably right for 1861 to 1865, but this is perhaps the wrong way to assess the impact of Black sailors with respect to the successes of the Navy. Perhaps a better perspective is to examine Gideon Welles' final statement to Congress on the number of sailors in service as a more accurate measure. If so, the percentage could be higher than that. Welles placed the final number of naval ranks at the

7. The Need for Army Contrabands and Its Fleet

end of the war at 51,500. With 18,000 Black sailors known to have served during all the war years, and because the majority of the fugitives enlisted during the last half of the war, the overall number at the end of the conflict could have been as high as 35 percent in 1865.

That is closer to the percentages calculated for the Black sailors that served with the Mississippi Flotilla, where the percentage of fugitive enlistees is thought to have averaged between 35 and 40 percent of naval crews. This is a higher percentage than what is thought to have served in the blue-water Navy. The increase is thought to be attributed to the easier and greater access of runaway populations to Union warships along the miles of river front of the southern Mississippi and its tributaries. In the future a thorough statistical analysis of Blacks in naval service might find that the percentage of brown- and blue-water Black bluejackets is statistically about the same during the last two years of the war. Whether or not such an analysis can be made, the fact is that the Union Navy desperately needed men, and Blacks were proud to serve. A half-year earlier Secretary Welles addressed the ongoing ramification of the draft act in a diary entry for 26 August 1864, noting: "Am harassed by the pressure on the enlistment question. A desire to enter the Navy to avoid the draft is extensive, and the local authorities encourage it, so that our recruiting rendezvous are, for the time being, overrun. The Governors and others are applying for more rendezvous in order to facilitate this operation. The draft for 500,000 men is wholly an army conscription. Incidentally it aids the Navy, and to that extent lessens the number of the army. I have been willing to avail ourselves of the opportunity for naval recruiting, but the local authorities are for going beyond this and making our enlistments a primary object of the draft. Because I cannot consent to this perversion I am subjected to much captious criticism, even by those who should know better."[8]

Welles' angst was directed in part at his own Department because his local recruiters were using posters that proclaimed in all caps, "THE CONSCRIPT BILL! HOW TO AVOID IT!! U.S. NAVY."

In the end, many wouldn't have a choice in avoiding it. By 1864, like it or not, many of those drafted into the Army after the introduction of conscription in 1863 with merchant marine, whaling or fishing experience were subsequently transferred to the Navy. Additionally, many of these Black and White drafted or enlisted soldiers after the introduction of conscription transferred to the Navy usually had notations on the Army regimental records noting that they had been "discharged and transferred to the Navy"; however, many also subsequently had the additional notation:

Black Sailors in the Civil War

"No service found on rolls of the U.S. Navy." For this reason, Navy counts are reasonably suspect for also undercounting, particularly with respect to Black naval service.

By the summer of 1864 there was also a concern in Congress that too many soldiers had been transferred to the Navy, depleting the ranks of the Army. The truth of the matter was that most of such transfers were expeditious, stopgap actions at best. Early on many of those that were transferred were going to man the Western Flotilla. In that case, some of those that were furnished to Flag Officer Andrew Hull Foote, as example, were offenders under military guards. In addition to being prisoners, whenever this was done, complained Welles, it was far from an ideal measure given the nautical expertise expected of seasoned sailors—skills that ordinary soldiers simply didn't possess. Black sailors were a far better alternative.

By 1863, contrabands became a critical necessity. To help ensure that warships were adequately manned, on 5 January 1863, Secretary Welles demanded that all ship commanders submit monthly reports of the contrabands employed on their vessels. Those that were sloppy in submitting their reports received a slap on the wrist from their commanding officers. Acting Master S.B. Gregory, commanding USS *Western World*, was one of those so chastised.

The advantages of successful deploying Black warfighters by the Union finally dawned on some military leaders in the South. Among them, Major General Patrick Cleburne proposed doing the same thing down South, emancipating slaves who were willing to bear arms for the Confederacy at the start of 1864. Cleburne's plan was roundly opposed by many vocal southerners. Former U.S. Congressman and Confederate Brigadier General James Patton Anderson, for example, called the idea "revolting to Southern sentiment, Southern pride, and Southern honor." It would be monstruous, Anderson insisted, to be "thus securing them to us as allies and equals." The South ultimately relented, but by then it was too late.

On the Mississippi River, the Army possessed its own fleet, including transports and gunboats, and it had an inkling of adding a flotilla of Army river rams too, vessels of the type envisioned by Colonel Charles Ellet. Ellet first proposed his ram idea to the Russian government in 1854 during the Crimean War as a way of breaking the British siege on Sebastopol. The following year he submitted his idea to the United States Navy. His scheme was simple. He proposed converting common steamers, such as tugs and ferryboats into battering rams that would fight without guns, but would win battles by momentum. Such conflicts, he suggested, would be short

7. The Need for Army Contrabands and Its Fleet

and sweet. "A hole only two feet square, four feet under water, will sink an ordinary frigate in sixteen minutes," he calculated. The Navy's response was discouraging. Ellet was advised that similar ideas had been proposed from time-to-time since the 1830s and that his plan "would introduce an entire change in naval warfare."

Undaunted, Ellet kept pushing his concept, citing collision damage reports to promote his case. If accidental collisions of small sailing crafts with larger ships at sea could sink the larger vessels, imagine what an intentional impact of a battering ram could do, he insisted. In the 1850s the Navy Department ignored his recommendations, as he thought it might, accepting that "people are accustomed to regard the art of naval warfare as the art of maneuvering cannon, and throwing shot and shell." When the war erupted, Ellet, who was then living in Washington, D.C., was in the perfect place and the perfect time to promote his scheme anew. The merits of Ellet's idea fully dawned on War Department planners when CSS *Virginia* sank USS *Cumberland* in a matter of minutes by using its ram. In short order, the Secretary of War commissioned Ellet as Colonel of Engineers and on 27 March 1862 Stanton directed him to acquire and convert suitable ships into river rams. This directive was followed up the next day with the instruction: "Lose no time."[9] Ellet quickly complied, purchasing five towboats at Pittsburgh and four river steamers at Cincinnati. The conversion of the rams was completed in short order. As an added touch, Ellet had his flotilla painted black to give them a more ominous appearance. Almost as soon as they were ready, he put them to the test. To prove her worth, Ellet ordered *Queen of the West's* engineers to lay on all

Most of the photographs of Black sailors from the Civil War are unidentified. This is attributed to the fact that, since many of them were illiterate fugitives, few could spell their names on the bottoms or backs of the photograph cards. (Library of Congress)

available steam and charge at her first victim, CSS *General Lovell: Lowell* was struck with such force that she sank within minutes. In backing *Queen of the West* away, Ellet's command ship was attacked by a pair of Rebel vessels.

In that exchange, Colonel Ellet was the only Union casualty. He was shot in the knee. In such cases, amputation was the normal course of action, but Ellet refused the surgery, preferring to take his chances with the possibility of a recovery. He lost that gamble on 21 June 1862. Command of the ram fleet devolved to Charles' brother, Alfred. In turn, Alfred gave command of two of the flotillas to his nephews, nineteen-year-old Charles Rivers Ellet and John A. Ellet. Having competing naval units on the river would take close coordination and constant communications to avoid conflicts. None of this made sense to Porter or Welles. The idea of competing fleets didn't sit well with Congress either. Rear Admiral Joseph Smith wrote a confidential letter to Foote on 11 July 1862 to say that things were a mess in Washington. "The Govt. is in a quandary about Army affairs," he noted and confided, "Congress has got the Navy Laws in a complete labyrinth."[10] Ultimately, Congress transferred the western gunboats from the Army to the Navy under an Act of 16 July 1862, but that law was unclear as to whether it also pertained to the Army's "U.S. Ram Fleet."

On 11 September 1862 Secretary of War Stanton asked for Welles' opinion on this matter. Welles responded on the 16th, citing the wording of the Act. The law, he said, stated: "that the Western Gun Boat Fleet constructed by the War Department for operating on the Western Waters, shall be transferred to the Navy Department." To his way of thinking it was therefore up to the War Department to decide whether that stipulation included the rams or not. Welles thought that it might be prudent only to transfer the gunboats for the time being and he told Stanton that the Navy was prepared to effect that transfer on 1 October, but within days he was forced to confide, "The Army has fallen in love with the gunboats and wants them in every creek."[11] Ellet, however, wanted to keep both classes of river craft. Unaware of this, on 21 October, Welles pushed ahead, informing Stanton that he believed the rams were indeed intended to be included in the transfer, but by 1 November, Welles wasn't sure that Porter still wanted them. Porter said that he did, telling his boss on November 3, 1862, "I am extremely anxious to get possession of [the Army's] Rams; they are the class of vessels I particularly want at this moment." Porter urged Welles, "Do settle the Ram business, and let me know by telegraph."[12] After so much time wasted on back and forth talks regarding the rams, where Porter and Welles tried flattering, convincing, cajoling and threatening

7. The Need for Army Contrabands and Its Fleet

to effect an outcome, then Stanton appeared to have begun having serious second thoughts. The Secretary of War appeared then to have taken to the idea of his own brown-water marine force, even though Congress ordered the transfer of all war vessels on the Mississippi to the Navy.

Welles' diary entry for 4 November notes that Stanton opposed the transfer as not being strictly within the letter of the law. At a White House conference later that month, attended by Welles and Stanton, the fate of the Army's ram fleet was thought to have been resolved by the President, but it hadn't been fully resolved. The ram fleet was supposed to become part of Porter's Mississippi Squadron; but making that a reality proved difficult. The unit's commander, Brigadier General Alfred Ellet, used his flotilla as he pleased, often helping his Navy colleagues. To assist Rear Admiral Farragut in joint riverine operations below Vicksburg aimed at blockading the Red River and harassing Rebel fortifications being built at Warrenton, Mississippi, Ellet ordered two of his rams—*Switzerland* and *Lancaster*—to run past Vicksburg and link up with Farragut, who had just dashed past Port Hudson with USS *Hartford* and *Albatross*. The attempted link-up was made before dawn on 25 March 1863. Each of the Army's rams was commanded by members of the Ellet family. *Lancaster*, commanded by Lieutenant Colonel John Ellet, was sunk in the attempt. *Switzerland*, under the command of Colonel Charles Ellet, made it past Vicksburg, but was in such sorry shape in doing so that the planned joint Army-Navy naval attack on Warrenton had to be called off. John Ellet survived the sinking by floating down river on a cotton bale, but is believed to have succumbed to an opium overdose on 16 October 1862 while on recuperative leave. Porter was keenly impressed with young Charles Ellet, telling Secretary Welles, "He will undertake anything I wish him to without asking questions, and these are the kind of men I like to command."[13]

By 16 April 1863 Welles forwarded a recommendation from Rear Admiral Porter to Secretary of War Stanton suggesting the Army's ram force be placed under his command as a naval anti-guerrilla unit. Otherwise, Porter suggested that it be merged back into the overall Army's command structure, severing its connection with the Navy, or abolished altogether. This didn't sit well with Alfred Ellet, who Welles described as being "full of zeal to overflowing; is not, however, a naval man, but is, very naturally, delighted with an independent naval command in this adventurous ram service."[14] "Father Neptune" as Lincoln dubbed Welles, also characterized Ellet as being from a family known for being "brave, venturous ... with many daring excellent qualities."[15] As expected, Porter's

An unidentified young Black sailor with a pair of unknown Union naval officers. (Heritage Auctions, HA.com)

7. The Need for Army Contrabands and Its Fleet

recommendations didn't go over well with Stanton. "Mars" as Lincoln called Stanton, relished having his own distinct naval force modeled after the Marines, and the general thought Porter was totally out of order in offering his suggestions to the Army.

Welles knew Porter was right, writing in his diary on 4 November 1862, "It is, however, a pitiful business on the part of Stanton and Halleck, who should take an administrative view and who should be aware there cannot be two distinct commands on the river, under different orders from different Departments without endangering collision." Despite the illogic of it, instead of giving up the rams, Stanton kept them and expanded his ram fleet in November 1863. It continued in service until August 1864. At that point the unit was disbanded, and the boats were turned over to the Quartermasters Corps for transport duties. With David Dixon Porter in command, on 1 October 1862, Welles reclassified the Western Flotilla as a Squadron.

8

From Overseers to Boatswains Mates

For contraband sailors, no longer would their lives be controlled by the overseer, the lash and the big horn or bell that marked the start and end of their days. Now commands were conveyed by the shrill pitch of the Boatswain's pipe. Now the Boatswain was their overseer. He conveyed the officers' orders to the men. He also taught new sailors what was expected and how they were to react when they heard his pipe calling out commands. He instructed them in proper dress, procedures, and protocols. He indoctrinated them with shipboard hygiene and normal operations. And he drilled them repeatedly until everything became mindless routine and flawless. A Boatswain demanded proficiency and perfection.

Shipboard routines began at 5:00 a.m., or earlier. Sailors rolled out of their hammocks and tied them up according to a strict protocol for stowing. Then there was holystoning or scrubbing the weather deck, eating, washing personal items, polishing the ship's brass, learning to tie the eight basic knots, splicing ropes with a fid and practicing defensive drills with a cutlass, rifle and pike. Then there were gun drills overseen by a Gunners Mate. These often were daily drills lasting 30 minutes, except on Sundays. Practice made perfect.

Everything followed a schedule. This was true on both sides. In the Confederate navy, clothes were typically washed on Mondays, Wednesdays, and Fridays. Hammocks were washed on the first and third Monday of each month and at that time all ship's bedding was aired out.[1]

As with most of this routine, a holystone was something not previously encountered by newly minted sailors. It was a block of soft sandstone that acted like sandpaper in removing dirt from the deck. It was called that because it was originally used on the sabbath.

For this, landsmen received $12 a month, plus $1.50 for grog money. After the use of alcohol aboard ships was abolished as of 1 September 1862, many sailors took up singing "Farewell to Grog" in mock protest. Officers

8. From Overseers to Boatswains Mates

didn't view this as an act of defiance to a naval regulation, since they were as upset over the ban as their sailors. Instead, the lyrics were viewed as a temporary way of blowing off steam. A cash allowance of five cents a day was added to sailors' pay for giving up their grog. Shanties like "Farewell to Grog," "Sipping grog one day at sea," or "O! Dear Grog thou art my Darling" utilized a "call-and-response" phrasing that is thought to have originated in West Africa to create a cadence for enslaved workers. For "O! Dear Grog," one verse, sung by a single sailor was:

> Now, if all the rest of Adam's race,
> Was assembled together in this place,
> I'd part withall [sic] without one tear,
> Before I'd part with you my dear.

The integrated crew of USS *Mendota*, photographed on 2 May 1864 on the James River. Several of her Black crew members are gathered on the right side of the deck. (Library of Congress)

Black Sailors in the Civil War

The chorus, which was sung in response to each verse by the entire crew, went:

> Oh, oh, Oh! Dear grog,
> Thou art my darling,
> I love thee well,
> Both at night and morning.[2]

Shanties also proved to be perfect for shipboard routines.

Ordinary seamen received $14 a month base pay. An ordinary seaman had to possess at least two years of prior nautical experience. A Seamen was an old hand aboard ship. He was paid $18 a month. For many freed sailors this was the first time they personally had ever received a working wage.

Young boys could serve as powder monkeys at age 13, with their parent's permission. This say-so was impossible for most runaway boys to get, so many commanders simply turned a blind eye to this regulation to get the young powder runners they needed and the first- or second-class boys they required. John Jackson was 13 when he enlisted on 6 June 1864. The four-foot-two-inch-tall runaway from Richmond, Virginia, was enlisted

Blue-water Black bluejackets aboard USS *Sacramento*. After the war, *Sacramento* was assigned to patrol the coast of West Africa. (Naval History and Heritage Command)

8. From Overseers to Boatswains Mates

as a second-class boy for a two-year term aboard USS *Pink,* a New York tugboat transformed into a gunboat.

Boatswains helped to ensure that, as with everything aboard ship, there was equality when it came to sleeping, eating, cleaning, drilling, fighting, and serving in the United States Navy.

9

Blue-Water Black Bluejackets

The Union Navy fought two water wars, one on the blue oceans and the other on the nation's muddy inland and coastal waterways. The latter was like the riverine war in Vietnam.

The majority of the Union's blue-water Navy was engaged in blockade duty. This service provided sailors with a few stark minutes of terror when faced with the prospect of, or actual combat at sea, sandwiched between days or weeks of sweltering boredom. Naval engineer Hiram Parker spoke of the monotony in a letter to his father of in 1862. "We are getting along about the same as we have been for the past few months," he wrote. "There is [sic] very few days something transpiring serving to keep up a little excitement—sometimes chasing a sailing vessel, sometimes a steamer."

The blockade was basically predicated upon a zone defense with two or three crisscrossing layers of blockaders patrolling offshore. For the three-layer scheme, the first line in the zone-like defense consisted of slower and smaller Federal ships or picket boats stationed close to the coast, vessels such as USS *Henry Brinker*. These would signal other larger and faster ships further out when they spotted a runner. The second blockade line was posted about 12 miles out and the third line cruised back and forth roughly 120 miles out. (If the scheme in use were for only two zones, the 120-mile zone was dropped.) The value of the zones was that any could be downsized or eliminated if ships had to be temporarily pulled off station. The use of crisscrossing zones increased the Navy's interdiction rates from roughly 20 percent to 50 percent. In all, about 1,500 vessels failed to elude the blockade.

Henry Brinker was hastily converted into a warship at Baltimore by initially adding a 30-pound Parrott gun. She was commissioned as a naval vessel on 15 December 1861. As a gunboat, USS *Henry Brinker* was assigned to the North Atlantic Blockading Squadron, where she provided valuable

9. Blue-Water Black Bluejackets

This rendering of USS *Henry Brinker* was prepared as a preliminary concept painting of *Brinker* by Patrick O'Brien. The rendering was the result of research by six maritime and naval historians based upon fragmentary data regarding what the ship may have looked like. No other drawings or photographs of *Brinker* are known to exist. What is known is that *Brinker* had to rely upon its Black sailors to stay afloat because the additional weight of her forward pivoting gun caused her hull planks to open, causing her to leak constantly. Her watchful crew had to keep her pumps going to keep her from sinking until she could be repaired. (Author's collections)

service in actions on inland and coastal waters. She participated in the capture of New Bern, North Carolina, where she enlisted her first fugitives.

Acting master's mate Thomas C. Barton served on the *Henry Brinker* after receiving the Medal of Honor for heroic actions in October 1862 while on board USS *Hunchback,* a New York ferryboat that, like the *Brinker,* was converted into a gunboat. Barton would help train *Brinker's* new sailors and she would have many of them. Although the precise number of sailors assigned to *Brinker* is unknown, an analysis of similar size and equally armed vessels indicates that her ship's complement was probably 57 sailors. This would mean that a typical watch would likely have consisted of at least 14 sailors; and, for much of the war, at least one-quarter of her Black sailors participated in each watch. During the entire war, *Brinker*

Black Sailors in the Civil War

was periodically assigned 23 different Black enlistees. Samuel W. Brigham, a 19-year-old from Westborough, Massachusetts, was one of them. A shoemaker by profession, he mustered aboard *Brinker* on 30 September 1863. Brigham was joined that September by James E. Gordon, Samuel Whiting, Moses Johnson, Anderson Ward, John Wright and Joseph Moseley. Three of these (Gordon, Moseley and Johnson) were from Norfolk. Four hundred nineteen Black sailors came from Norfolk during the war. In December 1863 a new crew of all Black sailors was mustered aboard *Brinker*, principally a blue-water warship, including Charles Granby, Andrew Ward, Cornelius Bell, Robert Langden, John Latimer, George Smith, and James Weaver; and, again, a large number of these were from Virginia. That fact isn't surprising when you consider that of the roughly 18,000 Black Civil War sailors who fought for the Union during the war, Virginia is currently known to have contributed 2,822 of them. Maryland is presently known to have contributed 2,332. According to the National Park Service's *Civil War Soldier and Sailor System* database, which contains the records of the approximately 18,000 Black Navy war veterans, those two States alone contributed nearly 29 percent of the total number of Blacks serving as sailors during the war.

All Black crews could be found aboard brown-water vessels too. Except for her ten officers, who were all White, the entire crew of USS *Petrel* was Black. *Petrel* was a brown-water gunboat that in April 1864 was operating on the Yazoo River. *Petrel's* commander, Thomas McElroy, was in search of cotton and glory. Near Yazoo City he had cut down a tree in search of firewood, when his ship came under attack from a pair of Rebel 12-pound Parrot guns. He immediately ordered the crew to cast off and make upriver to get away from the Confederate guns. In doing so, *Petrel* ran aground. Unwilling to let their prize escape, the Rebels moved the guns to within 400 yards of the hard-stuck Union ship. Their first shot severed *Petrel's* steam lines. Their second shot hit her powder magazine, which blew the legs off gunner's mate, Charles Seitz. Their third shot burst the ship's boilers. At this point McElroy ordered his crew to prepare to burn the ship. He also ordered the sailors to be armed. Then things got confusing. McElroy said he never ordered the crew to abandon ship, but his junior officers insisted that he did. McElroy's report noted that right after the boilers blew up, "the officers jumped on the bank, followed by the crew, and made a disgraceful run for the *Prairie Bird*, leaving with me the pilot, Kimble Ware, in the pilot house, and Quartermaster J.H. Nibbe, who stood his ground when all of the other officers deserted their flag." McElroy, Ware and Nibbe were taken prisoner.

9. Blue-Water Black Bluejackets

Petrel's executive officer, acting ensign M.E. Flanigan, reported a different version of events after the boiler explosion. "The vessel being disabled, and unable to work our guns, the captain gave the order to set the vessel on fire—which was done in three places—arm ourselves and jump ashore." Forty-four sailors made their way to the *Prairie Bird*, including firemen W. Thomas Waites and Morgan Cooper and seamen Ephraim Johnson, Harry West, Randal Morehead and Jerry Brown. Seven of *Petrel's* Black sailors were taken aboard the *General Price*, including firemen Nick Jones and James Monroe, and Adkin Whellis. USS *Covington* received 15 of *Petrel's* Black seamen, including Columbus Richardson, Wesley West and Ephraim Colton. The Black crew believed they were clearly following the lead of their White officers, which they had. Unlike commander McElroy's assessment that his officers and men acted disgracefully, according to acting ensign Flanigan's reporting of events to Rear Admiral David Dixon Porter on 23 April 1864, "during the engagement the officers and men acted most gallantly...."

The schooners *Henry Janes, William Bacon, Adolph Hugel* and *T.A. Ward* were other vessels purchased by the Navy in New York in 1861. All four were fitted out with 13-inch mortars and used by David Dixon Porter's mortar flotilla that shelled Forts Jackson and Saint Phillips below New Orleans and the fortifications and city of Vicksburg. These four mortar schooners were manned by an integrated crew, as shown here. (Library of Congress)

Black Sailors in the Civil War

To help conceal the firing locations of his mortar schooners, David Dixon Porter had trees lashed to their masts as camouflage. This pen and wash drawing was created by R.G. Skerrett in 1904. (Naval History and Heritage Command)

Much larger than *Brinker* and the mortar schooners, the steam sloop-of-war USS *Pawnee* was another example of the versatility of the Union's blue-water navy. She could operate both on inland rivers and coastal waters, as well as at sea, if she had sufficient water under her keel. *Pawnee* first saw service in the earliest days of the war protecting the nation's Capital. She was one of the few ships immediately available to defend Washington. Unfortunately, *Pawnee* was not highly manageable in heavy seas because of her wide beam and shallow ten-foot draft, but her 14-guns made her exceptionally valuable. Between May and August 1861 *Pawnee* served as the big guns of the Potomac Flotilla. She provided much of the inducement for the relatively peaceful surrender of Alexandria, Virginia, on 24 May 1861.

Pawnee saw action throughout the war. During that time her crews consisted of 76 known Black sailors.

The screw frigate USS *Minnesota* was substantially larger than USS *Henry Brinker* and USS *Pawnee*. Built at the Washington Navy Yard in 1854–1855, she was typical of a true blue-water warship. She was over 264

9. Blue-Water Black Bluejackets

feet long, with a 51-foot beam. Her draft was slightly under 24-feet. Her entire ship's complement was supposed to consist of 646 officers and seamen at any given time. Of these, during the war at least 352 were Black sailors. Twelve of them came from plantations in Lancaster County, Virginia, and most of them mustered aboard *Minnesota* on 1 January 1863, including Hiram and Solomon Blackwell, James Wednesday, Moses Marshall and Henderson Cruiser. One-hundred others were from Baltimore (59 Black seamen), Philadelphia (15), New York City (14) and Norfolk (12). Because of the array of armaments aboard—two 10-inch pivoting Dahlgren guns, 28 nine-inch Dahlgren guns, and 14 eight-inch Dahlgren guns—many of *Minnesota's* Blacks served on gun crews.

Minnesota participated in the battle on 8 and 9 March 1862 at Hampton Roads, Virginia, that revolutionized naval warfare. On the first day of the battle the iron-clad CSS *Virginia* steamed out of the Gosport Navy Yard, accompanied by CSS *Teaser* and CSS *Jamestown*. Within hours *Virginia* rammed and sank USS *Cumberland*, one of the Union warships blockading the Confederate port of Norfolk.

Virginia also destroyed USS *Congress*. While attempting to flee CSS *Virginia*, USS *Congress* ran aground. Under heavy bombardment, *Congress* struck her colors. Unable to take the Union ship as a prize, *Congress* was set ablaze using hot shot.

In attempting to escape the same fate, the Union's steam frigate *Minnesota* and sailing frigate *St. Lawrence* went aground too. With these wooden Union warships helpless, it appeared that the Confederacy had discovered the viable way of breaking up the blockade.

For much of the night of 9 March, the only hope for *Minnesota* and *St. Lawrence* was the *Dragon*. Despite her formidable name, USS *Dragon* was no winged monster. She was a lightly armed tug. *Dragon* was one of 418 vessels purchased at the start of the Civil War to establish and maintain the Union's blockade of the South. *Dragon* was purchased in New York in December 1861 and hastily fitted out for naval service at the Brooklyn Navy Yard. *Dragon* was ordered south to Hampton Roads to join the North Atlantic Blockading Squadron in late December, where she was assigned to the James River Flotilla. Part of *Dragon's* duties at Hampton Roads was to attend to the navigational needs of the Union's larger warships, including USS *Cumberland*, USS *Congress*, and USS *Minnesota*. When called upon, *Dragon* was also expected to serve as a patrol craft and dispatch ship. With fears growing in the North over the news of CSS *Virginia's* construction, in January 1862, *Dragon* and the tug *Zouave* were ordered to remain on constant duty alongside USS *Cumberland* and *Congress* in case of an attack by

Black Sailors in the Civil War

Virginia, ready to tow both Union warships to "an advantageous position" if attacked. As envisioned, the diminutive *Dragon* did indeed play a crucial role in attempting to save a Union vessel from CSS *Virginia*, only not the ones Flag Officer Goldsborough initially thought.

Instead of saving *Cumberland* or *Congress*, *Dragon* assisted USS *Minnesota* during the Battle at Hampton Roads on 8 March 1862. When *Minnesota* became grounded during the attack of CSS *Virginia*, the tug was called upon to pull the warship free. In attempting to extricate *Minnesota*, *Dragon* received a shot through her boiler, which exploded, causing extensive damage to the little vessel. If not for the timely intervention of USS *Monitor* the following day, both *Dragon* and *Minnesota* would have likely suffered the same fate as *Congress* and *Cumberland*.

As tiny as *Dragon* was, from 1863 to 1865 she had 27 Black sailors as part of her complement.

Blue-water crews took numerous prizes. Most were ships and their cargoes. Some were highly valuable, others were not.

In many cases sailors received little prize money because of the number of warships involved in a capture. A case in point was the seizure of the Confederate sloop *Secesh* at the entrance to Lawford Channel off Charleston on 15 May 1863. The Rebel ship was carrying 86 bales of cotton, one barrel of tobacco and a barrel of near worthless pitch. In informing Navy Secretary Welles of the capture on 16 May 1863, the captain of USS *Canandaigua* reported, "All of the vessels now composing the blockading force off Charleston will probably claim to share in the capture. Their names are as follows: US Steam frigate *New Ironside*, US steam frigate *Powhatan*, US steam sloop *Canandaigua*, US steam sloop *Housatonic*, USS *Flag*, USS *Stettin*, USS *Augusta*, USS *Unadilla*, USS *Huron*, USS *Paul Jones*, USS *South Carolina*, USS *Marblehead*, USS *Lodona*, USS *Wamsutta*, USS *Dandelion*, and US schooner *Para*." By the time the shares were parceled out with all these crews each sailor received pocket change as prize money.

Likewise, the crews of USS *Potomska* and *Pocahontas* received little from the sale of the 1,858 pieces of railroad track-iron they captured. The seizure didn't net much because T-iron, as it was known, was cheap and abundant in the North; but, in this case, it was particularly important that it was confiscated. In the South T-iron was precious because it was being used as a substitute armor for Confederate iron-clads. The seizure may have kept the Rebels from creating at least one or two new armored warships. Some southern rail lines were intentionally torn up just to reuse the T-iron for ship armor.

9. Blue-Water Black Bluejackets

During the war, *Pocahontas* was manned by 36 Black sailors. *Potomska* was manned by 47. Twenty-three of *Potomska's* crew were Black Marylanders. They likely came aboard while the ship was in Baltimore undergoing repairs in 1864. An especially large contingent mustered aboard on 30 September 1864, including James Taylor, Joseph Williams, Samuel Strikes, Daniel Thomas, Charles Brown, Levin Collins, Thomas Gross, Nicholas Cooler, James Jenkins, Robert Cavel, Robert F. Smith, James H. Johnson, Joseph Johnson and Robert Brown. Many of these Marylanders had been watermen before the war. Because of their experience as watermen, many of *Potomska's* sailors that mustered aboard in September 1864 were quickly reassigned to other ships.

Among the most successful prize takers was USS *Sagamore*, which took 20 ships trying to evade the blockade; USS *Kanawha*, which captured 16 vessels; USS *San Jacinto*, which seized 15 ships; and *R.R. Cuyler*, which also captured 15 vessels. Crewmembers each got a piece of the prize money from the sale of any properly seized ships. That was a unique experience for most Black crewmembers. "As the time come on the Black man gets to handle a little silver and greenbacks then he used to. Slaves didn't hardly ever handle any money long as he lives. He never buys nothing, he have no use for money," said Ambus Gray.[1] Frank Adamson from South Carolina couldn't agree more. "I seen some money, but never owned any then."[2] Now, Black sailors were receiving monthly pay, plus prize money. That meant a lot, as former South Carolina slave Ezra Adams observed: "I know from experience that poor folks feels better when they has food in their frame and a few dimes to jingle in their pockets."[3]

10

Brown-Water Black Bluejackets

There were downsides to brown-water service. Some operations—like Rear Admiral David Porter's Yazoo River Expedition—would be catastrophic. It was an ill-conceived attempt to discover a backway into Vicksburg by ascending the Yazoo River. In doing so, Porter risked his entire fleet because the upper Yazoo was basically a dense cypress swamp. On the river between February and April 1863 Flag Officer David Dixon Porter was hell bent on keeping his fleet moving despite the overgrowth. Porter knew his *City*-class gunboats were highly versatile, even using them on the Yazoo as tree extractors. To clear trees in the bayou, he had his ships ram any cypress trees that blocked the way.

Operating at three-knots, Porter's powerful ships bow-butted tree after tree, knocking each over on an angle on the first strike. The second strike knocked them down. Wrapped with a chain, the felled trees were yanked out like pulled teeth.

Porter's flotilla continued clearing trees in this fashion, ramming its way upriver. There was a downside to this method of tree clearing. Most of the trees were covered with critters and each boat strike brought down a shower of snakes, lizards, raccoons, and possums, as well as hanging moss and dead branches. Sweepers were stationed on the bows of the ships to clear the decks of the downed branch huggers.

The river became so dense with undergrowth that General William T. Sherman assured Porter that, "Before you fellows get through, you won't have a smokestack or a boat among you."[1]

As the Yazoo narrowed, Confederate raiders began sniping at Porter's boats. The Rebels also felled trees in front and behind to bottle up his boats. Instead of discovering a backdoor into Vicksburg, Porter realized he had steamed his fleet into a trap. Fearful of the worst, Porter issued instructions to button up his boats in anticipation of being boarded by Rebel raiding parties. He also issued orders regarding the potential destruction of

10. Brown-Water Black Bluejackets

Panther Swamp National Wildlife Refuge on the outskirts of Yazoo City, Mississippi, which illustrates what Porter had to contend with. (Library of Congress)

his fleet; in case it indeed became bottled up. He hastily retreated. One of Porter's principal accomplishments on the Yazoo was evacuating hundreds of slave families. Those refugees were dutifully reported to Washington. Many of Porter's officers—such as his station commandant at Cairo, Captain A.M. Pennock—didn't do this. Pennock and his station skippers were remiss in submitting reports of contrabands employed in naval service. Porter had to chide them to comply. "I have not received any report from any of the upper [river] vessels about the contrabands. Please attend to this, as the Department seems to be very particular. Send me a list of them; also those you have employed on [your] station." Because of such lax reporting, we may never know the full extent of Black service to the Navy.

All along the tributaries and main riverways, runaways in the South enlisted the first chance they got. That is what Virginia Davis' father, Isaac Johnson, did. She told an interviewer with the slave narrative project, "He tried to get in the Army and he did get in the Navy." "They said he was younger than he told his age," Ms. Davis recollected.[2] She said he enlisted for three years and served on the Mississippi River. The only Isaac Johnson listed in the National Park Service's Black sailor database who agreed to serve for three years said he was 21 when he enlisted on 29 June 1864 as

Black Sailors in the Civil War

a landsman at Washington, D.C. He served aboard USS *Ella* until the end of the war, but he never served on the Mississippi as his daughter thought.

Part of the Navy's Potomac Flotilla, *Ella* was a side-wheel steamer that was purchased second-hand by the Navy to serve as a dispatch and patrol boat on Virginia's tidal waterways. In that latter capacity, she would occasionally pick up runaways. *Ella* had a normal complement of 39 sailors and was based at the Washington Navy Yard. Entering service in 1862, throughout the war, *Ella* was manned by over 72 Black sailors. Most said they were either born in Virginia (29 enlistees), the District of Columbia (15) or Maryland (10). Isaac Johnson was one of those who said he was born in Washington, D.C. Commissioned as a warship in August 1862, the first Black seamen to muster aboard *Ella* were Isaac Cook, Nicholas Rooney, Francis Casey, Albert Mitchell and William Lewis. All five first came aboard in January 1863.

On the Mississippi, in addition to fighting, Federal gunboats had to protect commercial steamboats against guerrilla attacks. Such a thing occurred at Cole's Creek, Mississippi, on 18 February 1865, when the steamer *Mittie Stephens* was attempting to take on 100 bales of "properly permitted" cotton when she came under Rebel attack. Luckily, the *Mattie Stephens* was under the protection of USS *Forest Rose*, which opened fire on the Confederate raiding party as soon as the merchant ship was out of the line of fire. The firefight was lopsided, with the Union gunboat firing four 32-pound shells with five-second fuses, four 24-pound shells with three-second fuses, and six rounds of canister shot in a matter of minutes. The guerrillas barely had time to set fire to the cotton before being forced to flee for their lives.

The *Forest Rose* immediately landed sailors who extinguished the fire, saving all but five bales. At the time of this engagement, 28 of *Forest Rose's* sailors were Black. Some of these sailors were likely among the 70 refugees she picked up on the Mississippi River on 15 September 1864.

11

The Great Exodus in 1862 and 1863

One of the greatest exoduses from captivity occurred at the conclusion of the Union's disastrous Peninsular Campaign in the summer of 1862. After victories at Williamsburg and Yorktown Union forces steadily moved up the Peninsula between the James and York Rivers in a move to capture Richmond. Union forces got to within miles of the Confederate capitol following victories Williamsburg on 5 and 6 May, before being defeated at the battle of Seven Pines on May 31 and the Seven Days Battles between 26 June and 3 July. Believing that his Army was vastly outnumber by more than 200,000 Rebels, Union General George McClellan accepted the defeat as a sign of further disasters to come and ordered a retreat down the Peninsula to Harrison's Landing, with the Confederate hot on his Army's heels.

Located on the James River side of the Peninsula, Harrison's Landing was the site of a Union supply depot and the location of a United States Sanitary Commission field hospital operated by Frederick Law Olmsted. Olmsted, who served as the Commission's General Secretary from 1861 to 1863, was a genius at organizing complex operations. He and his fellow directors raised over $15 million to support wounded and injured Union soldiers. He was described as a leader who "directs everything in the fewest possible words.... He is a great organizer—and he is a great administrator, because he comprehends details, but trusts his subordinates...."[1] Black labor at Harrison's Landing was a key to Olmsted's success. There, 1,000 runaways were organized into labor gangs that quickly descended upon arriving transports, hospital ships, and supply barges.

According to the Union's Quartermaster General, Montgomery Meigs, these men "were most effective in landing stores from the transports, bearing fatigue and exposure in that unhealthy climate much longer than the White soldiers and laborers, who soon broke down alongside of them. Their assistance was there of the greatest value...."[2] To Meigs' way of thinking, "The labor of able-bodied [Black] men, with that of [Black] women able to wash for the [Harrison's Landing] hospital, has supported all who have come directly under charge of this department upon the Potomac."[3] Meigs went further in his praise. "Negro laborers have been of great value in the work of this department, and indeed at all points of the coast they have been a much-needed aid to its operations."[4] (Meigs always wished that President Lincoln had emancipated all slaves at the start of the war and used the massive enlistments of Whites and Blacks to steamroll the South into submission.[5]) Olmsted also deeply appreciated the help, and he was picky about those he opted to work with. "If they are good, he relies on them, if they are weak, there's an end of them," said Katharine Prescott Wormeley, one of his early volunteers. She was among the first of those who volunteered to serve with Olmsted's Sanitary Commission's Hospital Transport Service, which also had a base at White House on the Pamunky River in addition to its facilities at Harrison's Landing on the James River. Katharine Wormeley learned to hate both places. "May I never see the pretty poisonous Pamunky again," she told her mother towards the end of her tenure with the Transport Service in June 1862.[6]

At first blush, others thought White House and the Pamunky were idyllic. The approach to White House was described by war correspondent Joel Harris, who arrived there in May 1862, as possessing "[a] beautiful curve of a mile in length, the outer side of which was a low bluff surmounted by trees, changed the course of the river. In the centre of this curve was the White House and its grounds, and above it was the wharves and landings. Land and water blended to produce the scene; and the life given it by the moving craft on the river ... render the whole most picturesque." For volunteers like Katharine Wormeley, there was nothing charming about White House. It was a place of carnage, death, and cruelty.

These volunteers worked with field surgeons to help stabilize injured Union soldiers and then transport them to larger medical facilities often far from the battlefield in Washington or New York City using a fleet of second-hand transport ships furnished by the Army's Quartermaster's Department. The transports, of which the *Daniel Webster* was the first, served as floating hospitals. Each hospital ship was overseen by a surgeon-in-charge who had male nurses and a hopefully competent medical staff under them. The female volunteers were responsible for a ship's pantry and for preparing it to receive patients, including always having fresh linen and bedding and an ample supply of wholesome food to eat. During the last two months of that summer the hospital ships were furnished with nearly 43,000 new sheets and just under 50,000 new pillow

11. The Great Exodus in 1862 and 1863

cases. The most common foods served aboard the ships were beef bouillon, jelly- or butter-bread and milk-bread. Between 1 July and 31 August, the hospital ships utilized 634 pounds of liquid beef stock and over 1,000 pounds of solid stock, plus nearly 7,000 jars of jelly. Milk-bread was created by mashing up hardtack biscuits into buckets full of warm milk, plus an ample supply of sweetener. Of all the canned goods available to the ladies, nothing measured up to condensed milk. "Oh, that precious condensed milk, more precious to us ... than beef essence" (beef bouillon), wrote Katharine Wormeley to her mother on 5 June 1862, while the younger woman was in service aboard the *Wilson Small*.[7]

The arrival of any Sanitary Commission supply steamer or any commercial vessel was a thrill for the ladies of the hospital service. They'd be the first to board the supply ships and they'd requisition whatever they wanted.

"Essence of beef! We'll want all that," recounted Miss Wormeley of one raiding party on 23 May 1862.[8] While the volunteers were supposed to take what they needed from the supply ships, they began taking things from sutler's ships too. "Kleptomania is the prevailing disease among us. We think nothing of [distracting] the proprietor [from] some nicety ... and then pocketing the article," wrote Miss Wormeley to her mother. Stolen items included such things as corkscrews, nutmeg-graters and eating utensils. Miss Wormeley, admittedly, wasn't a very good thief. She confined her larceny to stealing tin pails, which she said she took, "with an abstracted air." The ladies justified their actions by telling themselves, as Miss Wormeley told her mother, "to us who remain here, such articles are as precious as if they were made of gold."[9]

Miss Wormeley confessed to acquiring other bad habits. "I drink coffee in excess," she informed her mother, "and whiskey [with quinine] occasionally, and eat alarming dinners."[10] Much of this overindulgence was undoubtedly to help dull the pain of what they witnessed each day.

The ladies were also responsible for seeing that every soldier was dressed in clean or new personal clothing. That summer the ladies of the Hospital Transport Service and the Sanitary Commission's store boats, which serviced healthy soldiers in the field, distributed over 48,000 new pairs of pants, approximately 89,000 shirts and almost 80,000 pairs of socks to those in their care. New attire was also furnished to any of the contrabands in the hospital ships service who served as stretcher barriers. They also prepared simple stimulants, such as brandy-water and spiked lemonade for the wounded soldiers. The ladies also oversaw an army of contraband laborers in doing the laundry and carrying out other simple chores.

Merchant crewmen and contraband relief workers at White House Landing. In May 1862 Black merchant seaman Samuel Granger enlisted at White House to serve aboard USS *Sebago* for a three-year term as a cook. Among *Sebago's* oldest Black bluejackets was Alex Cole, who enlisted on 5 July 1862 during the Union withdrawal from the Peninsular Campaign. At the time Cole was 44 years old and received an enlistment rating as a first-class boy. (Library of Congress)

Following every hostile engagement, the hospital ships were bursting with the wounded, often to a point where every available inch of deck space was covered by bleeding soldiers. During the voyages to the designated receiving shore hospitals, the ladies were busy preparing food, writing letters to loved ones, which many times were the man's last words home, or keeping pesky flies at bay by ensuring patients were covered by mosquito-netting if they were unable to swat them away themselves. The flies that summer were said to be of Egyptian proportion.

The ladies were also responsible for ensuring that the ship-board medical staffs had a constant source of hot water, and they would fill in

11. The Great Exodus in 1862 and 1863

when the shore field hospital staff had more than their hands full tending to the wounded. This support usually involved caring for excess soldiers placed in open fields awaiting care. During occasional rainstorms, it was left to the ladies and their contraband stretcher barriers to move hundreds of wounded men hastily from open fields into box cars of the Richmond and York River Railroad or other places of shelter.

Even though the ships assigned to the Sanitary Commission were provided by the Army's Quartermaster Corps, Navy vessels rendered great assistance to the medical teams. Among those that were highly supportive of the Hospital Transport Service's efforts was USS *Sebago*. This double-ended steamship was particularly helpful. Its crew furnished the Sanitary Commission Hospital Transport Service staff with a field tent that was converted into a massive field kitchen that could feed 4,000 men a week if necessary. *Sebago* crew of 156 sailors also lent 12 large caldrons and camp-kettles, plus two of its cooks and six seamen to help prepare the food for the sick. *Sebago's* crew also provided much of the food that was served; undoubtedly foodstuffs liberated by its crew from nearby farms. This field-kitchen could prepare a minimum of 20 to 30 buckets full of soup daily for the walking-wounded. All the meals for the hospital ships' bed-ridden patients were prepared separately by the ladies in galley kitchens, which were controlled by military cooks. To ensure that all the wounded men received a proper diet, the ladies had to use every trick available to them to convince the cranky cooks to cooperate. This was a constant frustration, as Katharine Wormeley noted to her mother, when she wrote, "We order, make ready, prepare; and then it is hard to find that the instant our backs were turned everything came to a standstill, and that dinner for the sick men can't be ready at the right moment without some superhuman exertion on our parts."[11] *Sebago's* crew occasionally volunteered to fill in for the ladies by taking the night-watch on the wards in place of the exhausted women.

Like *Sebago's* entire crew, Assistant Quartermaster Charles G. Sawtelle had a special sweet spot in his heart for the hospital service's ladies, frequently sending an orderly by with bouquets of magnolia, jessamine, and honeysuckle to brighten up their ship-board pantries and personal cabins. This was something southerners quickly noticed about the Yankees. They had a fondness for flowers. Francis Gaines Tinsley observed as much when she wrote: "the Yankees were perfectly devoted to flowers."[12] She noted that whenever she threw her withered ones out into her yard. The Union guards would quickly gather them up to take back to their camps. This gave her the idea of going into the bouquet business. She had her butler make-up bouquets which sold like hotcakes at the camps.

Black Sailors in the Civil War

Charles Sawtelle also furnished the ladies with baskets full of mint, and then showed up on their gangplanks to instruct them on the finer art of making mint-juleps. Katharine Wormeley called this an "improper thing," but she changed her opinion of his conduct after tasting one. She went on to assure her mother, "You may think it very vulgar but let me tell you it is very good; and you would think so too if you had been up all night, with the thermometer at 90 degrees."[13]

Sebago, with her single 100-pound Parrott gun and 11-inch Dahlgren gun, was there along with other Union gunboats, including USS *Galena*, which Katharine Wormeley thought was extremely ugly, and USS *Maratanza* and *Tioga*, to cover the Hospital Transports Service's withdrawal from White House only hours before Confederate forces occupied the place.

The Union Navy's prize ship—USS *Monitor*—also was on hand to furnish its fire support. Katharine Wormeley didn't think much of *Monitor*. It was tiny. Wormeley told her mother, "You don't imagine what a little

USS *Tioga*'s integrated crew in 1862. (Naval History and Heritage Command)

11. The Great Exodus in 1862 and 1863

tray of a thing she is,—I didn't." "She is literally nothing but a flat tray, a foot and a half out of water, with what looks like a small gasometer in the middle of her."[14]

What Miss Wormeley didn't realize at the time was the *Monitor* had only a half year left to live.

Between 1861 and 1865 the Union Navy employed 60 vessels just to supply its fleet a sea and its gunboats operating on rivers. These were called "supply ships," and among the earliest was USS *Supply*, USS *Rescue*, USS *Relief*, USS *Release*, and USS *Rhode Island*. Such ships had routine schedules to supply other ships on blockade duty or on riverine missions, but occasionally they were given specific assignments. The commander of USS *Cambridge* gave *Rescue* such an assignment in November 1861 when he ordered her to return immediately to Hampton Roads with a number of contrabands who had taken refuge aboard his ship. The contrabands were eating his ship out of house and home. According to the *Cambridge's* commander, William Parker, his guests "are rapidly consuming the provisions of this vessel, and it is very inconvenient to keep them here any longer, most of them being dirty, ragged, and lousy."

Rhode Island, as example, was purchased in 1861 especially for this purpose. She was a large side-wheel sea steamer of about 1,500 tons that acted principally like a floating naval supply depot. A typical supply run for *Rhode Island* was from New York to Key West and consumed 22 days. During that time, she often was required to service over 100 ships along the way. She was particularly capable of transporting large quantities of fresh beef and produce preserved in a massive onboard icehouse. Every vessel she visited customarily received two days' worth of refrigerated beef and vegetables per trip. A supply of ice was always distributed to each ship to keep the beef cold, and a little extra ice was always given out to the medical staff for treating the sick and injured. Such provision ships could also supply small amounts of coal, gunpowder, shot and shells of various sizes, medicine, clothing, bedding, and water as necessary. Personal and official mail was also picked up and delivered by the supply ships. Discharged and assigned sailors were also transported to and from the vessels on station, as were any captured prisoners. *Rhode Island's* usual complement was 257 sailors. Thirty-six Black sailors are known to have served aboard *Rhode Island* during the war, among them was John Joseph Blyden, Henry Francis, Joseph Clay, Joseph King, Josiah Clyett, Henry Lewis, and Cyrus Parkman.

On 29 December 1862, under the command of Commander John P. Bankhead, *Monitor* set out for Beaufort, North Carolina, to join the

Black Sailors in the Civil War

blockade. The voyage South was terrible. Under tow from USS *Rhode Island*, *Monitor* and her tethered partner were battered by a violent storm. On 30 December, the iron-clad began taking on water, particularly around the base of the turret, which had supposedly been well caulked with oakum that was gradually being washed out by the succession of violent waves that struck the ship. At first the water seeping through the small, yet widening opening, was handled well by the ship's Worthington simplex bilge pumps. Worthington steam pumps were state-of-the-art. Henry Worthington, their creator, was a valued colleague of John Ericsson, and his works were in Greenport, New York, where *Monitor* was assembled.

The pumps were furnished in January 1862. One of the pumps may well have been *Monitor's* Achilles' heel. In examining a pump following its recovery in 2001, the pump appeared to have failed because of a flawed casting. The cast plunger apparently broke under the pressure of pumping such a volume of water. With or without the factor of the broken plunger, as the storm intensified, it was clear that the Worthington pumps were unable to keep up with the rising water accumulating in the tossing vessel. In response, the ship's powerful Adams Centrifuge pump was employed. Hand pumps and buckets were used too, but nothing was working as the storm worsened. By 9:00 p.m. the water inside the ship was over a foot deep in places. With all the influx of water, within an hour *Monitor's* boiler fires went out, and created a critical condition. At 10:00 p.m. Commander Bankhead ordered a red distress lantern hung above the turret to alert *Rhode Island* of *Monitor's* plight. In her compromised condition, *Monitor* began transferring sailors to *Rhode Island* a few at a time. By midnight, most of the sailors were safely aboard *Rhode Island*. Some refused to abandon ship, fearing they'd be swept into the churning ocean. A few already had been. The reluctant sailors preferred to take their chances with the *Monitor*, dimly hoping that she might somehow weather the storm. Bankhead came off at about 12:30 in the last rescue boat, begging those who refused to leave to join him. *Monitor* was bobbing up and down like a heavily weighted cork in the unrelenting troughs and swells. Her red distress lantern, hoisted high above her turret, successively appeared, then disappeared, to those aboard *Rhode Island*. Each time the red lantern appeared, there was hope that the ship might survive. Finally, at about 1:00 a.m., on 31 December, the signal light vanished. The ship had foundered off Cape Hatteras, North Carolina, taking 16 sailors with her.

Navy Secretary Gideon Welles was greatly affected by the news of *Monitor's* loss, recording in his diary for 3 January 1863, "She is a primary representative of a class identified with my administration of the

11. The Great Exodus in 1862 and 1863

Navy. Her novel construction and qualities I adopted, and she was built amidst obloquy and ridicule. Such a change in the character of a fighting vessel few naval men, or any Secretary under their influence, would have taken the responsibility of adopting."[15] Two days later, after conferring with Commander Bankhead about the loss of *Monitor*, Welles' diary entry notes: "For months I have been berated and abused because I had not more vessels of the *Monitor* class under contract. Her success with the [*Virginia*] when she was under the trial as an experiment made men wild, and they censured me for not having built a fleet when she was constructed. Now that she is lost, the same persons," who Welles dubbed "factious fools" and "officious blockheads," "will be likely to assail me for expending money on such a craft."[16] In this case, Welles would prove to have the last word, writing in his 1865 report as Secretary of the Navy: "On a public appeal to the mechanical ingenuity of our countrymen, this want was supplied by the *Monitor*, a turreted vessel, which as soon as completed, vindicated its capability, and the model thus projected has been adopted and extensively copied abroad. This class of vessels stands as the undoubted and acknowledged best defence [*sic*] of our shores against any naval armament at present in existence."

Barges used to remove contrabands from White House Landing. (Library of Congress)

Black Sailors in the Civil War

At White House on the Pamunky River, any White shore-people wishing to leave were placed aboard steamships. The Navy also furnished numerous barges for hauling away Sanitary Commission and Army supplies. It also had a small armada of vessels on hand to provide the barges with the necessary tows down river. Barges were also thoughtfully provided to handle the expected exodus of hundreds of contrabands, who swarmed to White House with everything they could carry.

Separate barges were provided for Black men and for women and children. No one who wished to leave was left behind. All were towed away in the nick of time. Katharine Wormeley was on one of the tow boats. Her last vision of White House was the smoke bellowing up from its burning frame over the treetops as she steamed to safety down river. "The smoke at White House is growing denser and denser, and we hear cannon,—which we take to mean that the gunboats are getting a chance at the enemy," she wrote home on 27 June.[17]

By mid–July 1862 the Hospital Transport Service was disbanded. Its hospital ships were turned back to the Quartermaster's Division and its faithful and by then worn-out volunteers, such as Katharine Wormeley, were sent home.

The second great exodus occurred on 2 June 1862 in an operation that was led by Moses (Harriet Tubman) and Colonel James Montgomery. It involved sending a raiding part up the Combahee River in South Carolina to free slaves held on the Blake, Lowndes, Middleton, Nemours, and Heyward rice plantations. The Navy provided

Harriet Tubman as photographed by Harvey B. Lindsley. (Library of Congress)

11. The Great Exodus in 1862 and 1863

three gunboats for the operation and the Army assigned African American soldiers from the Second Regiment of South Carolina Volunteers to the task.

The military purpose for the expedition, known as the Combahee River Raid, was to destroy southern supplies, bridges and Rebel railroad rolling stock, as well as clear Confederate mines from the river.

Tubman knew where the mines were planted thanks to her network of slave-spies. The slaves' underground network had also alerted the workers of Moses' coming, and as soon as the gunboats arrived hundreds flocked to the shoreline with everything of value. While some of the Black soldiers formed a protective perimeter, others descended upon the plantations—setting fires and creating general chaos that caused the owners to flee. Simultaneously, the Navy landed boats to take on as many runaways as was safely possible, but those waiting on shore for a chance at freedom grabbed onto the boats and would not let them go for fear of being left behind. Harriet Tubman tried to assure them that all would be taken out of bondage, but their hands still clung tightly to the boats. Colonel Montgomery called to Tubman with a solution. "Moses, you'll have to give them a song," he shouted, and she sang:

> "Of all the whole creation in the East or in the West,
> The glorious Yankee nation is the greatest and the best.
> Come along! Come along! Don't be alarmed,
> Uncle Sam is rich enough to give you all a farm."[18]

At the end of her verse the runaways on land threw up their hands in praise and shouted out "glory, glory." As soon as the hands were held on high the oarsmen pushed off. All and all, nearly 800 contrabands were ultimately taken aboard the gunboats that day, including a pair of pigs that were quickly dubbed "Jeff Davis" and "P.T.G. Beauregard." The raid was a stunning success, but went unreported until the story broke in *The Commonwealth*, a Boston abolitionist newspaper, on 10 July 1863 when it reported:

> "Col. Montgomery and his gallant band of 300 black soldiers [the number was actually 170], under the guidance of a black woman, dashed into the enemy's country, struck a bold and effective blow, destroying millions of dollars' worth of commissary stores, cotton and lordly dwellings, and striking terror into the hearts of rebeldom, brought off near 800 slaves and thousands of dollars' worth of property, without losing a man or receiving a scratch. It was a glorious consummation."

What was oddly coincidental about this exodus was that when the Spanish first charted the Combahee in 1520, they named it the "River

Black Sailors in the Civil War

Jordan." Now, a new Moses had led her people out of bondage on the river Jordan.

Most Union naval officers relied on Blacks as spies, including Rear Admiral John Dahlgren. While operating off Georgetown, South Carolina, he ordered a subordinate officer to furnish transportation for several Black men, telling the officer, "I send the colored men, Fred, Williams and Billy, by *Geranium*, and desire you will land them at such point and at such time as they desire. Furnish them with whatever they ask for to assist them. They will inform you where they will return and have a boat about the spot every night the weather permits. I desire that particular attention shall be given to the matter, as I expect these men, particularly Williams, will bring me useful information."

Many runaways weren't spies, but they knew an awful lot. Kent Newton was one such font of nautical knowledge. He was picked up by USS *Monticello* on 30 December 1861 and gave the ship's commander, Lieutenant Daniel L. Braine, a great deal of vital intelligence about what was happening in and around Wilmington, North Carolina, at the time. Newton had worked for several years on the ferryboats that serviced Wilmington and, as result, he was fully aware of what was happening all along Wilmington's 19-mile channel, including the fact that the Rebels had just sunk four large stone cribs as obstacles around New Inlet. This knowledge effectively bottled up that section of the channel to any ships with a draft greater than a nine-foot, including their own. In effect, the South had blockaded their own port access in this area. Originally from North Carolina, Newton was the first contraband to serve aboard USS *Monticello*. He enlisted in the Navy in January 1862. He ultimately was one of two Black sailors to serve aboard *Monticello* in 1862. He reenlisted multiple times, serving on *Monticello* and several other vessels throughout the war, including USS *Wabash*, *Powhatan*, and *Wanderer*. Within a matter of days, another recruited runaway sought sanctuary with the Navy off Wilmington. Hamilton Davis was taken aboard USS *Chippewa* on 11 January 1862. According to Lieutenant Andrew Bryson, commanding *Chippewa*, Davis confirmed everything Newton had said to Lieutenant Braine.

According to Bryson's official report to Flag Officer Goldsborough, published in Series I, Volume Six of the *Official Records of the Union and Confederate Navies in the War of the Rebellion*, Davis signed aboard *Chippewa* for one year at a compensation of $10 a month. Unfortunately, Davis' service does not appear in the National Park Service's Black Sailors Database. Only one Black sailor—Edward Hewitt—is listed as serving aboard *Chippewa* during the war. What happened to Davis is unclear,

11. The Great Exodus in 1862 and 1863

but regardless of this, Newton and Davis were clearly among the earliest self-emancipated Americans to enlist in naval service during the war.

While *Mount Vernon* and *Chippewa* were steaming north for repairs the remaining Union vessels off Roanoke Island attacked and captured Elizabeth City, North Carolina, on 10 February. In that action two sailors died and seven were wounded. James A. Young, a 42-year-old Black sailor from Maryland, was among the injured. He was wounded by flying wood splinters and his neck and face were burned while serving aboard USS *Valley City*. Young was among the first three Blacks of the 54 Black bluejackets that ultimately served aboard this vessel during the war.

12

Seizing the Lower Mississippi: David Farragut, the Minority Flag Officer

While the Peninsular Campaign was a fiasco for the Army, and the Combahee River Raid was a success for both the Army and the Navy, not every operation went well. Nowhere was that more apparent than with the capture of New Orleans. While the capture was a stunning naval success, the aftermath was a naval embarrassment. It showcased just how ill-equipped the Navy was at holding towns and cities. Judging from the angry crowds and defiant mood that greeted the Union Navy at New Orleans, no one there was happy to see anyone dressed in Navy blue. The fall of New Orleans demonstrated how ill prepared the Navy was to serve as an occupying force. Hostile crowds booed and jeered the Federal Navy's initial landing parties. The attempt to raise the American flag over the former United States Mint building was met with angry mobs. That flag flew for a matter of minutes before it was torn down by William Mumford, a local card shark and hothead, who allowed it to be dragged through the streets.

Instead, the Louisiana state flag flew over city hall. Over the course of several days, the mayor, John Monroe, had a clash of wills with Flag Officer David Farragut over the fate of New Orleans. When Farragut asked Monroe for the city's surrender, the mayor refused, saying it was an idle and meaningless ceremony because he wasn't a military man and he lacked the authority to surrender anything; but he advised Farragut on 26 April, that even if he had the authority, he wouldn't do it. "The city is yours by the power of brutal force, and not by any choice or consent of its inhabitants," Monroe insisted.[1] Farragut then demanded that all flags except that of the United States' should be taken down. The mayor replied that no one in his city was willing to do that either. Farragut said he expected the city's inhabitants to respect Union authority. The mayor said he couldn't guarantee the loyalty or respect of any of his citizen except to that government

12. Seizing the Lower Mississippi

which his constituents pledged their allegiance—the Confederacy. Farragut said that if there were any outbreak of hostilities within the area over Union authority, he'd have no alternative but to shell the city, and the shelling might accidently breach the levees. As a precaution, Farragut recommended that the mayor evacuate all women and children from New Orleans within 48 hours to ensure their safety. The mayor called Farragut's threat of shelling the city "utter inanity."[2] Monroe responded that the population in New Orleans numbered over 140,000, and that the town was largely full of women and children with nowhere to go. He assured Farragut that any shelling would kill most of them because none was willing to leave their homes for fear of Union looting. In their back and forth the mayor closed with a response on 28 April that included an even more defiant tone: "We will stand your bombardment, unarmed and undefended as we are. The civilized world will consign to indelible infamy the heart that will conceive the deed and the hand that will dare to consummate it."[3]

By then, Farragut had enough of Monroe's insolence. He advised Monroe that if he wished to communicate any more with him he could have someone signal for a parlay with a handkerchief from the docks.[4] The 29 April 1862 edition of the *New Orleans Bee* characterized Rear Admiral David Farragut as either the "green soldier who caught a Tartar or the luckless gentlemen who drew an elephant at a lottery," concluding that he would soon discover the ferocity of his unbowed prize. New Orleanians mocked the idea of Farragut as a military governor and the notion of naval occupation. Farragut was clearly no civil administrator. Fortunately for Farragut, that role was ideal for Benjamin Butler, who arrived in New Orleans at the head of a Federal Army of occupation the very next day. Butler immediately took charge of the city. The Louisiana state flag came down from city hall and the American flag was hoisted over the old Federal customs house. Butler had Mumford hanged in front of the U.S. Mint on a charge of treason. Under Butler's administration, much of the population was quickly cowed. In short order, anyone who wouldn't take the oath of allegiance to the Union was forcibly expelled from New Orleans. The exiles were able to take few possessions with them. Hundreds of families were sent packing for Confederate lines.

After a woman tried to dump a chamber pot on David Farragut, Butler ordered that any female caught being disrespectful to a Union officer, sailor or soldier was to be treated as if she were a common prostitute. Butler's "Woman Order," (*General Order 28*) was issued on 15 May 1862. The proclamation was applauded in the North and considered an outrage in the South. One outcome of the order was that women in New Orleans stopped spitting in the faces of Union officers. However, for these, and other harsh measures taken while ruling New Orleans as its military governor, Butler earned the nickname "Beast." Jefferson Davis was so outraged by Butler's treatment of southern women that he authorized any Confederate officer who might catch him to hang him. The British government was also outraged by Butler's actions.

Despite being characterized in the South as a despicable Yankee, as a military governor, Benjamin Butler was naturally compassionate. He found New Orleans in need of nearly everything. Its population, which at one point had comprised nearly three-quarters of a million mouths, was on the verge of starvation. Fewer than 30 days' worth of food was available at best, and most of the poor had no means to acquire it. Nearly one-quarter of the recipients were considered destitute. Most of the population was unemployed. In a penniless city, general taxes could not be raised, but much of the cotton on hand was said to be owned by foreign nationals from Spain, France and Prussia (Germany), who claimed that, since it was neutral foreign property, their cotton could not be seized. As a result, Butler imposed a cotton

Uncle Abe: *"Hell! Ben, is that you? Glad to see you!' Butler: "Yes, Uncle Abe. Got through with that New Orleans Job. Cleaned them out and scrubbed them up! Any more scrubbing to give out?"* While General Benjamin Butler was the brunt of many Northern cartoons he was loathed in the South, where one of his various unflattering nicknames was, "Spoons." This label was given because of his petty seizure of a set of personal silverware from a woman fleeing New Orleans. Butler confiscated her family silverware and ordered her held on a charge of smuggling because her permit to leave town only allowed her to take her clothing. This cartoon appeared in the 17 January 1863 edition of *Harper's Weekly*. (Seth Kaller, Inc.)

12. Seizing the Lower Mississippi

brokers' tax. This enabled Butler to raise sufficient funds to employ 1,000 of the city's poor on public works, such as cleaning the city's streets or working on the docks. He also launched a free food program for more than 30,000 people, through the distribution of thousands of pounds of pork, beef, bacon, split peas, and bread. A large percentage of the recipients were Black families, while more than 1,000 of the families receiving food charity were also families of Confederate soldiers. Food shortages affected everybody, especially slaves on the run with little or no cash. Cato Carter learned that all too well. He didn't want to flee, but had no other choice. He recounted his escape this way: "They was a [field hand] workin' in the fiel' and he kept jerkin' the mules and Massa Oll got mad, and he give me a gun and said, 'Go out there and kill that man.' I said, 'Massa Oll, please don't tell me that. I ain't never kilt nobody and I don't want to.' He said, 'Cato, you do what I tell you.' He meant it. I went out to the [worker] and said, 'You has got to leave this minute, and I is, too, 'cause I is 'spose to kill you, only I ain't and Massa Oll will kill me.' He drops the hanes and we run and crawled through the fence and ran away. I hated to go, 'cause things was so bad [during the Civil War], and flour sold for $25.00 a barrel, and pickled pork for $15.00 a barrel. You couldn't buy nothin' lessen with gold. I had plenty of 'federate money, only it wouldn't buy nothin'." Abusing a farm animal was one of the common plantation rules that could be punishable by death.

Additionally, Butler established five asylums for indigent widows and orphans and established a charity hospital.

When several of the consuls of the aforementioned foreign countries in New Orleans complained about Butler's conduct, he was ready to respond with devastating proof of their complicity with the enemy. He promptly presented evidence that all had taken the Oath of Allegiance to the Confederacy, most had contributed cash to the Rebel cause, many had helped raise troops for the South, and many had accepted commissions in the Confederate Army. His evidence was damning. In the case of the Prussian consul he informed Secretary of War Stanton in October 1862, "I find also the house of Richard & Co., the senior partner of which is General Richard in the rebel army, the junior partner, Mr. Krutteschuitt, the brother-in-law of [Judah P.] Benjamin, the rebel Secretary of War, using funds in his hands to purchase arms and collecting the securities of his correspondence before they are due to get funds to loan to the rebel authorities, and now acting Prussian consul here, doing quite as effective service to the rebels as his partner in the field."

Butler had an extraordinary intelligence network. In short order he was able to obtain messages that the French consul in New Orleans attempted to smuggle contraband through the lines. Butler informed Secretary Stanton that "I immediately set about making inquiries through my secret police and finding it a matter of very grave import as affecting the relations of the French consul here, I undertook a personal examination of the subject." Stanton always appreciated Butler's thoroughness. Butler prepared irrefutable dossiers on each subject he investigated, including sworn statements, affidavits and documentary evidence that demonstrated intent if not downright guilt.

Where there were doubts, Butler would seize any questionable property and let the courts ultimately decide its intended use by the Confederacy, even if that took years. Without hesitation, he seized a warehouse full of blankets he believed were destined for the Confederate Army that were hidden in New Orleans. The blankets were promptly distributed to a hospital, but he promised to pay for them at a fair price, if the courts someday decided that they weren't contraband.

Farragut was glad to be rid of the role as New Orleans' military mayor. His comfort zone was standing on the deck of a ship. Prior to Welles' appointment, Farragut was a long shot for command. At the start of the Civil War, he was 76th on the Navy's seniority list. He was a southerner by birth, having been born on 5 July 1801 in Campbell's Station in eastern Tennessee. He was living in Virginia and married to a southerner, named Virginia, so his loyalties were suspect. Despite these impediments, Secretary of the Navy Gideon Welles promoted Farragut ahead of many of Farragut's rivals, appointing him to command the newly formed Southern Blockading Squadron. What was different about Farragut was that he possessed all the qualities that truly mattered to Welles. He avoided politics, intrigues, glorification in the press, and the common propensity of his peers to blame others for his actions if he made a mistake, which was a rare quality in an officer. Most of all, he wasn't a self-promoter, unlike so many of his contemporaries. At the start of the war this made him a relative unknown, but his actions soon earned him fame and honors recognition which he oddly didn't crave. What he was above all else was a detail-oriented hard-charger—a leader who led from the front of his forces. Because of all his estimable qualities, if John Dahlgren was President Lincoln's darling, David Farragut was Gideon Welles' favorite Flag Officer. Commissioned as a midshipman in 1810 under the tutelage of his adopted father, Captain David Porter, Farragut served during the War of 1812 onboard USS *Essex*. Captain Porter already had two sons of his own. Like their father, both William "Dirty Bill" Porter and David Dixon Porter

12. Seizing the Lower Mississippi

became naval officers. Neither of the Porter boys was close. At the time of the Civil War "Dirty Bill" hadn't spoken to his brother in roughly 15 years. Their foster brother, David Farragut, wasn't particularly close to William either. "Dirty Bill" was a fitting nickname for William.

As a younger man, William David Porter had a relationship with a servant that produced an illegitimate child. His father disinherited him. And, after his father died in 1843, "Dirty Bill" began signing documents fraudulently by using his father's name after dropping his own first name. William Porter's son joined the Rebels. A letter from the senior Porter to his son was published in which he said that while the decision to go South was a mistake, he expected his son to do his duty in serving the Confederacy. When Secretary Welles learned of the letter, he recalled the father to Washington. Sheepishly reporting to Welles, Dirty Bill disavowed the letter, claiming it was a fake and that its publication was meant to hurt his career. William Porter told Welles that he was estranged from his son and didn't share his southern sentiments. Welles was certain that William Porter wrote the letter. "William had, not without reason, the reputation of being very untruthful," wrote Welles on 20 August 1862.[5] A lack of candor was a family curse, thought Welles, one that afflicted William's brother, David Dixon Porter, too. "I did not always consider David to be depended upon if he had an end to attain, and he had no hesitation in trampling down a brother officer if it would benefit himself," thought Welles, adding, "He had less heart than William."[6] Despite his doubts, the Secretary supported William Porter because of his meritorious service on the Mississippi, saying, "whatever the infirmities of the man, I recognize his merits as an officer."[7] Welles discussed his feelings with the President, whose opinion was that whatever Welles decided to do would be okay with him. "I will stand by you, come what may," said Lincoln.[8]

Weighing all the facts, Welles decided that there might be a grain of truth in William Porter's claim of innocence. He promoted Porter to the rank of Commodore based upon his exceptional bravery and service. Years after the fact, Admiral Farragut assured Welles that he was certain that the letter was indeed a forgery intended for mischievous purposes. But worse was yet to come for the hapless Commodore. While "Dirty Bill" was lingering close to death at Saint Luke's Hospital in New York City, he had to defend himself against allegations of misrepresentation and insubordination, charges preferred by his adopted brother for writing an offensive letter aimed at his military colleagues. This time, Welles had to do something. He ordered Commodore Porter to present himself to the retirement board. Since December 1861, the Navy's legislatively mandated retirement policy called for officers who had served 45 years or reached the age of 62 to be retired from active duty and placed on the retirement lists at the grade they attained at the time of their retirement. This law would be applied to William Porter. In making that decision, Welles wrote in his diary, "Like all the Porters, he is a courageous, daring, troublesome, reckless officer."[9] William Porter died of heart disease in New York on 1 May 1864.

David Farragut, whose birth name was James, but changed his name to David in honor of his adopted father, David Porter, was given his first command at the age of 13, when he was made the prize master of British ship *Alexander Barclay*.

Farragut continued to advance in his naval career, albeit slowly as the fledgling Navy often had more officers than available berths on ships. After serving in the Caribbean combating piracy, he was finally promoted from midshipman to lieutenant in 1825. Farragut also spent much of his career on shore duty and managed the building of Mare Island Navy Yard in California. Farragut married twice, first in 1823 to Susan Marchant, until her death in 1840. (Susan Marchant Farragut was the sister of William D. Porter's first wife, Jane Marchant Porter, who died in 1835.) In 1843, Farragut married again, taking Virginia Loyall of Norfolk, as his wife.

Despite his home in Norfolk, his southern birth, and his southern wife, Farragut announced he was "sticking to the flag" and moved his family to New York after Virginia seceded in 1861. Navy Secretary Welles initially had doubts about Farragut's loyalty, but gave him a chance to prove himself, giving him command of a blockading squadron and ordering him to capture New Orleans. Farragut accomplished that on 25 April 1862.

After capturing New Orleans, Farragut faced another challenge—getting past Port Hudson on his way to Vicksburg. With his typical thoroughness, Farragut planned every manageable aspect of the passage. Each of his warships was to be tethered to a gunboat. Farragut made it clear in his orders to his officers that the object of their mission was to run past the batteries at Port Hudson with the least possible damage, so that the ships could get above the town to assist the Army in taking Vicksburg. This wasn't to be a broadside shootout. It was to be a mad dash, with Farragut ordering, "well directed fire from our guns, shell and shrapnel at a distance, and grape when within 400 or 500 yards." Farragut's *General Order 135* directed his officers to focus on the enemy's batteries, causing the greatest damage possible at the least possible cost to their ships.[10] For

12. Seizing the Lower Mississippi

Music brought crews together more than almost anything else. Sailors who could play an instrument were highly prized and many were Black sailors, which is why this seaman is front and center. By March 1864 the Union Navy had 34,000 Black and White seamen in service, but instead of coming predominantly from northeastern maritime communities, as might be expected, the average White sailor was about 26 years of age and was from an urban working-class background. Of Black sailors, most were largely from the mid–Atlantic States, including a majority who had no naval traditions either. This placed most novice Navy men on an equal footing. Because all the men were at similar levels of inexperience, integrating crews was not as difficult as it might have been. Music became a great past time aboard ships and bands were comprised of Black and White sailors. It was a tremendous unifier and great diversion. USS *Hartford*, as example, had a fife rail at the base of her mainmast where a sailor with a flute would whistle out tunes while the men worked. (Library of Congress)

the commander of the *Wissahickon*, a shootout was the least of his concerns. This was going to be *Wissahickon's* first combat action and her crew, including 21-year-old Black sailor Robert Benson, were untested. Just surviving the run past the pair of forts would be Lieutenant A.N. Smith's primary concern. *Wissahickon* was a small gunboat that was part of Farragut's fleet. She mounted one 11-inch Dahlgren gun and a single 20-pound gun, plus a pair of 24-pounders for protection. Speed was going to be

Black Sailors in the Civil War

Wissahickon's principal weapon. She could make over 10-knots if challenged, and this was going to be a race for her life. This little steamer went on to fight at Grand Gulf in June 1862 and take part in Farragut's actions against Vicksburg. The ship would go on to fight off Charleston and along the South Carolina and Georgia coast for the remainder of the war.

Farragut held a council of war with his commanders on the morning of 14 March 1862, aboard USS *Hartford* before getting underway, coordinating all the details with his Army counterpart, Major General Nathaniel P. Banks, so his troops could attack Port Hudson on land as the Navy attempted to force its passage that night. Banks was certain his troops were ready to take Port Hudson. During that morning meeting Union mortar schooners began shelling the Rebel batteries to soften them up. By about 10:00 p.m., Farragut's fleet was on the move. As usual, Farragut in *Hartford* took the lead, tethered to USS *Albatross*; followed by USS *Richmond*, secured to USS *Genessee*; and USS *Monongahela*, lashed to USS *Kineo*. USS *Mississippi* occupied the lone sweep position.

The rush up river faced an array of major problems from the start, including: The Confederates' positions along the river were well fortified and their aim was deadly; once past Port Hudson, Farragut's ships had to turn sharply to the west to navigate a bend in the river and just before that bend the Rebels positioned their largest caliber guns, eight- and ten-inch Columbiads, each weighing 9,240 and 15,400 pounds respectively; the river's current was extraordinarily swift and unpredictable, at points swinging some of the Union's ships nearly sideways; and, the main channel was heavily silted, making navigation difficult. Additionally, several of Farragut's ships, such as *Mississippi* and *Richmond*, drew too much water for that portion of the river, without significantly lightening them. To make matters worse, there was no breeze that night to clear away the accumulating gun smoke which soon hung thick as fog. Over a dozen of *Richmond's* crew were Black bluejackets who all were transferred to her in October 1863. Most had come from USS *Brooklyn*, so they knew how to work well together and formed a tight brotherhood, one that included Victor Martell, who served as a sailmaker; Levi Brinkley; Richard R. Morse; Scott Brown; Aaron Smith; Manuel Johnson; John Albert; David H. Smith; Henry Taylor; Joseph Miller, Beverly Ashton; John H. Pettyford; and Thomas Henry. Henry had previous maritime training, having served as a merchant seaman before the war. Born in Scotland, Henry enlisted at Boston and received a rank of seaman. John Hart had transferred to *Richmond* from USS *Hartford*.

In the lead, *Hartford* took heavy fire and ran aground in the current.

12. Seizing the Lower Mississippi

She was freed with help from her lashed partner. *Richmond* was disabled by shots to her engine room and was forced to turn back with help from *Genessee*. *Monongahela* ran aground directly across from a Confederate battery and was riddled for nearly 30 minutes before *Kino* was able to get her off and moving; unfortunately, mechanical problems forced *Monongahela* and *Kino* to drop down river out of range of southern guns.

Monongahela was mauled. Her mizzenmast was struck three times and was unfit for service. Her mainmast was severely damaged. Her main trysail gaff was broken. The starboard hull was penetrated eight times. Six crew members were killed and 21 injured. All of *Monongahela's* 22 Black sailors signed on board after this action.

Only *Mississippi* was left to run the gantlet. In trying to avoid *Richmond* coming back down river, *Mississippi* ran aground too, but in that situation, there was no partner to help pull her off. *Mississippi's* crew tried frantically to lighten the ship in attempting to break her free from the suction of the mud, as the vessel was attacked by Rebel gunfire. Fires soon broke out in multiple places aboard *Mississippi*. The ship was abandoned. Finally breaking free from the muck as she burned, the flaming hulk drifted down river, and exploded the following morning. Only *Hartford* and *Albatross* made it above Port Hudson.

Certain that his wife would read all about the action at Port Hudson, and be deeply concerned, Rear Admiral Farragut wrote her, saying, "I passed the batteries of Port Hudson with my chicken [USS *Albatross*] under my wing. We came through in safety." Farragut wasn't sure about the safety of his other shipmates, telling her: "Would to God I only knew that our friends on the other ships were as well as we are! We are all in the same hands, and He disposes of us as He thinks best.... You know my creed: I never send others in advance when there is a doubt; and, being one on whom the country has bestowed its greatest honors, I thought I ought to take the risks which belong to them. So I took the lead...." Secretary Welles wasn't displeased with the attempt, congratulating the crew of *Hartford* upon their gallant passage past Port Hudson. On 16 March 1863, Welles responded to Farragut's report of the events of that week, saying, "Although the remainder of your fleet were not successful in following their leader, the Department can find no fault with them. All appear to have behaved gallantly, and to have done everything in their power to secure success. Their failure can only be charged to the difficulties in the navigation of the rapid current of the Mississippi, and matters over which they had no control."[11] All of Farragut's ships, except for *Mississippi*, were ultimately repaired.

Black Sailors in the Civil War

Banks' initial attack in March on Port Hudson failed and his forces pulled back into siege positions. Despite his having only a fraction of his force available above Port Hudson, Farragut immediately set about harassing the enemy with the force that he had. *Hartford* and *Albatross* shelled the Confederate batteries at Grand Gulf on 19 March. The duo then began operating between Grand Gulf and Warrenton, which is just below Vicksburg. Running low on coal and provisions, Farragut requested a shipment from General Grant, who sent barges floating down the river, where Farragut retrieved them just below Warrenton. Farragut also was having trouble maintaining his two ships. He advised David Dixon Porter on 25 March 1863, "I can not get to a machine shop, or obtain the most ordinary repairs without fighting my way to them."[12]

Farragut was temporarily trapped, and it greatly troubled him. He wrote to his friend, Rear Admiral Theodorus Bailey, on 21 April 1863, "My disaster in passing Port Hudson was a misfortune incidental to battle, but the damage, with the exception of the loss of *Mississippi* was nothing: the smoke was so thick that the pilot could not see. I worked through by the compass as I did [elsewhere] and had my pilot in the mizzentop." What troubled Farragut most, he told Bailey, was, "I have now been absent from my command six weeks and know nothing of what is going on below.... They say no news is good news, and I hear of no disasters, and therefore hope for the best."[13] Farragut's waiting game ended in July with the fall of Vicksburg. Secretary Welles recording in his diary on 17 July 1863, "The surrender of Port Hudson is undoubtedly a fact. It could not hold out after the fall of Vicksburg." Port Hudson had surrendered on 9 July 1863.

None of what transpired on the lower Mississippi River during those months between Farragut's passage at Port Hudson and its final fall bothered Secretary Welles, nor diminished his opinion of Rear Admiral Farragut.

Welles reflected in his diary in 1864, "no cheering response was made to the appointment of Farragut. Some naval officers said he was a daring, dashing fellow, but they doubted his discretion and ability to command a squadron judiciously."[14] Members of Congress questioned Welles' wisdom in appointing him. A later diary entry for September 1864 notes, "Neither the President nor any member of the Cabinet knew [Farragut], or knew of him except, perhaps Seward, but he was not consulted and knew nothing of the selection until after it was made." Welles realized and accepted that Farragut lacked a showy name, didn't have much in the way of scholastic attainments, wasn't wealthy, and had few courtly talents. These otherwise seemingly significant impediments were ideal because they indicated that Farragut wouldn't be a meddlesome, intriguing, primadonna.

12. Seizing the Lower Mississippi

To Welles' way of thinking, Farragut became a marked man to everyone else the minute they heard that he was from the South, married to a southern wife, and had resided in the South at the start of the war; but none of these circumstances mattered to him, because Farragut had declared himself for the Union, abandoning Virginia and moving North as soon as Virginia seceded. "This firm and resolute stand caused me not only to admire the act, but led me to inquire concerning the man," recalled Welles.[15] By the early fall of 1864, Welles knew he had picked a true winner. Farragut had proven to be an honest naval hero, but the truth was that by September 1864, Farragut was a broken man. Major General Henry Halleck received an assessment of the Admiral's physical condition from Edward R.S. Canby on 30 September 1864, saying: "Farragut has been ordered to Port Royal. His health is so much impaired that he contemplated asking to be relieved but on being advised of contemplated operations and the Sherman might possibly come in at some point on the Gulf at once relinquished the idea and determined to remain. He feels himself that he is not at present physically equal to any new task of magnitude and that while he can be of service here he would break down in the new assignment." Despite the lack of cheers when Farragut was first appointed, when he walked off *Hartford* for the last time, every man was at the rails or on the spars to honor their commander. After his string of stunning victories, Admiral David Farragut was allowed to return to New York to recover his health. Farragut became the Navy's first Vice Admiral. His appointment was a certainty. His nomination was prepared as soon as the bill authorizing the rank was approved by Congress. Gustavus V. Fox sent the nomination request to John Nicolay on 20 December 1864. Fox's transmittal began: "Learning that the Bill authorizing a Vice Admiral had passed both Houses, I have prepared, in anticipation of the President's approval, a nomination for Rear Admiral Farragut to fill that position—The dates are left blank, to be filled with the dates of the approval of the Act by the Presd."

In 1865, Farragut had the painful duty of serving as one of President Lincoln's pallbearers at the White House funeral service on 19 April 1865. In 1866, Vice Admiral Farragut, who was the first to hold that rank, reached another career milestone when he was promoted to full Admiral, the first such title conveyed by the Navy. Welles had a definite affection for the nation's first Admiral. Farragut stayed with Welles during the first week of June 1867, receiving his orders to take command of the European Squadron while he was Welles' guest. Under those orders, Farragut planned to sail for Europe within two weeks. In departing Washington, the Secretary recorded in his diary on 7 June, "In bidding him good-bye I was more affected than he was aware, and I perceived that he was to some extent similarly affected. We have both reached that period of life when a parting of two years may be a parting forever on earth. Circumstances have brought us together, and we are under mutual obligations."[16] Welles praised Farragut's service, his heroic qualities, and his unassuming modesty, concluding that day's diary entry by writing: "I consider him the great hero of the War, and am happy in the thought that I was the means of carrying him to the head of his profession, where he had an opportunity to develop his power and ability."[17]

The European Squadron was the Navy's most important peacetime command. Accompanied by his wife, Virginia, and Gideon Welles' two youngest sons, one of whom served as the Admiral's private secretary and the other served as an aide to the captain of USS *Franklin*, Farragut embarked on a goodwill cruise to Europe. Of arranging for his sons to accompany Farragut, Welles wrote in this diary, "I know no better man to intrust [sic] them."[18] In Europe, Farragut was received as a naval hero in every port of call. Farragut retired from active duty due to his failing health at the end of the European tour. Always staying true to his calling as a naval officer, he refused attempts to put forth his name for nomination as a presidential candidate. While visiting a friend in Portsmouth, New Hampshire, Admiral Farragut suffered a stroke and died at the age of 69 on 14 August 1870. He had spent almost 60 years in the Navy. Public funeral ceremonies were held locally in Portsmouth and later in New York City, where a procession of 10,000 Black and White soldiers and sailors, military officers, and official dignitaries, including President Ulysses Grant, escorted the coffin to the train station. The funeral train was decked in black for its final journey to Woodlawn Cemetery outside New York City, where Farragut was laid to rest with full military honors. Admiral Farragut's legacy only increased after his death. Monuments and statues were erected in multiple cities, and schools, parks, and streets all took his name. Farragut had become the greatest naval leader of the Civil War.

This pleased Gideon Welles greatly, for years earlier he had recorded in his diary, "Had any other man than myself been Secretary of the Navy, it is not probable that either Farragut or Foote would have had a squadron. At the beginning of the rebellion, neither of them stood prominent beyond the others. Their qualities had not been developed; they had not possessed opportunities."[19] Welles' instincts about Farragut had proven correct. Despite the questionable condition of his star player, Welles' overall optimism of the Navy's conduct in the war was increasing. In his

12. Seizing the Lower Mississippi

diary entry for 15 October 1864, he characterized the state of the rebellion as "exhausted" and hoped that in not too many months it might well be totally suppressed altogether, reflecting to himself, "Not that there may not be lingering banditti to rob and murder for a while longer, the offspring of a demoralized state of society, but the organized rebellion cannot long endure."[20] Of Farragut's many accomplishments, perhaps the capture of Mobile Bay was among his crowning achievements, but that would come later in the war.

13

Capturing the Upper Mississippi: Andrew Hull Foote, the Union's Pious Sailor

Securing the upper Mississippi for the Union was Flag Officer Andrew Hull Foote's greatest accomplishment during the war, but it would cost him his life. John Dahlgren and Andrew Hull Foote were long-time friends. Their relationships spanned 20 years, beginning when both were shipmates aboard USS *Cumberland* in the 1840s. Over the course of their friendship, the two were said to have never quarreled. And, when Foote died in 1863 from complications from a foot wound suffered while attacking Fort Donelson on the Cumberland River in Tennessee in command of the Western Gunboat Flotilla in 1862, Dahlgren's face was one of the last Foote saw. Dahlgren recorded his friend's final moments with him, writing: "Next morning after my arrival in New York, my first care was to visit my old and dearly beloved friend Foote. Alas! He was delirious—a few words rallied the fast departing senses—the wondering eye rested on me for a brief moment, and he uttered my name distinctly—even remembering my boys—then he relapsed and another day ended in this world the life of a brave and as good a man as ever served any country. No one better knew his virtues than I—no one prized them more dearly. We had been bosom friends for 20 years and never a cloud between us. What a loss to the country!"[1] It was also a loss for his Black bluejackets.

Foote was truly a righteous sailor. He supported the establishment of temperance movements aboard Navy ships, with those electing to abstain being allowed to add the savings in grog money to their monthly pay. He helped form a Sailors Association to care for seamen on shore. He functioned as an unofficial chaplain, providing weekly religious services to all who were willing to listen. He led missions to combat piracy in the West Indies. He supported the suppression of the slave trade on the high seas; and, he was an ardent abolitionist, writing an influential abolitionist

13. Capturing the Upper Mississippi

publication, *Africa and the American Flag*, in 1854. Foote was not initially drawn to religious thoughts and righteous actions. The grandson of a stern New England Congregationalist minister, as a young boy Foote chafed at the idea of honoring the Sabbath, which for the God-fearing Foot family (Andrew added the "e" to the end on his family name), ran from before sundown on Saturday until you could see at least three stars on Sunday evening. According to family lore, the "three star rule" was frequently broken, a fact that was confirmed by Andrew's brother, John, who admitted, "Very certain I am that the play sometimes commenced before I could see any stars; and I am equally certain that he never, in after-life, watched for them in a storm at sea, or on a lee shore, more anxiously than when a boy, on a Sunday evening, he watched for them as a license to begin his sports."[2] Andrew also loathed having to sit through lengthy church services. However, all that changed when, as a young officer serving aboard USS *Hornet* in 1827, he had a religious epiphany while talking with a spiritual lieutenant. For the next few weeks, he immersed himself in his Bible—looking for answers to what he said was causing him "great agitation of mind." After intense reflection, Foote declared that henceforth he was dedicating himself to God, "to be Thine ... wholly Thine." Foote returned home a changed man. He married Caroline Flagg in 1828. In addition to being a committed Christian, Foote was now a totally devoted sailor.

In 1837 Foote embarked aboard USS *John Adams* on a voyage around the globe. While he was away on this three-year odyssey, his wife died, leaving his infant daughter to the care of others. Shortly after his return home, he remarried, this time to his second cousin, Caroline Augusta Street. During this period, he served as the officer in charge of the Naval Asylum in Philadelphia.

From 1843 to 1845 Foote served as the executive officer aboard USS *Cumberland*, which was part of the Navy's Mediterranean Squadron. During the Mexican War, Foote was idled at the Charlestown Navy Yard. In 1849 he was back at sea in command of USS *Perry*, serving off West Africa as part of the Navy's anti-slavery patrol. Although the United States withdrew from the transatlantic slave trade in 1808, slaves continued to be illegally trafficked in American flagged ships. The Navy's fledgling role in stopping the slave traffic began in 1820 when warships were deployed off West Africa to catch American slavers. Enforcement of the slave trade ban was sporadically enforced until a permanent African Squadron was deployed in 1842. On 6 June 1850 a boarding party from USS *Perry* seized the slaver *Martha* just hours after she had taken on 1,800 slaves from Angola. Initially *Martha's* captain, Henry Merrill, thought that *Perry* was a British warship. Immediately, he hoisted the American flag, because U.S. law prohibited foreign navies from stopping American flagged ships on the high seas. This caused Merrill to think that he was safe from search and seizure; but, unfortunately for him, upon closer examination, he spotted a U.S. naval officer stationed on *Perry's* deck. Realizing his mistake, he hastily hoisted a Brazilian flag in an effort again to hide his true identify. This ploy didn't work. *Martha* was boarded and seized. *Perry's* commander, Lieutenant Foote, sent *Martha* to New York City as a captured prize. An admiralty court subsequently condemned *Martha* and its first mate was convicted and imprisoned for two years. Henry Merrill skipped bond and escaped justice. The following year Foote commanded USS *Portsmouth*, which bombarded the fortifications blocking the Canton River in China in retaliation for attacks on the American flag.

The outbreak of the Civil War found Foote commanding the Brooklyn Navy Yard. The war reunited Foote and his new boss, Navy Secretary Gideon Welles. Welles was an older schoolmate at the Rev. Tillolson Bronson's Cheshire, Connecticut, Episcopal Academy. The decision to replace Commodore John Rogers with Foote was an easy one. Knowing Foote as he did, Welles selected him to take command of the Navy's riverine force because he knew that Foote would get along well with his Army counterparts. Foote's brother officers said he was non-combative and highly aggressive—an overachiever in battle. Foote was said to pray like a saint and fight like the devil. Rogers knew Foote well, calling his replacement a bulldog.

In going out west, Foote confided to his friend John Dahlgren, "I expect of course to be shot by a Kentucky rifleman; but I mean to die game, as there must be a providence in all these things." Foote's premonitions proved accurate, but it wasn't a sharpshooter that would ultimately kill him. It would be a splinter of wood. Although he was basically a deep-sea sailor at his heart, Foote threw himself into standing up an effective riverine force. The task was daunting. Foote needed pretty much everything, calling the western river theater a "wilderness of naval wants."[3]

Upon arriving on the Mississippi River, Foote initially discovered that he had an improvised fleet of timber-clad gunboats, and very few seasoned sailors. Desperate for sailors, he requested 1,000 seamen from the Navy Department, but was granted only 500. The remainder, he was told, were to be supplied by the Army, an arrangement that didn't really work well. He also cabled his friend John Dahlgren for additional help and Dahlgren dispatched as many sailors as he could spare. Unwilling to wait

13. Capturing the Upper Mississippi

until he had everything he might want, he simply made do and moved on. Because of these manpower shortages, Foote could only muster seven partially manned gunboats instead of the 11 fully manned vessels he wanted.

Making do with what he had, he sent three gunboats up the Cumberland River and two up the Tennessee River on 13 January to begin threatening southern forces. Foote's crews were predominantly raw and inexperienced, especially when it came to gunnery. On 15 January he admonished the commander of USS *St. Louis*, urging him to impress upon his officers that they were to carefully watch every shell being fired to ensure that none were being wasted in gauging height and distance. The first shot was sufficient for that, thought Foote. Any more was wasteful and only convinced the enemy that Union naval gunners could not aim very well, he would later say. That same week seven powerful new gunboats joined Foote's growing force. These armored, shallow draft vessels were the Union's first brown-water iron-clads. They were nicknamed "Pook's Turtles," because of their turtle-like appearance and the fact that they were the brainchild of Samuel Pook. Officially, however, the new warships were designated as the Navy's *City*-class of gunboats because each was named for a city, including *Cairo, Carondelet, Cincinnati, Pittsburgh, Louisville, Mound City* and *St. Louis*. With these, Foote believed he was ready to begin effectively all-out offensive operations.

Between February and April 1862, Foote was constantly on the attack. In January Foote notified Gideon Welles, "I am using all possible dispatch in getting all the gunboats ready for service. There is great demand for them in different places in the western rivers."[4] Despite the disparate needs, Foote's first target was Fort Henry on the Tennessee River. By the end of January, the decision to move against Fort Henry was made, and Foote telegraphed Washington on February 1, saying, "I leave tomorrow with four armored gunboats on an expedition cooperating with the Army."[5] Although the investment and capture of Fort Henry was to be made by a joint Army-Navy expedition, the fort was captured on February 6 by naval forces alone. General Grant's force was delayed by heavy rains, forcing the gunboats to attack unsupported. Foote's strategy was to make a mad dash directly at the fort. He did this to inspire terror among the defenders, and it worked. Taking to heart Admiral Foote's admonishment to his officers regarding the need for accuracy, the northerners' well directed naval gunfire disabled all but four of the Confederate garrison's guns, forcing the Fort's surrender to the Navy.[6] Foote's and Grant's next combined target was Fort Donelson on the Cumberland River. By 14 February Fort Donelson was under joint Army and Navy attack. Originally,

Foote wanted to wait for the arrival of mortar boats so the Navy could shell the Rebel fortifications at a greater range, but that would have added three days to the overall operation. Foote's request was overruled by General Henry Halleck, who—to steal Grant's glory—had imposed himself into the operational command-and-control. While this was against Foote's better judgment the naval force followed orders and went in at a far closer range.[7] This was a costly mistake for Foote and his fleet. In the exchange of gunfire with the Fort, Foote's flagship, USS *St. Louis*, was hit 59 times, losing her steering, and drifting out of formation. In the battle, Foote was also struck in the foot by splinters. Unconcerned with his personal injury, he carried on the fight. In a letter to Secretary Welles after the fighting, Foote said, "our fire had so demoralized their troops that they could not afterwards be brought up to their work, and the Commander of the fort actually went down to Capt Davis in the 'Louisville' & offered to surrender the Fort to him as my representative."[8]

Immediately after the fall of Fort Donelson, Foote's gunboats were on the move again, this time attacking Clarksville, Tennessee, which the Confederates evacuated on 19 February. Without hesitation, Foote urged his superiors to allow him and General Grant to move immediately against Nashville, telling them, "The Cumberland [River] is in good stage of water and General Grant and I believe we can take Nashville." Given the green light, Nashville was occupied by Union forces on 25 February.

Foote always liked to boast that a local Nashville newspaper said that it couldn't believe what was happening, reporting, "We had nothing to fear from a land attack, but the gunboats are the devil."[9] The devil was also playing out physically inside of Foote's foot. By 8 March 1862, it was clear that his injury was not healing properly. His doctor reported that there was little improvement because Foote wasn't taking care of his wound properly. What he needed was absolute bed rest and the whole extremity immobilized. However, undeterred by his festering ailment, Foote craved more action. On 12 March, he wrote to Secretary Welles that his flotilla, including seven gunboats and ten 13-inch mortar rafts, was heading for Island Number 10.[10] The Confederate linchpin position was on an island that formed a natural chokepoint at a series of sharp bends in the Mississippi River not far from New Madrid, Missouri. Federal troops under Brigadier General John Pope captured New Madrid on 14 March, leaving the fortifications at Island Number 10 as the key to unlocking control of the river around the junctions of Missouri, Tennessee, and Kentucky. Foote and Pope wanted to own that key, but that wasn't going to be easy. The land around the island was swampy, making any land approach impossible,

13. Capturing the Upper Mississippi

except for an access road on the Tennessee side of the river that ran from Tiptonville, Tennessee, to the riverbank opposite the fort. Unfortunately, Pope's force was on the wrong side of the river to take advantage of the pathway to victory. To attack Tiptonville, he needed several of Foote's gunboats to cover his river crossing from the Missouri side of the river. None of Foote's captains were keen to run the gauntlet past the island and the Rebel batteries on the riverbank to get to New Madrid, about six miles downriver. Foote didn't like the prospects either, especially since he had promised Welles that he'd be cautious with his squadron, as the loss of it "would turn the whole tide of affairs against us."[11] Finally under cover of a severe thunderstorm, USS *Carondelet* attempted to make a run down the river. It succeeded in safely getting past the island's fort and the Confederate river batteries. Several days later, USS *Pittsburgh* tried the same move, again under cover of a heavy downpour. It, too, succeeded. General Pope now had the protection his troop transports needed to cross the river safely. Union troops hastily crossed the Mississippi, bottling up the defenders on Island Number 10, which surrendered on 8 April. That day Foote wrote to his wife about the fall of the Island, saying he was exhausted after "intense mental anxiety for 23 days." He said that what he needed most is a good night's sleep, but that his foot was causing him fits.[12]

Thanks largely to Foote, the upper Mississippi River was then mostly under Union control. For his hand in this winning trifecta—the captures of Fort Henry and Fort Donelson and the fall of Island Number 10—Congress awarded Flag Officer Andrew Hull Foote a vote of thanks from a grateful nation. Despite this honor, Foote was gradually losing the battle with his foot. During the early stages of the Island Number 10 campaign, Foote promised Secretary Welles that he would strive to stay on the best of terms with his Army counterpart, Brigadier General John Pope. "I will & have not shown jealousy against the army," Welles was told. True to his word, Foote maintained a strong friendship with Grant, and his cooperation in the capture of Island Number 10 with Brigadier General Pope, secured a large portion of the Mississippi River and its upper tributaries for the Union. For Pope's actions in capturing New Madrid and Island Number 10, he was promoted to the rank of Major General. Foote further cemented his relationship with Grant by assisting in saving his Army at the Battle of Shiloh. On 6 and 7 April 1862, two of Foote's gunboats—USS *Lexington* and USS *Tyler*—helped stave off a Union defeat of Grant's Army at the Battle of Pittsburg Landing (Shiloh) on the Tennessee River by anchoring the Union's line along the River during the first day's fighting. Each of Foote's engaged gunboats served as formidable water-borne castles moving their powerful naval batteries along the riverbanks where they could throw in shot and shell as needed to cover Union troop movements.

For a time, the Union Army literally sheltered under the protection of the two ship's guns. These same gunboats also helped ensure ultimate Union victory on day two of the fighting by shelling the Rebel positions all night long, giving the enemy little chance to rest. Grant was deeply grateful for the Navy's role in snatching victory from the jaws of possible defeat, but he was shocked by what that contest cost in blood. He had witnessed bloodbaths before, but not on this magnitude. Nearly 24,000 men were killed, wounded, or captured on both sides. This was slaughter on a whole new scale. It was the bloodiest battle of the war to that point. For Grant, the fighting at Fort Donelson, which was hard fought, was nothing compared to the butchery at Shiloh. At Shiloh, the wholesale carnage of war began assuming new dimensions that would last until its end. Foote was fast becoming another fatality of that war. On 14 April his naval force began bombarding Fort Pillow in Tennessee. By then, he was forced to rely on crutches.

In a letter to Gideon Welles, he confessed that "the effects of my wound have quite a dispiriting effect upon me, from increased inflammation, and swelling of my foot and leg, which have induced a feeble action, depriving me of a good deal of sleep and energy. I cannot give the wound that attention and rest it absolutely requires, until this place is captured." In addition to his rapidly failing health, three days later he had to admit to Welles that he wasn't all that confident of capturing Fort Pillow, owing to the foot-dragging by General John Pope, who was leaving him in the lurch by moving his troops from where he needed them to be. Foote was also thinking of his reputation regarding the current operation. He told Welles that while he was ready to die for his country, he wasn't sure what posterity might think. He begged Welles to ensure that "if disaster comes you will vindicate my memory."[13] Within a few more days, Foote was confined to his cabin. He told Welles of his declining condition while USS *Benton* was still lying off Fort Pillow on 24 April 1862. He ended his letter with a postscript saying: "my foot goes on from bad to worse. I certainly stood up against it to the very last, but disease has prevailed."[14] His letter implied that he wished to be relieved, as his health continued to deteriorate. He was exhausted both physically and mentally. By late April, his injury had made him nearly immobile. Foote was spent. If he were to have any chance of recovery, he needed time off to heal. After word of his need to be relieved made it into print, Foote insisted that he *never* asked he be replaced. In fact, on 29 April he made that abundantly clear to Welles—saying that that

13. Capturing the Upper Mississippi

wasn't the case and asking that the Navy Department insist that the newspapers had gotten it wrong. This put Welles in a pickle. Foote had indeed asked to be relieved, saying that he was suffering too much to command properly, but the Rebels then really feared him. Rebel deserters were invoking Foote's name as one of their reasons for deserting. Foote was deeply flattered by what he called the newfound prestige of his name. Any replacement would lack that well-earned fear factor, but Foote was in dire shape.

Fearing for his subordinate's wellbeing, Welles finally ordered Foote to take a break. Although Foote was allowed to retain nominal control, Captain Charles Davis assumed operational command of the Western Gunboat Flotilla on 9 May. Under Davis' leadership, the Western Flotilla continued to wrestle control of the Mississippi River aggressively from Rebel forces. The Confederates evacuated Fort Pillow in early June 1862, following a sustained naval bombardment, and Memphis, Tennessee, surrendered on 6 June. Davis' nominal appointment as commander of the gunboat flotilla became permanent on 17 June; but Davis' tenure was short-lived. Throughout that summer, Welles found that Davis was more of a scholar than a fighter, recording in his diary that he "has gentlemanly instincts and scholarly acquirements, is an intelligent but not an energetic driving, fighting officer, such as is wanted for rough work on the Mississippi; is kind and affable, but has not the vim, dash—recklessness perhaps is the better word—of Porter."[15] By fall 1862, Davis was relieved by David Dixon Porter, but Porter wasn't the ideal choice either. In appointing Porter, Welles recorded a lengthy assessment of the good and bad traits of his pick in his diary, writing: "Porter is but a Commander. He has, however, stirring and positive qualities, is fertile in resources, has great energy. Excessive and sometimes not over-scrupulous ambition, is impressed with and boastful of his own powers, given to exaggeration in relation to himself—a Porter infirmity—but not generous to older and superior living officers, whom he is too ready to traduce, but is kind and patronizing to favorites who are juniors, and generally to official inferiors. Is given to cliquism [sic] but is brave and daring like all his family. He has not the conscientious and high moral qualities of Foote to organize the flotilla and is not considered by some of our best naval men a fortunate officer; has not in his profession, though he may have personally, what the sailors admire, 'luck.'"[16]

In giving Davis' command to Porter, Welles accepted that John Dahlgren would be disappointed. Command was his pathway to promotion, and Welles recognized that being overlooked would be a severe blow. "Dahlgren, whose ambition is great, will, I suppose, be hurt that Porter, who is his junior, should be designated for the Mississippi Command; and

Black Sailors in the Civil War

the President will sympathize with John Dahlgren who he regards with favor, [feeling incomplete without someone to share his ideals or work] while he has not great admiration or respect for Porter," wrote Welles.[17]

In reality, Dahlgren had his eyes more set on the capture of Charleston, but this was also the posting Du Pont had in mind for himself. This time around, Dahlgren would be disappointed on both counts. Porter was assigned the Western Flotilla, while Du Pont was given the South Atlantic Blockading Squadron.

The effectiveness of Porter's Western Flotilla depended largely upon Black sailors.

Porter's appointment wasn't popular with all the squadron's officers. Several thought they were better suited for the post, including one self-promoting candidate who tried to ply Welles with outside political pressure. This backfired in the worst possible way, with Welles telling the offending officer, who otherwise had a fine battle record, "Local and party appeals for promotion and command are the usual resorts of inferior minds and I regret that one so capable and who rendered such eminent service should adopt them." Welles softened his closing, as he typically did. This was Welles' way. Even when he rapped a sailor's knuckles, which he frequently did, he would typically close his corrective notes with words

View of the Western Squadron on the Mississippi River at Mound City, Illinois, in 1863. Mound City was a major embarkation point for Union troops fighting in the West and a key supply center. Union vessels on the western waters were a hodge-podge of types—including cotton-clads, timber-clads, tin-clads, and iron-clads—all manned by large numbers of Black sailors. (Naval History and Heritage Command)

13. Capturing the Upper Mississippi

Initially part of the Army's fleet, USS *Essex* was transferred to the Navy in October 1862. Formidable in appearance, *Essex* was an overdone makeover of a common riverboat. Seemingly always in trouble, *Essex's* conversion was undertaken by her onetime commander, William "Dirty Bill" Porter, without authorization. Over the course of the war, *Essex*, photographed here at Baton Rouge, Louisiana, where she helped repel a Confederate attempt to retake that city, was manned by 118 Black bluejackets, most of which mustered aboard in July 1863. Many of her Black sailors remained aboard *Essex* for their entire terms of service. *Essex* had a normal complement of 124 sailors, so a significant portion of her crew towards the end of the war were Black. During the war *Essex's* sailors shared in the prize money paid out on the capture of 2,204 bales of cotton. (Naval History and Heritage Command)

of praise, encouragement or forgiveness. After giving Lieutenant Commander Seth Ledyard Phelps a lengthy tongue lashing over his claim of being Porter's better, Welles closed by saying: "With whatever emotion this letter may be received I am confident that if your life is prolonged the time will arrive when you will be convinced it is prompted by the best of motives to yourself as well as for the service." Phelps' ambition-driven antics and his politically charged criticism of the Navy's seniority system threatened his further promotion potential.[18] Welles was haunted by the thought that he had, perhaps, made a mistake. By March 1863, Welles was wondering if perhaps Porter was right for the post. Porter's reports were full of verbosity that wasn't backed by satisfactory results. Welles expressed his frustration in his diary on 17 March 1863 by recording, "Porter has capacity and I am expecting much of him, but he is by no means an Admiral Foote."

Black Sailors in the Civil War

Starboard view of USS *General Grant* on the upper Tennessee River. This was one of several gunboats named after prominent Union general officers. Others included *General Sherman*, *General Thomas*, *General Bragg*, *General Lyon*, *General Price*, and *General Burnside*. Twenty Black sailors are known to have served aboard *General Grant* during the war. Most of these Black bluejackets mustered aboard in September 1864. This is an amazing number given that this gunboat was only commissioned in July 1864. As a result, she was basically manned almost entirely by Black sailors. *Grant* was highly effective in suppressing guerrilla actions on the Tennessee River. (Library of Congress)

Andrew Hull Foote was appointed Rear Admiral in 1862. This reward for extraordinary service was a hollow honor, because it was accompanied by the loss of three of his five children to illness, including his blind daughter whom he loved very much.

After several months of inactive service, in July 1862, Foote was placed in charge of the Bureau of Equipment and Recruiting. Foote disliked such desk jobs. He was also greatly frustrated by the failings of some of his fellow officers and urged his superiors that he be considered as a replacement for them. Sensing he was miserable, Welles promised him another posting once he was ready. Foote's wife had her own set of reservations. She advised her husband to accept any other assignment, except the Mississippi Flotilla. There was little glamour in it. As the riverine fleet grew, trained sailors had to be spread out, making experienced crews thinner and thinner in number. New sailors on the river tended to be an odd lot, comprised largely of scrawny youths, city hooligans, runaway slaves,

13. Capturing the Upper Mississippi

USS *Red Rover* was the Union's first hospital ship. She was captured during the Battle for Island Number 10 in April 1862 and converted for medical duty. *Red Rover* had a normal ship's complement of 47 sailors. Throughout the war 105 Black bluejackets served aboard *Red Rover*. Many of her Black sailors mustered aboard on 1 October 1863. While *Red Rover* served injured and sick sailors on the Mississippi River and its tributaries, Elm City, a companion 500-bed hospital ship operated by the Hospital Transport Service in conjunction with the United States Sanitary Commission's field relief work, served Union sailors on eastern waterways. (Library of Congress)

and undisciplined immigrants. The boats tended to be hellholes: airless, hot and stinking; sickness was commonplace, with as many as 40 percent of crews down with illnesses in the summer months. Foote's wife wanted none of this for her husband.

As Welles' frustration with Porter in the west grew in March 1863, so did his impatience with Du Pont in the East outside Charleston. While Welles labored hard to get Du Pont every available resource, Du Pont kept postponing decisive actions, husbanding whatever he received for some distant showdown. This was precisely the problem that the Navy Secretary had witnessed with the Army under McClellan, and he was adamant that the Navy would not make a similar mistake in its leadership. Part of Welles' problem during the month of March was that he was seriously ill, but he nevertheless showed up at work for all but one day. That was the

Black Sailors in the Civil War

A tin-clad, USS *Cricket*, was manned by 41 Black bluejackets during the war. Her normal complement was 50 sailors. *Cricket* was commissioned in January 1863. Many of her Black sailors mustered aboard in December 1863. *Cricket* was principally engaged in confiscating cotton, suppressing guerrilla activities, and transporting troops. *Cricket's* crew was especially good at seizing cotton. Her sailors shared in the prize money paid out on the capture of 2,212 bales of cotton during the war. Her crew also shared in the adjudication of two steamers they captured. (Naval History and Heritage Command)

only day he'd taken off sick since the start of the Administration. He was clearly fatigued—exhausted and out of sorts—which might help explain his great dissatisfaction with Porter and Du Pont. But Du Pont's and Porter's shortcomings were obvious to others, including the President. Lincoln stopped by Welles' home on 2 April 1863 and during a lengthy session expressed his doubts of Porter's plans on the Mississippi and Du Pont's resolve. That night Welles recorded in his diary that Lincoln said that Du Pont was like McClellan, always calling for more and more regiments, only in his case he wanted "more ships, more iron-clads." Du Pont had been given the best of everything. "As regards the Navy," wrote Welles on 8 April, "we have furnished Du Pont the best material of men and ships that

13. Capturing the Upper Mississippi

The Union iron-clad river monitor USS *Osage*. Thirty-six Black sailors served aboard *Osage* during the war. The majority mustered aboard in two waves, one in May 1863 and the other in January 1864. These crewmembers shared in the distribution of a portion of the prize money earned on the seizure of 2,357 bales of cotton during the war. (Naval History and Heritage Command)

were ever placed under the command of any officer on this continent and, as regards officers, unequalled anywhere, or at any time." Unfortunately, that wasn't enough. By the end of April, Welles was disgusted with Du Pont, saying: "I fear he can be no longer useful in his present command, and am mortified and vexed that I did not earlier detect his vanity and weakness."[19] Porter got a reprieve when he captured Grand Gulf, below Vicksburg, in early May. Du Pont remained in the hot seat. Du Pont had talents and capabilities, but Welles saw neither playing out at Charleston. What he was witnessing mirrored what he was seeing within the Army. "The old army infirmity of this war, dilatory action, affects Du Pont," recorded Welles towards the end of May.[20] Enough was enough. By 23 May, Welles concluded that the capture of Charleston by such a commander was out of the question. On 4 June 1863, Welles selected Foote to replace Rear Admiral Samuel Francis Du Pont in command of the Southern Atlantic Blockading Squadron. Du Pont received little notice of the switch. He was officially advised of the change only the day before. By then Welles didn't think Du Pont really cared. "He makes no suggestions, gives no advice, presents no opinion, says he will obey orders," Welles noted in his diary on 3 June 1863.²¹ In preparing to assume this command, Foote moved to New York City, taking up residence at the Astor House. Suddenly he was prostrated again by his recurring ailment, and the prognosis looked bleak. Welles was now deeply concerned. Welles' diary chronicled his childhood friend's decline. On 18 June, Welles noted, "Have information that Admiral Foote is quite ill at the Astor House."²² While Welles was recording that in his diary, C.A. Stetson was telegraphing Gustavus V. Fox the opposite message. "Admiral Foote is better. Will telegraph again before night."

On 19 June, Welles' diary entry was: "[t]he illness of Admiral Foote is serious. I fear fatal. Our first intelligence this morning made his case almost hopeless...."²³ For 20 June, Welles recorded, "Tidings from New York are sad respecting Admiral Foote. I fear he cannot recover and that his hours upon earth are few."²⁴ The following day, Sunday, 21 June, Welles wrote, "Dahlgren, who left New York yesterday, says the case is hopeless, that Foote told him it was the last of this world and he was prepared for the event."²⁵ In talking with Dahlgren on that Sunday, Welles told him that he would be taking Foote's place in commanding the South Atlantic Blockading Squadron. On 24 June, Welles noted, "Admiral Foote still lingers, but there is no hope of recovery."²⁶ That same day, Dahlgren left to assume his post with the South Atlantic Squadron. On 27 June, Welles noted, "A telegram last night informed me of the death of Admiral Foote." As a mark of respect for his childhood friend, Navy Secretary Gideon Welles issued *Naval Order Number 16* on 27 June 1863. This order required flags at Union naval installations and aboard all squadron flagships, lowered to half-mast in Foote's honor. Thirteen minutes of gunfire were to accompany the flag lowering ceremonies. These tributes to Foote were to occur at noon following the receipt of Welles' order. Andrew Hull Foote was buried at his hometown—New Haven, Connecticut—in the Grove Street Cemetery, the first planned cemetery in America.

In a further sad twist for the Foote family, the Admiral's second wife, Caroline Augusta Foote, died at New Haven on 27 August 1863, two months after her husband.

In July 1862, a fellow officer paid him the ultimate compliment when he penned a postscript to a letter to his friend calling him "a model man of the times."

14

Vicksburg: The Gibraltar of the Confederacy

If the capture of Mobile, Alabama, was David Farragut's passion, the fall of Vicksburg, Mississippi, was President Lincoln's. Lincoln would get his wish first. Gideon Welles was the first Cabinet member in Washington to learn of the fall of Vicksburg. As such, he broke the news to the President. Welles received the news from David Dixon Porter on 7 July 1863, while listening to a delegation from New England plead for increased coastal protection against Confederate marauders. Welles immediately excused himself and rushed to the Executive Mansion, where he found the President looking over a map of General Grant's movements around Vicksburg, highlighting strategic points with Treasury Secretary Salmon Chase and several others. Lincoln was highly impressed with Grant's audacity, calling his campaign "one of the most brilliant in the world." Welles blurted out the news of Vicksburg's surrender three days earlier, which immediately electrified Lincoln. "He seized his hat, but suddenly stopped, his countenance beaming with joy; he caught my hand, and throwing his arm around me, exclaimed: 'What can we do for the Secretary of the Navy for this glorious intelligence? He is always giving us good news. I cannot, in words, tell you my joy over this result. It is great, Mr. Welles, it is great,'" recorded Welles in his diary.[1]

The only one miffed by Welles' announcement that day was Secretary of War Stanton, who tightly controlled the news coming out of his department and believed that he should have been the one to break the news. Stanton blamed Porter for heralding the news ahead of General Grant, and before it could be confirmed, but his real complaint was that his control of the War Department's telegraph office had failed him, with Welles getting word first. There had been a tradition between the branches of the armed forces of a mad rush to see which would be the first to announce a major victory. In this case the Navy won the race. Welles confided in his diary on 8 July, "The telegraph office is in the War Department Building, which has a censorship over all that passes, or is received. Everything goes

Black Sailors in the Civil War

under the Secretary's eye, and he craves to announce all important information." Part of Stanton's upset was valid since twice before news of Vicksburg's fall had been bogus; but what made this particular news worse was that Porter had allowed Welles to beat Stanton to the punch before. Back on 8 May 1863, Welles received a telegram from Porter saying that the Navy was in possession of Grand Gulf, allowing him to be the first to break that news to Lincoln. This pleased Welles no end, who recorded in his diary, "The news was highly gratifying to the President, who had not heard of it until I met him at the Cabinet-meeting."[2] In both cases, Stanton's process had failed him because Porter grasped the promotional value of being the one to convey good news. To ensure that he was the one to convey the news, as soon as Vicksburg fell, he dispatched one of his swiftest gunboats to Cairo, Illinois, so that the news could be quickly telegraphed to Welles. The news of Vicksburg, and the victory at Gettysburg, created instant jubilations in the North. It also set up the perfect opportunity to promote "acting Rear Admiral" Porter to the rank of Rear Admiral, which Welles proposed on 13 July. Lincoln gladly assented, although Stanton was unforgiving of Porter's perceived misstep in superseding Grant in announcing the capture of Vicksburg, characterizing him as a "gas-bag, who makes a great fuss and claims credit that belongs to others."[3] Welles didn't agree with Stanton's characterization, but he did write in his diary on 13 July: "I am aware of [Porter's] infirmities. He is selfish, presuming, and wasteful, but is brave and energetic."

Lincoln's mood towards the Army soured the following day during the Cabinet's meeting, when Stanton was asked about the whereabouts of the Confederate Army and whether they were or had crossed back into Virginia. Stanton said curtly that he didn't know. In an instant, Lincoln fired back, "I do!" rebuking Stanton with an icy expression. Lee's Army had been allowed to escape unmolested across the Potomac River to safety in Virginia, and Lincoln knew it. The President abruptly adjourned the meeting, saying that he was in no mood for any further deliberations. Stanton left the meeting abruptly. Welles left slowly. Lincoln easily caught up to Welles walking to the Navy Department. In stopping to talk, Welles was struck by the depths of the President's depression, recording in his diary, "He said, with a voice and countenance which I shall never forget, that he had dreaded yet expected this; that there has seemed to him for a full week, a determination that Lee, though we had him in our hands, should escape with his force and plunder [taken from Maryland and Pennsylvania]...." In frustration Lincoln confided to Welles, "What does it mean, Mr. Welles?" "Great God! What does it mean?" To this diary entry, Welles added, "On only one or two occasions have I ever seen the President so

14. Vicksburg: The Gibraltar of the Confederacy

troubled, so dejected and discouraged."[4] Later that day, Stanton asked Welles to join him in reviewing the reports from Vicksburg. At the War Department Welles found the President stretched out on Stanton's sofa completely overwhelmed with bad news from the Army of the Potomac. The only good news that afternoon was the report of the prisoners taken at Vicksburg—almost 30,000 of them.

By August 1864, Confederate Lieutenant General Richard Taylor had to report that having forces cross the river in any strength was now impossible. "Accurate observations have been made of the enemy's gunboats between Red River and Vicksburg," he told General Kirby Smith, "and from the strictness of the guard maintained no success can be anticipated."[5] The South was now effectively divided in half. The triumph on the Mississippi was a long time in coming.

Two years earlier, in August 1862, Welles was deeply troubled by the Navy's Mississippi progress, noting in his diary, "Am sorry that better progress is not made in the war upon the Rebels. Our squadrons are paralyzed everywhere by inactivity and dilatory movements of the Army. Vicksburg should have been taken by the first of June, but no adequate cooperating military force was furnished, and as a consequence our largest squadron in the Gulf and our flotilla in the Mississippi have been detained and injured." By January 1863 nothing had changed. Welles blamed Henry Halleck, who had been the Army's senior commander in the western theater and was by then the Union's General-in-Chief, for the missed opportunities and foot dragging, writing on 9 January 1863, that if the Army had only supported Farragut and Davis back in the Summer of 1862, Vicksburg might already have been taken. At that time, Vicksburg was tightly sandwiched between Farragut's Gulf Squadron and the Davis' Western Flotilla, which was just above it. But, Halleck, who was nicknamed "Old Brains" as an insult, claimed he had no support to spare. This was basically true, given all the competing requests he had for troops, especially for the Army of the Potomac, which was like an unquenchable sponge. Porter's and Farragut's forces began shelling the city that summer and continued through much of June and July, at one point requesting that the mayor surrender, but he refused, saying that he didn't know how and wasn't about to learn. That opportunity evaporated by 24 July 1862, when falling water levels on the Mississippi forced Farragut to withdraw down river.

In Welles' eyes, Halleck, who was made General-in-Chief in July 1862, was the architect of that earlier failure, and now, nearly a year later, was the current stumbling block to Porter's movements. Welles castigated Halleck as "dull, stolid, inefficient and incompetent."[6] At one point, Welles wrote,

"Stanton seems stupid, Halleck always does."[7] To Welles' way of thinking, Halleck had accomplished nothing and had lost all public and administrative confidence. As bad as that characterization was, Welles said worse, saying Halleck "organizes nothing, anticipates nothing … plans nothing, suggests nothing, is good for nothing."[8] "Halleck scolds and swears about him as a stupid, worthless fellow. This seems his way to escape censure himself and cover his stupidity in higher position," wrote Welles.[9] "The army has no head," Welles penned in his diary on 3 September 1862. By then, Lincoln's opinion went farther, once, according to John Hay, likening Halleck to serving as little better than "a first-rate clerk."[10] There was no Navy counterpart to Halleck. The Chief of Naval Operations position wouldn't be created until May 1915. As a result, Welles held direct command and control over his officers.

To blockade the mouth of the Red River, Porter sent USS *Indianola* below Vicksburg on 12 February, but her duty there would be short-lived.

USS *Indianola* was lost to a superior Confederate naval force on 24 February 1863. According to the Confederate after action report, *Indianola* succumbed to a nighttime raid where she was repeatedly rammed. Mortally struck below the waterline, and sinking, she was surrendered. To make her easier for the Rebels to raise, and to keep her from being reclaimed by Federal troops, two of her attackers towed her to the eastern side of the Mississippi. Before fully reaching the shoreline, *Indianola* sank up to her gun deck. The *Indianola* was a real loss for the North. Brand new, she had joined the Mississippi Squadron in January 1863. As an ironclad gunboat, she was equipped with dual paddlewheels and twin propellers. Her armor consisted of three-inches of iron, backed by 32-inches of wood. She mounted two 11-inch Dahlgren guns in her forward casemate and one 9-inch gun on each side. The loss disturbed Secretary Welles greatly. He wrote to Porter on 2 March by encrypted telegram reminding him that "The disastrous loss of the *Indianola* may, if she has not been disabled, involve the most serious results to the fleet below [Vicksburg]." Porter had to hastily ensure that *Indianola* was either fully destroyed or was somehow salvaged by his sailors. Letting her fall into Confederate hands was unthinkable. Porter responded that, "There is no use to conceal the fact, but this has, in my opinion been the most humiliating affair that has occurred during this rebellion.... My only hope is that she has blown up."[11] She hadn't blown up. *Indianola* had been rammed and beached herself. And, the South had every intention of raising *Indianola* and adding her to its growing armada on the Mississippi. Porter had to think fast.

14. Vicksburg: The Gibraltar of the Confederacy

When it came to confounding the enemy, Porter proved he could be a true trickster. In just 12 hours he had his sailors create a dreadful-looking facsimile iron-clad that totally fooled the Confederates into destroying *Indianola*, a brand-new, yet just captured Union iron-clad. That was an ideal swap. The 300-foot long faux "gunboat" was built from the waterline up on an old coal barge. The dummy was created using scrap lumber to construct the casemate and wheelhouses and Tobacco hogsheads to emulate two massive smokestacks. Big iron pots were used under each smokestack to burn tar and oakum to simulate its belching black smoke. An array of fake broadside "guns" protruded from its sides and a single deadly looking main gun, created from a giant log, extended from its forward casemate. The whole vessel was covered in tar and black paint to give it the appearance of being clad in thick iron. As added touches, Porter had a skull and crossbones pirate flag flown from its bow post and the dread words, "Deluded Rebels, Cave In!," were ominously painted on the wheelhouses.

At midnight the fake gunboat was towed just above Vicksburg and set adrift. Immediately Confederate batteries opened fire on the lone monster slowly descending the river. Confederate cannons did no real damage despite the amount of gunfire that was unleashed. Once safely below Vicksburg, whenever the dummy boat ran up on the western shore, she was pushed free by Union soldiers. As the barge boat descended the river the awesome looking monster was spotted by the Rebel boat *Queen of the West*, which was heading up to Vicksburg to get pumps and salvaging gear to raise *Indianola*. The *Queen* immediately turned tail and raced back down river, leaving the work party attempting to salvage the sunken *Indianola* to fend for themselves. Despite not appearing to be in any hurry to attack the Confederate salvage team, the Rebels were unwilling to wait around for the Union boat to unleash that formidable looking forward gun on them. They destroyed *Indianola* to prevent any subsequent Union salvage efforts, and fled, but not before liberating all the ship's wine and liquor. Those are the only things of value the Rebels came away with. The dummy iron-clad seemed to hover in the immediate area. The following day a small party of curious Confederates rowed out to see why the iron-clad wasn't moving and didn't seem to have a crew. They found the boat that they so feared was a fake that was stuck on a sandbar.

When word of the ruse got out, the southern press had a field day rubbing Rebel noses in it. The incredulous *Vicksburg Whig*, reported on 5 March: "We stated a day or two since that we would not then enlighten our readers in regard to a matter which was puzzling them very much.

Black Sailors in the Civil War

We allude to the loss of the gunboat *Indianola*, recently captured from the enemy. We were loth [sic] to acknowledge she had been destroyed, but such is the case. The Yankee barge sent down river last week was reported to be an iron-clad gunboat. The authorities, thinking that this monster would retake the *Indianola*, immediately issued an order to blow her up.... It would really seem we had no use for gunboats on the Mississippi, as a coal barge is magnified into a monster, and our authorities immediately order a boat—that would have been worth a small army to us—to be blown up." The *Whig* wanted to know, "Who is to blame for this piece of folly?" Porter quoted from this news clipping in telling Welles about this exploit. But Welles was already well up on Porter's dummy gunboat trick, having learned about it from a Confederate newspaper from Richmond. That paper said its readers should "Laugh and hold your sides, lest you die of a surfeit of derision," explaining how what it called "a flat-boat or mud scow with a small house taken from the back yard of a plantation put on top of it" was floated down the river in the guise of being a Federal iron-clad monster. Welles wasn't the least bit amused by the article or by the trick. His department had just lost a brand new, state-of-the-art river iron-clad. This time, Porter had barely saved his skin through a hoax.

By April 1863, Welles wanted to see some serious action on the Mississippi. This view was shared by David Farragut, who told Porter, "The whole country will be in arms if we do not do something." For Welles' part, he told Porter that he desired an end to what he called "side-issues and by-play,"[12] an apparent reference to General Grant's vain efforts to divert the Mississippi away from Vicksburg either by digging a canal or blasting out new channels that would bypass the place, thus neutralizing its military and strategic importance. The canal was among Grant's biggest side-stepping schemes. Four thousand of his soldiers and 2,000 freed slaves engaged in digging the canal, which was nicknamed "the ditch," at the Tuscumbia Bend in the Mississippi. The canal would have short-cut cross the western peninsula opposite Vicksburg. Grant's big dig was basically flawed from the start. Southern guns on the eastern side of the river could simply move further South to overlook the proposed southern mouth of the canal. Additionally, Mother Nature didn't cooperate. The river contributed more silt to the effort than erosion. The canal idea was abandoned. What is interesting about the canal is that Welles proposed it back on 25 June 1862, when he instructed Flag Officer Charles Henry Davis, commanding the Western Flotilla, to consider "the narrow neck of land opposite Vicksburg formed by a bend in the Mississippi River, the width of which is probably not more than three quarters of a mile. The

14. Vicksburg: The Gibraltar of the Confederacy

water sometimes flows over this, and it is through that, by opening a ditch, the river will soon form a channel through, sufficient for purposes of navigation, and thus obviate the necessity of passing Vicksburg."[13] Welles' instruction to Davis was to explore the feasibility of this measure in supporting Farragut's efforts to gain control of the Mississippi in 1862. Without sufficient Army support, with Porter and 12 of his mortar boats pulled away from Farragut and repositioned to Hampton Roads in accordance with a confidential telegram from Welles on 5 July 1862, any hope of opening the entire Mississippi in 1862 was lost. As disappointing as this was for Farragut, and Welles realized that it would be, he instructed his faithful Flag Officer to "Let there be no delay. Answer by telegram."[14] A few days later, Farragut was instructed to proceed with his fleet to the Gulf for the purpose of conducting operations at some point or points on the coast. This order was tartly amended on August 12 with Farragut being advised of Welles' "serious mortification" over the escape of the CSS *Arkansas* from his naval force. "It is an absolute necessity that the neglect, or apparent neglect, of the Squadron on that occasion should be wiped out by the capture or destruction of the *Arkansas*, which I trust will have been effected before this reaches you," Welles chillingly told Farragut. Welles closed this order with another stern expectation: "It is not to be supposed that you will leave Vicksburg until this is accomplished."[15] On 19 August, Welles was elated to send his congratulations to Farragut upon learning of the destruction of the dreaded *Arkansas*.

Weeks earlier, Welles sent a subtly written letter to Secretary of War Stanton underlining the importance of the river and the pressing necessity of possessing Vicksburg at all costs, but, that doesn't appear to have been its true intensions. In the letter, Welles didn't personally blame the Army for a lack of support, but he furnished extracts of a letter from David Dixon Porter to David Farragut that did, introducing it with the notation, "Excuse these suggestions which are made unpleasant in transmitting the extract from Com. Porter's letter.... I would invite special attention to the remarks in relation to General Williams and his force and the opinion expressed that he can go anywhere 30 miles into the interior below Vicksburg, and supported by the gunboats destroy the enemies stores, capture the cattle they have grazing, and be instrumental in keeping open the river."[16] Welles told Stanton that he placed great value in Porter's observations and urgent convictions, which was why he was induced to forward them to the War Department. Welles added a further bit of insult to injury by telling the Secretary of War, "The long detention of so large a Naval force before Vicksburg in consequence of the absence of a sufficient land force to cooperate with the Navy in taking and holding the place, is I am aware a source of regret to you, as well as to myself."[17] The bottom line, which Stanton clearly got, was that the Union could have taken Vicksburg if only the Navy had gotten adequate support from the Army. Such an unflattering transmission, attributed to Porter, put the naval commander in Stanton's crosshairs and had the potential for driving a wedge between any further relationships Porter, a recognized plotter and intriguer, might try to forge with the Secretary of War outside of Welles' knowledge.

Nearly two years later, Welles told Porter to stop subordinating himself to the Army and start suppressing his feelings of inferiority. He was to start acting independently, if necessary, instructed the uncommonly stern Secretary. Welles anticipated that his message might prove hurtful to Porter, but the Secretary was under pressure to provide people with some serious success. Appearing to feel slightly guilty over his tone, Welles unburdened his mind a short time later in his diary on 17 April, writing, "he cannot misunderstand, and which, I will not, I hope, wound his pride."[18] Welles was also concerned that such side-shows, like the operations on the Yazoo River, were unnecessary distractions. The idea was to force a passage on the Yazoo, known as the Steele's Bayou Expedition. Welles thought the operation was insignificant, with little in it to lift spirits at home, and little to be gained militarily. What Welles hadn't maybe been adequately told was that in some respects it made perfect sense as the Yazoo region was considered the "granary of Vicksburg." The region was so far untouched by the war. Barnyards were full and fields were planted. Sheds along the river were also full of two year's worth of cotton. All this bounty wasn't going to be easily surrendered. Almost as soon as Porter's sailors began scavenging for cotton and foraging for food, Confederates, backed by irate planters, began burning whatever cotton the Federal hadn't yet claimed. Cotton fires blazed everywhere, often on both sides of the river. Livestock was driven inland, and poultry was scattered. Trees were felled in the waterway making movement insufferably slow.

Rebel sharpshooter began sniping at any sailor that moved. At one point the shots got so close to Porter that an old salt presented him with a piece of tattered old iron smokestack to use as a shield.

Despite such scares, Porter lived well on the river. His personal pantry was always well stocked with good liquor and fine food. He had a cow for milk and coops on board for his personal waterfowl and chickens. He had a piano and a collection of dogs for entertainment. And, it is said that he had a propensity for surrounding himself with witty sailors and those who had a knack for scrounging cotton. In his leisure time, he often

14. Vicksburg: The Gibraltar of the Confederacy

penned burlesque cartoons of those around him or people who were on his mind. Gideon Welles and Assistant Secretary Fox were said to be frequently the brunt of his unflattering artworks.

Porter advised Welles that he was just following orders, saying: "In this operation I act in obedience to the orders of the Department to cooperate with the army, and shall do my best to make them successful." To others he wrote, "Our people are too insatiate for success."

In any event, guilt-racked or not, Welles hoped his acerbic April message might work, recording in his diary, "I hope we may soon have something favorable from that quarter."[19] That month the pieces of the joint Army-Navy operations against Vicksburg were coming together. Porter advised Welles of Grant's overall strategy, informing his boss, "[Major General Grant] proposes to embark his army at Carthage, seize Grand Gulf under fire of the gunboats, and make it the base of his operations.... The squadron will pass [Vicksburg's] batteries and engage them while the transports go by in the smoke, passing down, of course, at night...." Porter told Welles that Grant was taking his army below Vicksburg to invest Vicksburg from the rear, after first taking Jackson, Mississippi.

To make this strategy work, Porter had to run elements of his squadron, and the Army's transports, past the city's fortifications. He didn't really like that idea, because once his gunboats were South of Vicksburg there was no chance of coming back upstream against the river's strong currents. Any return passage upstream against the flow of the river would make his gunboats, which could barely make four to six knots if they were lucky, sitting ducks while under the sights of the enemy's guns. As it was, it was going to be hard enough going downstream with the current flowing in their favor. While Porter fretted over how best to get past Vicksburg, the survival of Vicksburg alarmed Confederate Secretary of War James Seddon, who had replaced Judah P. Benjamin, when Benjamin became the South's Secretary of State. Seddon's fears prompted him in May to consider stripping some military units from Charleston to avert what he saw as a possible disaster on the Mississippi.

This decision was sharply opposed in South Carolina, but Seddon defended his decision, writing to the objectors: "I beg you to reflect on the vital importance of the Mississippi to our cause, to South Carolina, and to Charleston itself. Scarce any point in the Confederacy can be deemed more essential, for the 'cause of each is the cause of all,' and the sundering of the Confederacy [on the Mississippi] would be felt as almost a mortal blow to the most remote parts." Whatever help he could provide wouldn't prove to be enough to stave off the inevitable. Oddly, at about the same time, Lieutenant General John C. Pemberton, the overall commanding officer of Confederate forces in the Vicksburg area, considered lending some of his troops to other commanders elsewhere because he was under the false impression that General Grant had given up on the idea of taking Vicksburg and was heading back North to Memphis. Porter's gauntlet downstream was slated for the night of 16 and 17 April. Porter prepared a number of vessels for what he feared would be a murderous dash, covering them with wet bales of hay and soaked cotton to help snuff out any potential fires and covering them with additional layers of logs wherever possible. These protective measures were later described by Porter as "an excellent defense." Additionally, barges, each containing 10,000 bushels of coal, were lashed alongside all the ships, except for *Benton*, as useful shields. Instead, *Benton* was tethered to USS *Ivy*, a tug, which served as General Grant's dispatch boat. USS *Lafayette* was the only ship to lose her coal barge in the run past the Confederate batteries. That night there was no moon, and the ships were to run without lights. The vessels began floating downstream shortly after 11:00 p.m., at little better than the speed of the river's current, only adding slight steam to provide sufficient control against the river's erratic current and eddies, which could spin a ship around uncontrollably like a hydroplaning car, if not careful. Porter took the lead in USS *Benton*, his flagship. *Benton* was like a floating castle. Mounting 16 guns, she was considered the most powerful of the Navy's "river-clads." *Benton* was followed USS *Lafayette*, which was trailed by USS *General Price*. With 50-yards separating each vessel, the line included four of Porter's "turtle-style" gunboats, *Louisville, Mound City, Pittsburgh* and *Carondelet* (these were the Union's first brown-water iron-clads); three transports (*Forest Queen, Silver Wave* and *Henry Clay*). USS *Tuscumbia* served as the sweep ship. *Tuscumbia's* placement in the pack was in part because she was extremely powerful, mounting three 11-inch Dahlgren smoothbore guns in her forward casemate. She was also fast, capable of making eight-knots if fine-tuned because she had a pair of screw propellers plus paddle wheels; unfortunately, she wasn't highly reliable because of her mechanical sophistication and her poor construction. If she faltered along the way, her wide 72-foot beam could create a deadly bottleneck, so she needed to come last.

Luckily for Porter, many Confederate officers were attending a gala that evening hosted to celebrate what they thought was Grant's departure, so there was a slight chance that the Union's riverine armada might slip by undetected. Unfortunately, the fires used by Confederate pickets illuminated the slow-moving ships. In short order the night came alive with

14. Vicksburg: The Gibraltar of the Confederacy

Confederate gunfire. As soon as shots were fired the Union vessels added steam. Because the river's channel cuts in close to the city, many of the harassed ships hugged Vicksburg's shoreline, which caused Confederate gunners on the bluffs to overshoot some targets. After two-and-a-half hours, the passage was completed. Although the Union ships endured 68 hits, all but one, the transport *Henry Clay*, made it safely downstream. Wisely, as a precaution, Porter had ordered members of the Army aboard his armored gunboats for their safety during the evening's escapade. The transport ships were carrying rations and supplies.

Once safely past Vicksburg, Grant put his land campaign in motion, with successive battles at Grand Gulf on 29 April, Port Gibson on 1 May, Raymond on 12 May, Jackson on 14 May, Champion's Hill on 16 May and Big Black River on 17 May. This put Grant's Army, now numbering roughly 70,000 strong, at Vicksburg's back door by 18 May. What ensued next was a month-and-a-half long siege. Grant and Porter proved to be a good team. Whenever Grant needed naval fire support he got it, and whenever his command needed water-borne transportation, he received that too. Grant returned the favors, including lending Porter 800 bluecoats when his squadron was faced with a manpower shortage resulting from routine naval discharges. Contrabands were also exploited, with Porter pressing 600 freed slaves into his naval units. These were trained to man the Navy's big guns because they were accustomed to strenuous work and proved better suited than the recruits he was receiving from the North, who he said were mostly young boys. Porter repaid Grant. He had USS *Cincinnati's* guns removed and transferred to the Army, which erected a shore battery for them. *Cincinnati* had been sunk on 27 May 1863, when it was hit by plunging fire from the river's bluffs. *Cincinnati* was commanded by Porter's nephew, Lieutenant George Bache, who beached his ship before she sank. While many were safely taken off the ship, unfortunately, she broke free and began drifting down stream forcing those who remained aboard to swim for it. Many of those who could not swim, like Bache, were saved by the few crewmates who could. For their actions six swimmers of the crew received the Medal of Honor. Forty of the crew weren't so lucky, killed, wounded, or drowned in the action. Plunging fire was the greatest threat to Porter's fleet because his ships weren't particularly designed to deflect this type of gunfire. In the case of *Cincinnati*, logs and hay had been used to increase her protection, but these proved ineffective, with the ship's commander reporting, "The shots went entirely through the protection—hay, wood, and iron." *Cincinnati* was raised in August 1863 and resumed duty.

Porter also transferred 10 heavy naval guns, including six 32-pounders, that would effectively be used in the rear of Vicksburg. Several of these big guns were even manned by sailors. Porter also furnished trained gun crews to man a significant number of 8-inch howitzers borrowed from the Navy. The Navy also supplied the necessary shot and shell for the howitzers, furnishing the Army with roughly 6,000 rounds of ammunition.

On the river, at first, naval fire support against the city's upper batteries proved daunting. Because Vicksburg and her upper batteries were situated on typically 200-foot-high bluffs it was almost impossible to elevate the Navy's broadside guns high enough to prove effective in hitting the city or its fortification. Porter solved this by placing three 11-inch guns in the bow of each of his gunboats and elevating them as high as possible, which made them far more effective. During the siege the Navy's gunboats expended roughly 4,500 shot and shells. Additionally, the Navy's mortars proved extremely effective. Porter's mortar vessels, typically sailing schooners that were purchased at the start of the war and modified specifically for duty in the mortar flotilla, pummeled the place with approximately 7,000 massive 13-inch mortar shells. Porter loved using mortars

Illustration of one of David Dixon Porter's 13-inch mortar schooners in action on the Mississippi River, as depicted in *Harper's Weekly*. Although the illustration shows an entirely white crew, likely at least half were Black bluejackets. (Naval History and Heritage Command)

14. Vicksburg: The Gibraltar of the Confederacy

because he could conceal his mortar boats around bends in the river well outside Confederate sight and cannon range and rain shells down on targets with impunity. He particularly liked using his mortars at night to annoy the enemy, denying them any rest. He told Secretary Welles, "The mortars keep constantly playing on the city and works.... Not a soul is to be seen moving in the city, the soldiers lying in their trenches or pits, and the inhabitants being stowed in caves or holes dug out in the cliffs."[20] These 200-pound mortar shells were timed to explode overhead, forcing most residents and defenders alike to live underground like mole people.

Grant was impressed with Porter's mortar ships too, writing him on 2 July, "the firing from the mortar boats this morning has been exceedingly well directed on my front. One shell fell into the large fort, and several along the line of the rifle pits. Please have them continue firing in the same direction and elevation."[21] Those inside Vicksburg were being slowly pulverized with an average of 150 mortar shells dropping on them each day. This rate of shelling amounted to about two every minute both day and night. The incessant shelling, followed by the eerie lulls, only added to the terror.

If incoming mortar fire was abundant, food inside Vicksburg was not. Confederate soldiers were on constantly shrinking subsistence rations, including a form of barely edible bread made from peas. By the end of June some civilians were consuming birds, cats, dogs, and mules as part of their survival diets. Many realized the end was near. One Confederate officer wrote his wife, saying: "All seem to think that Saturday or Sunday will tell the fall of Vicksburg."[22] The letter was intercepted on Monday, 29 June. The Sunday referred to was 2 July 1863. The sender, General Martin Smith, was off by two days. Lieutenant General Grant was laudatory of Porter's role in the fall of Vicksburg, saying: "The Navy under Porter was all it could be during the entire campaign. Without its assistance the campaign could not have been successfully made with twice the number of men engaged." Thinking back on the victory, Porter wrote: "What bearing this will have on the rebellion remains yet to be seen, but the magnitude of the success must go far towards crushing out this revolution and establish once more the commerce of the States bordering on this river." Lincoln best tied Grant's and Porter's thoughts together on August 26, when he applauded the resumption of Union control of the Mississippi River by saying: "The Father of Waters again goes unvexed to the sea.... Nor must Uncle Sam's web feet be forgotten. At all the watery margins they have been present. Not only on the deep sea, the broad bay, the rapid river, but also up the narrow muddy bayou, and wherever the ground was a little damp they have been and made their tracks." Taking control of the Mississippi helped make Welles' year. His diary entry for the end of the year summed up his mood going into 1864: "The year closes more satisfactorily than it commenced. The War has been waged with success, although there have been in some instances errors and misfortune. But the heart of the nation is sounder and its hopes brighter. The national faith was always strong, and grows firmer."[23]

15

Prizes and Problems Along the Red River

Not all prize money came from capturing ships and track-iron, as the Black and White seadogs involved in the Red River Expedition would discover. This joint Army-Navy Red River Expedition, between 10 March and 22 May 1864, should have wrecked Rear Admiral David Dixon Porter's naval career. It was the largest such joint riverine operation of the war, involving a combined Army-Navy fleet of 90 vessels ... and it was an absolute fiasco.

The expedition had multiple ambitious purposes, including the capture of Shreveport, Louisiana, a rail hub to Vicksburg and potential gateway to Texas. In addition, the campaign was to counter the growing influence of the French, which had installed Austrian Archduke Maximilian as emperor of a puppet Mexican empire. Thousands of French troops were fighting to overthrow the government of Benito Juarez under the pretext of collecting Mexican debts owed to France. The South supported the French. It was using Mexican facilities at Matamoros to traffic its cotton to Europe and to bring in contraband supplies, slipping them across the border for use throughout the South. The United States knew this was going on. It was obvious. In his 1887 work, *The History of the Confederate States Navy*, J. Thomas Schart notes, "That the final destination of the trade between England and Matamoros was Texas and the Confederacy, was too plain to deceive...." It could not go unnoticed. The little city of Matamoros, which before the war might have had six to eight ships at any time in port, now had between 180 to 200 vessels often stacked up at the mouth of the Rio Grande ready to off-load and take-on illicit cargoes. Trans-shipping of cotton through Matamoros was a convenient, albeit illegal, way of keeping southern cotton out of Federal hands. Union textile merchants and shippers were exploiting the Matamoros loophole too. "Goods are received and cotton exported by this route under our own, as well as foreign flags," noted Welles in his diary during the Spring of 1863.[1] Welles wanted such

Black Sailors in the Civil War

access stopped, but Secretary of State Seward thought that forcing the issue would only further sour relationships with France more than necessary. The United States was timidly supporting Juarez because it was in no position to risk war with France. In the chaos of America's war, Union leaders feared that Napoleon III might be contemplating annexing parts of Texas as part of this greater Mexican empire. By July 1863, Secretary Seward told his Cabinet colleagues that there was mounting evidence that Louis Napoleon was indeed planning to make a play to get Texas. Welles urged the Cabinet to take immediate steps to occupy Galveston, Brownsville or Indianola to thwart those plans. Galveston had been brought under Union control in the summer of 1862, at least as much of it as could be covered by Federal artillery, but it had been lost again in January 1863.

Following that Cabinet meeting, Welles and Seward went to see Secretary Stanton and Major General Halleck to discuss possible military actions in Texas. "Halleck, as usual, was heavy, sluggish, not prepared to express an opinion," penned an exasperated Welles in his diary.[2] Halleck dragged his heels. In September 1863 an expedition was finally launched, but not against Galveston or Brownsville. Instead, it was against Sabine Pass. This was the second attempt to invade Texas there. An effort a year earlier there also failed. In his diary entry for 24 September 1863, Welles recorded, "I am more [despondent] than I care to acknowledge.... Heigho! The Sabine Pass?" This effort failed too, despite the Union's use of 22 transports, five gunboats and an estimated 15,000 men. For one thing, the Confederates had learned a vital lesson on the eastern side of the Mississippi. There, the Union confiscated or destroyed everything they could find. It wouldn't be that way on the western side of the river. There, everything of value would be moved out of the Federal's way. On 13 September 1863 Lieutenant General E. Kirby Smith instructed Brigadier General Henry McCulloch on "securing negroes and stock as our troops retire before the enemy. It is our policy to strip the country and leave it bare of supplies as we fall back." The herding of Blacks away from Union hands left many beyond the grasp of freedom. By September 1863 numerous southerners in the western theater were learning too. They realized it was worthless to take Confederate currency in payment for anything. To combat this trend the Confederate Headquarters of the Department of the Trans-Mississippi issued a *General Order* on 16 September 1863 from Kirby Smith saying: "The lieutenant-general commanding regrets to learn that citizens within the department, demoralized by speculation and the love of gain, persistently refuse to receive Confederate money in the sales of supplies and in payment of debts." Smith's remedy was to declare anyone unwilling to

15. Prizes and Problems Along the Red River

accept Confederate currency "an alien enemy, his property sequestered, and himself sent without our lines."

Gideon Welles was taking drastic measures too. Taking matters into his own hands, Welles did what he could to disrupt shipments to Matamoros under the doctrine of "continuous voyage," also known as "ulterior destinations," meaning where it is going to ultimately end up. The fact was that items were coming through a neutral Mexican port wasn't the ultimate destination. The Confederacy was the final point of consumption. As such, all such shipments were contraband. Welles ordered naval officers to step up their searches of Matamoros shipping. He also authorized the selective seizure of the mails coming out of Matamoros. Much of the Confederacy's official correspondence with Europe was sent or received by way of Matamoros. In single-handedly disrupting the mails, Welles was guilty of doing what he loathed in his fellow Cabinet members. He hated it when Seward or Stanton acted as if they were the Secretary of the Navy.

Now, it was Welles who was intruding upon the administrative realms of two of his Cabinet colleagues by assuming the prerogatives of the Secretary of State and the Postmaster General in ordering the interdiction of the mails. Seward believed that this was in strict violation of a special directive annunciated in August 1862 by the President regarding the mails. According to the Secretary of State under Lincoln's order Union naval officers were prohibited from opening any mail they might find on board a captured vessel. Instead, they were to surrender such mail to any appropriate representative of the government for which the mail was intended with the understanding that they might open the mail and determine what might be contraband or evidence that might prove invaluable to a prize court. Welles' actions deeply upset Seward, who sent him a note on 31 October 1862 saying, "in case of capture of merchant vessels suspected or found to be vessels of the insurgents or neutral power duly certified or authenticated as such, shall not be opened or searched, but be put, as speedily as may be convenient on their way to their designated destination." Welles recorded the receipt of this note in his diary on 4 November 1862, observing, "Seward sent me ... a singular note, supercilious in tone, in relation to the mails captured on blockade-runners, telling me 'It is deemed expedient that instructions be given to our naval officers' that such mails should not be opened, but that as speedily as possible they be forwarded." This missive miffed the Navy Secretary. Welles' reasoning in responding to Seward was that if a suspected blockade-runner was captured, regardless of its country of registry; and if the ship's cargo was seized, regardless of questions over who owned what portions of its cargo; and if the vessel's crew was taken prisoner, regardless of their nationalities; then the mail being transported aboard a captured ship must also be taken, especially if it might contain correspondence from those who were insurrection against the United States or prove that the ship was indeed a blockade-runner.

In this way he had the seized mails included in the prize court submission for adjudication. The most important part in Welles' logic was the thought that the captured mails might also contain germane correspondence that condemned the ship as a blockade-runner, information that may be useful to the prize courts. What Welles didn't say is that he saw captured mail as an intelligence treasure trove too. Captured mail *was* being opened and mined for tidbits of useful information. A case in point is a man's letter from Charleston, dated 16 January 1863, to his wife in which he recounted a grand dinner for the officers of a visiting French frigate in which the talk centered around what the letter writer described as the pending "alliance, offensive and defensive, [that] has been made or will very shortly be made by our Minister, Mr. Slidell, with the French Government." In passing this intelligence along to Secretary Seward on 3 February, Welles was clearly spilling the beans on the Navy's reading of captured mails, but the Navy's Secretary thought Seward needed to know, and that the letter writer also reported talking with visiting officers of the British warship *Petrel*, who said they were confident their government would shortly recognize the Confederacy. Seward was shocked to hear that mail was being read, but this wasn't foreign mail. It was Rebel mail and since they were Americans in rebellion it was American mail. Besides, in April 1863 Welles bluntly told Seward that he and the President were wrong to not use all the means available to them to protect the Union, including opening suspect mail.

In his April letter to Seward, Welles called the prohibition "so repugnant to my own convictions that I came to the conclusion it was only a passing suggestion, and the subject was therefore dropped."[3] The *Peterhoff*'s mail was in this category. *Peterhoff* was a sleek side-wheel steamer that belonged to Pile, Spence & Company of London. The ship was engaged in trade between England and Matamoros, when it was inspected by USS *Alabama* inbound for St. Thomas in the Virgin Islands. *Alabama*'s commander believed that the merchant ship's papers were in order. A short time later Charles Wilkes thought otherwise. He was commanding USS *Vanderbilt*, which had been transferred to the Navy by Commodore Vanderbilt on 9 September 1862 and was subsequently fitted out as a proper warship. It arrived on the scene just in time to follow *Peterhoff*'s departure from the harbor. While still within sight of St. Thomas, *Peterhoff* was boarded again by sailors from USS *Vanderbilt* and seized as a prize

15. Prizes and Problems Along the Red River

on 25 February 1863. Wilkes seized the international mail aboard *Peterhoff* based upon Welles' instructions. According to Secretary Seward that act prompted Lord Richard Lyons, the British Ambassador to the United States, to demand the mail back. That was a reasonable requirement, but some hoped for more. Many in the South wished that the *Peterhoff's* seizure would push England off its ledge of its faux neutrality and cause it to openly side with them. Such a step would dramatically destabilize the United States. And, even if that didn't happen it was hoped that it would at least be enough to cause the current government in England to become an even stronger or more aggressive proxy against the United States. As a Confederate surrogate, Great Britain was already doing a lot, despite its claim of neutrality. Instead of being impartial, its shipyards were building Confederate commerce raiders. Its commercial interests were furnishing the South with much of the means needed to maintain its Army, including arms, ammunition, and ordnance. Its merchant ships were openly serving southern ports. Its merchant sailors were manning many of the Confederacy's warships on the high seas. Its financial houses were extending credit or accepting cotton bonds in lieu of cash. And its government officials willingly turned a blind eye or a deaf ear to the actions of Confederate agents such as James Bulloch. They also were snail paced in reacting to urgent pleas from Lincoln's government to curb southern actions in British territories, but were quick to insult, wrong or badly treat American naval officers for carrying out their duties off British territorial waters.

Great Britain was the only nation that could challenge the Union's massive military build-up at sea. And, up through December 1863 this fact enabled it to militarily intimidate the North into accepting sanctions and conditions, thus forcing Lincoln into making concessions or apologizing for every perceived offense. Welles was also miffed at the way the United States had to cow-tow to the French too. Such groveling grated on Welles. He accepted that in 1862 the United States was in no condition to fight a war with Great Britain, but he also believed that England wasn't in any better shape to fight one with us either. In September 1863, Lincoln and Welles had a frank and lengthy written exchange of views regarding neutral vessels and relations with Britain. Welles assured the President that he was aware of his desire to keep Great Britain on friendly terms and that "in this feeling I cordially participate." "But," noted Welles, "my earnest conviction is that we shall best command the respect, which insures peace by firmly, but not offensively, maintaining our rights and in no way can amicable relations with Great Britain, and all others, be so surely maintained as by our claiming only what is right, by surrendering nothing that is already and indisputably our own; and by referring always the question of what just rights are to those tribunals of Prize; which are instituted by the consent of nations to adjudicate those points under the laws of nations...."

The need for such an exchange digressed in the fall of 1863 when it was announced that six Russian warships would winter at New York, Philadelphia, Boston, and Washington, and six would visit San Francisco. Publicly, the precise reason for this visit was uncertain. It appeared to be a simple visit of friendly convenience, but there was far more to it than mere gracious expediency. Over a quiet dinner in New York City between David Farragut and a friend from earlier years, Russian Rear Admiral Stepan Lesovski, the two prior friends discussed why the Imperial Navy was going to be port-bound for so long. To Farragut, the degree of idleness for so many ships seemed odd. Lesovski was somewhat evasive towards his old acquaintance. He said he had sealed orders from the Czar that he couldn't discuss unless something specific happened. Before long the Russian came clean, explaining that he was to open the Czar's orders if England or France declared war on the United States. If that happened the American Civil War would become a global war, with Russia and the United States as allies.[4]

The flagship of the Russian naval squadron visiting New York was the 57-gun frigate *Alexander Nevsky*, commanded by Rear Admiral Lesovski. Other frigates in the flotilla included *Peresvet* and *Oslyabya*. Lesovski also commanded two steam-powered corvettes—*Varyag* and *Vityaz*—and a steam-powered clipper, the *Almaz*, mounting seven cannons.

Gideon Welles was overjoyed by the Russian government's decision, noting in his diary, "It is a politic movement for both Russians and Americans, and somewhat annoying to France and England."[5] Although ideologically at odds with each other, Russian sentiments in the 1860s sided with the United States, as it had for over a half-century. This affinity was because the Czars saw the United States as the only nation that was capable of truly checking British naval dominance. That was convincingly reinforced to the Russian nobility during the War of 1812. In an editorial the *New York Herald* emphasized this fact in its 28 September 1863 edition by assuring its readers, "The Emperor Alexander of Russia has not and will not depart from the policy of his predecessors, because he is aware that we alone can, as a maritime Power, curb the arrogance and insolence of Great Britain, and because he must know that we cannot for a century or two in our ongoing march come athwart the progress of the great Russian empire." The *Herald's* opinion was the Czar could dominate Europe if he

15. Prizes and Problems Along the Red River

wanted to do so, but the United States only wanted to remain unmolested by any of the empires in the Old World so that it successfully put down the insurrection in the south.

Russia was in the same boat. It was contending with its own rebellion in Poland, which put it in a somewhat similar position against potentially identical foes as the United States—England and France. In the summer of 1863 Britain asked the United States to join with it in condemning Russia for its treatment of the Poles, but Secretary Seward flatly refused. He was unwilling to abandon a longstanding friend for a fickle one. It was clear the American-Russian relationship was more than one of mere convenience. Instead, the announced Russian naval visit was seen for what it was ... an alliance.[6] Clearly the greed of British merchants in wanting to sell to the South was the root cause of the souring of U.S. relations with Great Britain. If these merchants hadn't been so insistent on running goods and war material illegally through the blockade, there wouldn't have been a problem. Parliament realized that its merchants were at fault for not observing the neutrality insisted upon by the Queen's government; but instead the fault was tacked onto the naval officer whose actions brought much of the issue into sharp focus—Charles Wilkes. *Punch*, the popular British satirical magazine, poked fun at the man it believed was behind much of the international upset. *Punch* said it would like to commend Charles Wilkes to Parliament, suggesting he should receive some sort of a medal for giving it so much to joke about during what might have otherwise been a dull season. The fruits of his follies graced many of the publication's pages from 1861 to 1863. During that time Wilkes had become Uncle Sam's most infamous naval officer of the era in Europe. By the summer of 1863 he had racked up complaints from the governments of Spain, Denmark, Mexico, and Great Britain.

Wilkes' antics aside, it didn't take long to sense which way the winds were beginning to blow. By the end of September Welles was sensing "a better tone and temper in England, and I think in France also."[7] As a further olive branch Britain's ambassador, Lord Richard Lyons, joined Welles and Seward at a diplomatic dinner, accompanied by what was said to be the first British admiral to visit the United States in 40 years. The admiral, Sir Archibald Berkeley Milne, couldn't have been more gracious towards Welles. He "[c]omplimented the energy we had displayed, the forbearance exercised, the comparatively few vexatious and conflicting questions which had arisen under the extraordinary condition of affairs, the management of the extensive blockade, and the general administration of our naval matter," wrote Welles.[8] Milne's charm offensive worked. "It is, I

Black Sailors in the Civil War

think, the harbinger of a better state of things, or rather of a change of policy by the English government," he wrote that October.[9] Anglo-American relations appeared to be improving, and perhaps just in time. Where war with England wasn't thinkable in 1861 or 1862, by 1863 the United States had turned the balance of naval power on its head with the visit of the Russian fleet and the Union's own naval build-up. It had also made great refinements in tested iron-clad technology and now had proven experience with heavy naval ordnance.

These innovations made wooden sailing ships obsolete. The United States had also gained a great deal of practical experience with the deadly use of exploding shells against actual armored vessels and fortifications, more than almost every other country, and that would give it a distinct advantage against any foreign enemy. And, it had a growing understanding of naval mine technology. Additionally, by 1863 the North had successfully mobilized its manufacturing capacity to sustain a war effort and it had a large, rapidly expanding navy. The nation also had a large standing army, which was rapidly expanding, thanks to the addition of colored troops; and, it had state militias in its border states that might elect to invade Canada. That was one of the nice things about the United States in the 1860s, it had no overseas territories to protect. Great Britain had many protectorates, and most were vulnerable to coastal naval attack. The Palmerston Government had to weigh all these factors. It also had to consider what the British war debt might be if it decided to declare war against the United States over its interdiction of illegal blockade-runners in its war against the slave holding south.

Was it worth that added financial cost? In addition to the financial price tag, England was tired of fighting wars. She fought a disastrous war in the Crimea against Russia (1853–1856), she put down the bloody Sepoy Mutiny in India (1857–1858), and she fought an opium war in China (1856–1860) all in the previous decade. Were the British willing to endure another decade of bloodshed? For the United States in the early 1860s, the real struggle was over the enforceability of the blockade more than getting back at England for its blatant hand in facilitating Confederate blockade-running and commerce raiding; and, its open promotion of southern naval and commercial interests, despite declaring itself neutral. By 1863 what Welles wanted most was for England to accept that the United States would "command the respect which ensures peace, by firmly, but not offensively, maintaining our rights...."[10] Those "rights" were now far broader than just the blockade. He reasoned that you cannot claim your country is neutral and then allow your countrymen to do what they've been allowed to do. Instead, he wanted the British government to

15. Prizes and Problems Along the Red River

curb that country's substantial aid to our nation's enemy or run the risk of war. "Having been permitted to aid the insurgents without hindrance from the government, the English ship builders and others have undoubtedly plunged into the matter of furnishing aid to the Rebels to an extent that is becoming alarming to that government, and which, if fully carried out, must lead to hostilities between the two countries," Welles told Secretary Seward in January 1863.[11] In early 1863, Welles was hawkish on the prospects of war with England, while the nation's chief diplomat didn't wish to ruffle any European feathers and certainly not make any fly in anger. Welles accepted Seward's dovish nature as a reflection of Lincoln's desires. He was fully aware of the President's wish to placate Great Britain and make all reasonable concessions to her to preserve the peace. He just didn't agree with what was always considered "reasonable." He told that to the President at the end of September 1863, when the atmosphere in Europe was highly uncertain.

Nikolai Demidoff was a Russian sailor on *Almaz*, one of two Imperial warships that visited the United States Naval Academy at Annapolis, Maryland, in February 1864. Regrettably, he was killed over a drink in a local tavern. The Provost Marshal forbade the serving of alcohol to men in uniform. Whether that pertained to foreign military personnel wasn't clear, but the barkeeper refused to serve Demidoff. A fight erupted during which the sailor was mortally shot. To placate the Russians, Demidoff was buried with full military honors after a Russian Orthodox funeral mass at the Naval Academy's Chapel. He was interred in the Academy's National Cemetery.

The *Peterhoff* case is an amazing study of the political wills of Welles and Seward at work. "Seward is in great trouble about the mail of the *Peterhoff*, a captured blockade-runner. Wants the mail given up. Says the instructions which he prepared insured the inviolability and security of the mails," Welles recorded in his diary.[12] Welles strongly disagreed with Seward's "instructions," prompting Seward to make a house call on Welles on Saturday, 11 April 1863, to try to resolve their personal impasse. Seward insisted that the mail was sacred, and said that he had personally made arrangements with the British legation to have it returned to the British postal service. Again, Welles disagreed, saying the matter was now beyond the Navy's control. Instead, he said it was a matter for the prize court to decide. Over this issue, Welles became uncharacteristically feisty, asking Seward if he truly had the authority to make such a promise to the British legation, and asked whether his agreement constituted a treaty, and if so, had it received confirmation by the Senate. In his diary Welles recorded that during their meeting, he "[t]old him the law and the courts must govern in this matter," pointing out that "the Secretary of State and the Executive were powerless. We could not interfere."[13] Welles also made it clear that the Navy didn't take orders from the State Department. On 13 April, Welles wrote a lengthy letter to Seward outlining the issues of the case, making it a point to say that "the idea that our Naval officers should be compelled to forward the mails found on board the vessels of the insurgents—that foreign officials would have the sanction of this government in confiding their mails to blockade-runners and vessels contraband, and that without judicial or other investigation, the officers of our service should hasten such mails, without examination, to their destination, was so repugnant to my own convictions that I came to the conclusion it was only a passing suggestion, and the subject was therefore dropped."[14]

Seward fired back with a nasty letter of his own, dragging the President into the argument. Seward's reproach had the opposite effect than hoped. Instead of getting the Navy's Secretary to kowtow, Welles dug in deeper, writing in his diary, "The President may be induced to order the mail to be given up, but the law is higher than an Executive Order, and the judiciary has a duty to perform. The mail is in the custody of the court."[15] Seward pressed Welles to comply, reminding him of the President's position back in August, but when Welles pursued this with Lincoln, he couldn't recall making any such ruling. In the Navy's letterbook for 20 April 1863, alongside a copy of Seward's letter to Welles, is the penciled notation: "The President said he did not recollect having approved this [unintelligible] nor did he remember it being ever brought to his notice, but he presumed it had been because Mr. Seward said so." Welles stuck to his guns, insisting that the prize court was the proper place to decide such questions. He also frankly told Seward that if the *Peterhoff*'s mail had been opened, and if her capture proved to be an error, then reading her mail might have been an illegal act. In the meantime, he said the mailbags are in the possession of the prize court and that was the appropriate place to decide their fate. Lincoln told both men that he was no expert on either subject, but that something had to be done. Neither Welles nor Seward would give in. During the next few days both sent nasty letters to the other. Lincoln realized this petty quibbling had to end. As usual, his principal objective was to "keep the peace" within his Cabinet, as well as in this instance, with the British, who according to Seward, were insistent they get their mail back. With that aim in mind, on 21 April the President addressed a joint letter to both his feuding Cabinet members, informing them: "It is now a practical question for this Government whether a government mail of a neutral power, found

15. Prizes and Problems Along the Red River

on board a vessel captured by a belligerent power, on charge of breach of blockade, shall be forwarded to its designated designation, without opening; or shall be placed in custody of the prize court to be in the discretion of the court opened and searched for evidence to be used on the trial of the prize case. I will thank each of you to furnish me. Firstly, a list of all cases wherein such question has been passed upon, either by a diplomatic or a judicial decision. Secondly, all cases wherein mail under such circumstances have been without special discussion either forwarded unopened, or detained and opened in search of evidence. I wish these lists to embrace the reported cases as well in the books generally, as the cases pertaining to the present war in the United States. Thirdly, a statement and brief argument of what would be the danger and evils of forwarding such mails unopened. Fourthly, a statement and brief argument of what would be the dangers and evils of detaining and opening such mails, and using the contents, if pertinent, as evidence. And lastly, any general remarks that occur to you or either of you." Welles dutifully responded to the President's directive on 27 April, submitting a carefully prepared 31-page legal-sized brief. According to Welles' diary, "It has occupied almost every moment of my time for a week."[16] Welles was aided in preparing his position paper by several outstanding attorneys and Attorney General Bates.

He also shared his brief with Massachusetts Senator Charles Sumner and Salmon Chase, who concurred with his position. Seward basically argued the "sanctity of the seal," a longstanding domestic and international postal standard that said that under normal circumstances mail was not subject to censorship or search. Welles countered that this was not a normal circumstance, it was a wartime measure, and mail had never been seized from a blockade-runner before so the application of that standard should not apply. Welles' statement wasn't true. In early January 1863 Du Pont furnished Welles with Rebel mail intercepted off Charleston from a Confederate vessel. A Rebel officer aboard the ship dutifully threw a weighted mailbag overboard as the bluecoats were boarding to keep it from falling into Federal hands, but the bag he tossed was empty. The ship's master, whom Welles had previously sacked for drunkenness, switched the contents to another sack to save his bacon. The opened letters, including some from the southern Secretaries of the Navy, Treasury and State Departments, were provided to Welles, who distributed some of the more interesting missives to his Cabinet colleagues on 13 January. Lincoln pondered every point in Welles' submission regarding the *Peterhoff*'s mail. He was struck with its comprehensive and compelling arguments, but was plagued by its singular flaw in one very crucial piece of persuasion—had the courts ever actually opened the mails of a neutral government taken from a captured prize? On 15 May, Lincoln went to see his Navy Secretary to discuss this important question mark. Welles emphatically said that this *always* happened when mails were captured on board a good prize. Lincoln insisted that if that was, so he wanted to read examples of where that was indeed the case. He wanted to see the proof of that statement. Welles didn't have it. Instead, he told the President that the subject never had been questioned before, and that as such, "The courts made no report to me whether they opened or did not open the mail." As a lawyer, Lincoln wasn't buying such evasion. If a court used the mails as evidence in a case, there should be some record of that evidence having been presented, Lincoln insisted. Welles was told to find such evidentiary records. He couldn't. This one critical flaw in Welles' argument, known as a "rat" in Navy parlance, might have proved sufficient to drown his otherwise thoughtful position, except for what happened over the course of the next few days. The President talked with Senator Charles Sumner during a casual White House visit on 27 April and the conversation got around to the *Peterhoff* situation. Lincoln said that the United States could ill afford to fight a war over some silly letters. Sumner shared this conversation with Welles, saying he wasn't sure if this was the President's real thought, or his affected ignorance. Welles said he had no doubts that the President was sincere in his concern, but that such fear-mongering was being imposed and reinforced by Seward's constant wailing in his ear. "The President is thus led away from the real question, and will probably decide it, not on its merits, but on this false issue, raised by the man who is the author of the difficulty," he confided to his diary on 28 April. Knowing what he now knew, Sumner would prove to be the key to resolving this matter. At a reception hosted by the Spanish Minister to the United States the following evening Senator Sumner had an occasion to talk with Lord Lyons about the *Peterhoff*'s mail. Sumner said that he deeply regretted that Great Britain hadn't made its demands in such a way as to avoid giving offense to the United States and bringing things to the brink of war. The British diplomat was stunned over this. There had never been any demands by his government, the ambassador insisted. That had been studiously avoided.

Seward had turned this into a crisis. He had imposed made-up demands, not Great Britain, Lyons insisted. And, to prove this point, Lord Lyons said he'd authorize Sumner, who was chairman of the Senate's Foreign Relations Committee, to see all his legation's correspondence regarding the mail taken from *Peterhoff* if he wished. The following day Sumner reported all this to the President, who was dumbfounded. "I shall have to

15. Prizes and Problems Along the Red River

cut this knot," he reportedly told Sumner. Neither Welles nor Sumner was sure what the President meant by "cut this knot," but it sounded positive.[17] Ultimately, Welles' decision to disrupt the mails would be upheld, as would his assumption that the mail of belligerents could be detained and searched. The opinion of the prize court judge, Samuel Rossiter Betts of the Southern District of New York, was rendered in 1864. Betts' court presided over roughly half of all prize cases presented during the war, so the process was slow, but deliberative. Betts' opinion was that *Peterhoff* was indeed a blockade-runner based upon its cargo, which included large quantities of army boots, gray blankets, and four-horse artillery harnesses with side saddles, along with large quantities of quinine, calomel, morphine and chloroform, all of which were desperately needed by the Confederacy. The United States Navy subsequently purchased the *Peterhoff*. As a Federal warship USS *Peterhoff*'s service was short-lived. She was commissioned in February 1864 and assigned to the North Atlantic Blockading Squadron. In taking up her position off New Inlet, North Carolina, she collided with USS *Monticello* on 6 March 1864 and sank. To ensure that the South could never salvage her, *Peterhoff*'s hulk was used for gunnery practice by USS *Mount Vernon* the following day.

After the war, the Supreme Court overruled the prize court's ruling on the *Peterhoff* case, ordering the Federal government to make plaintiff compensation for its loss. A partial synopsis of the high court's key point in its 1866 opinion was that: "a belligerent cannot blockade the mouth of a river, occupied on one bank by neutrals with complete rights of navigation; and, that a vessel destined for a neutral port with no ulterior destination for the ship, or none by sea for the cargo to any blockaded place, violates no blockade. Hence trade, during the late rebellion, between London and Matamoros, two neutral places, the last an inland one of Mexico, and close to our Mexican boundary, even with intent to supply, from Matamoros, goods to Texas, then an enemy of the United States, was not unlawful on the ground of such violation."

While not unlawful, for the South Matamoros proved to be an expensive port of importation. By 1863 a pair of army shoes that should have cost $2.25 almost anywhere else were being invoiced at Matamoros for $9, payable in cotton at a rate of 12.5-cents a pound. (The going rate for cotton elsewhere within the South was averaging 30-cents a pound.)

At the time of the *Peterhoff*'s seizure, Charles Wilkes was out hunting CSS *Florida*, which had eluded Union blockaders in broad daylight, boldly sailing past a Federal warship commanded by Captain George

Black Sailors in the Civil War

H. Preble, who only offered a meager challenge since the ship was flying British colors as it entered the port of Mobile. Welles was livid over Preble's performance, calling it "sheer pusillanimous neglect."[18] In truth Welles wished it had been someone else. Preble was from a distinguished and decorated naval family, and he was well connected with many powerful people, but in this case, Welles realized that simple slap on the wrists would do no good.

If Welles amply rewarded success he was equally heartless in cases of feebleness and indecision. His diary entry for 20 September 1862 records: "The time has arrived when these derelictions must not go unpunished." Welles anguished over what to do. He consulted with Secretary Seward and Attorney General Bates, each of whom advised dismissal. He also talked the matter over with the President, who recommended letting Preble go if Welles thought it wise. Lincoln said he'd do it if the choice was up to him. Preble was sacked. The Navy Secretary informed Preble's commanding officer, David Farragut, on 21 September 1862, saying "Enclosed, herewith, is an order of the Department dismissing Commander Preble from the service." But Welles went further, ordering copies of a *General Order* regarding Preble's conduct to be read aloud on the quarter-deck of each vessel in Farragut's squadron. Within days Preble began mobilizing sufficient support for his possible reinstatement. A delegation from Maine led by Senator William Fressenden petitioned the President to restore Preble and overturn his dismissal for neglect of duty. Welles responded to Fressenden on behalf of the President on 9 October 1862, assuring them that the President had reviewed their petition and felt compelled to sustain his decision to remove Preble. But Preble wasn't finished in his attempts to regain his position. In response to subsequent efforts by Preble, Welles was forced to convene a three-member naval board of inquiry, headed by Rear Admiral Andrew Hull Foote, to review the case. The board concluded that he had indeed failed "to perform his whole duty as senior officer of the force blockading Mobile, and further, that he did not do his utmost to prevent the passage of the steamer 'Oreto' [CSS *Florida*] into the harbor."[19] Preble acknowledged that he made an error and the board asked as an act of "grace and clemency that he be restored to the Naval service." During the proceedings Preble blamed Farragut for his failure, saying his commanding officer never forwarded adequate instructions on how to prevent blockade-runners. Also, while the board was meeting, Senator Fressenden repeatedly asked the President and Secretary Welles to reconsider their decisions. He even got the Naval Committee of the Senate to request that Preble be reinstated. The White House and the Navy Department also

15. Prizes and Problems Along the Red River

received countless testimonials telling of Preble's bravery and great service to the nation. All of this came to a head in February 1863. Based on such entreaties from Fressenden and others, and the naval board's recommendations, Welles was worn down. On 3 February, Welles submitted a lengthy report to the President outlining all the proceedings for his consideration and decision "should you deem it proper to re-nominate Commander Preble to his former position in the Navy." Based upon the President's favorable decision, reluctantly Welles accepted Preble back into the Navy family but assigned him to Portuguese waters in command of an old sailing sloop. As the flap over Preble was unfolding Secretary Welles was dealing with additional upset created by Secretary Seward. Seward had passed on the contents of an unofficial British complaint to Welles on 10 October 1862, over the seizure of the steamer *Bermuda*.

The ship had been purchased by the South in September 1861 and captured on 27 April 1862 by USS *Mercedita*, but according to Seward, the British wanted her back prior to her condemnation as a prize and being taken into Union naval service. Seward told Welles that "such a measure would afford ground for serious complaint on the part of the British Government which, under the existing circumstances, it is desirable to avoid." Welles didn't care. He responded to Seward on 15 October reminding him in a multi-page letter precisely how such captured vessels are correctly adjudicated. He also expressed shock over the British attitude regarding the taking of the *Bermuda*. "I cannot forbear the expression of my surprise at the interposition of her Majesty's representative in behalf of a vessel captured with such an amount of contraband of war on board intended to afford assistance to Rebels who are waging war upon this government. Her cargo of guns, shot, shell, powder, etc., is a perfect magazine of munitions designed, as you and I well knew before she left the shores of England, for those of our countrymen who are in insurrection." *Bermuda* became USS *George Meade*.[20] Throughout this period of Seward's and Welles' distractions over ships and mail, the threat of French intervention in Texas remained. Maximilian soon begin offering disaffected Confederates opportunities to start over in Mexico rather than face occupation by their northern aggressors, further supporting the possible idea of expanding the French colony into Texas. In addition to blunting any attempt to take Texas a further underlying aim of the Red River campaign was to get at the estimated 100,000 bales of cotton reportedly held along the Red River. In this latter regard, for both Porter and his Army counterpart, this became purely and simply a glorified cotton grab. Cotton had been the South's ace card, but playing it hadn't panned out. Before the war, South Carolina Senator James

Black Sailors in the Civil War

Henry Hammond gave a speech before the United States Senate in which he declared: "Without firing a gun, without drawing a sword, should they make war on us, we could bring the whole world to our feet.... What would happen if no cotton was furnished for three years?.... England would topple headlong and carry the whole civilized world with her save the South. No, you dare not to make war on cotton. No power on the earth dares to make war upon it. Cotton is king." He was right at the time.

Before the war, cotton represented nearly 60 percent of the total exports of the United States. Cotton literally balanced the national debt. Many believed cotton was indeed America's economic "king." That phenomenon was the result of the Indian Removal Act, which became law in May 1830. That Act opened millions of acres of Indian tribal lands to cotton cultivation because of the forced relocation of the Creeks, Choctaws, Osages, Cherokees, Pawnees and other southeastern tribes. The "Trail of Tears" for one race became a source of wealth for another, and a legacy of pain, suffering and slavery for a third. Access to these lands, and the corresponding attempts to extend slavery into these territories, was a catalyst for transforming Welles from a loyal 30-year-long Democrat into an avid Republican. The debate over what to do with Kansas and Nebraska was a turning point in his life. His view was that: "If the Compromise of 1820 is swept away, now can that of 1850 stand? Broken compacts and violated promises invite contempt, and lead to anarchy. Some of our Southern friends, I apprehend are not aware of the seed they are sowing; but they may have to gather the thorns that they plant. I say this in no bad or taunting spirit, but they should recollect that the vibrations of the popular pendulum are to extremes. One extreme follows another as they will find should the act of 1820 be repealed. I am no apologist or admirer of the Missouri Compromise, but the circumstances attending its enactment and acquiescence of the whole country in it, reaffirmed and acknowledged as it has been on repeated occasions as a solemn compact and agreement, impart to it more than ordinary legislative sanctity. Repeal it and the whole public mind will be roused. No northern man who votes for it can sustain himself—he will sink where plummet will never find him. Nor will the public indignation be appeased with these victims only. It will demand more, and it will have more...."[21] For Welles the debates of the 1850s was more than merely allowing for "popular sovereignty." He believed that this was a case of potentially breaking a three-decades old binding national compact to appease southern interests. The resulting Kansas-Nebraska Act of 1854 greatly disappointed Welles. It allowed the settlers in those territories to decide to allow slavery within their borders or not. It also repealed

15. Prizes and Problems Along the Red River

the Missouri Compromise of 1820, which forbade slavery above latitude 36°30'. Unfortunately for the South, Great Britain found alternative sources for cotton in India and Egypt, destroying "King Cotton's" reign by 1862.

During the war years, northern textile mills also desperately needed cotton. Contraband cotton occasionally came on the northern market, as when 60 bales of Sea Island cotton was offered for sale at auction on 10 April 1862 by order of the government. This sale also included 23 bales of superior Gulf cotton. The sale, by Burdell, Jones and Company at Wall and Front Streets in New York City, was advertised in the 7 April edition of the *New York World*. At the same time jute, flax and hemp yarn were being promoted as substitutes for cotton yarn. In late 1862 the need for cotton drove the Federal government to consider issuing special exemptions for trading with southern planters for cotton. Secretary Welles strenuously opposed the idea of such "trade permits" as a simultaneous scheme to both fight and feed the enemy.

The British attitude in 1862 was that its textile manufacturers simply didn't wish to wait to see which side would win out in the American Civil War, deciding instead to buy cotton from India. These are cotton bales at Bombay, India, in the 1860s awaiting shipment to England. (Library of Congress)

Black Sailors in the Civil War

Permits or not, unscrupulous northern brokers intended to get their hands on southern cotton any way they could. And such northern cotton shipments from southern territory were tempting targets for Rebel guerrillas. On 7 November 1863, as example, the *Allen Collier*, a merchant ship attempted to illegally load up on cotton destined for the North, was taken over when she landed at a point less than a half-mile from a Federal gunboat. Rear Admiral Porter told Secretary Welles that this loss was "in consequence of disobedience of orders prohibiting vessels landing at any point except under cover of a gunboat." It also was a consequence of an illegal transaction. What the *Allen Collier* was doing was landing at designated locations and trading with locals, food or cash in the form of greenbacks or various southern banknotes, whatever the sellers would take, for cotton. These transactions were conducted without any government approval. In the case of the *Allen Collier*, the gunboat USS *Eastport* was within sight of a merchant steamer when she tied up to make the trades.

Regrettably, *Eastport's* boilers were being cleaned at the time of the attack and she was down to about 250 bushels of coal, so she was unable to furnish immediate assistance. The Rebel boarding party burned the *Allen Collier* at Whitworth's Landing, Mississippi. In reporting the incident on 12 November, Porter advised Welles, "I am not surprised at the burning of the steamer, and only wonder that we have not more of it, as there is a most extensive system of smuggling going on up and down the river out of sight of the gunboats, the Rebels frequently going on board and regaling themselves, a perfect understanding existing between them and the people on board." A somewhat similar thing occurred at Cole's Creek, Mississippi, on 18 February 1865, when the steamer *Mattie Stephens* was attempting to take on 100 bales of "properly permitted" cotton when she came under Rebel attack. This time however, the *Mattie Stephens* was under the protection of USS *Forest Rose*, which opened fire on the Confederate raiding party as soon as the merchant ship was out of the line of fire. The firefight was lopsided, with the Union gunboat firing four 32-pound shells with five-second fuses, four 24-pound shells with three-second fuses, and six rounds of canister shot in a matter of minutes. The guerrillas barely had time to set fire to the cotton before fleeing for their lives. The *Forest Rose* immediately landed, and sailors extinguished the fire, saving all but five bales. The following year southern planters, who by then were financially strapped and awash with cotton, suggested designating New Orleans and Baton Rouge as special free trade zones, called "cotton depots," where bales could be exchanged for northern greenbacks. Secretary Welles was okay with this idea, believing it might be a good way of perhaps opening

15. Prizes and Problems Along the Red River

the whole country west of the Mississippi River above New Orleans to the benefits of peaceably returning to the Union; this time General Grant opposed the thought as adverse to the interests of the Army. He feared Army units would become more interested in searching for cotton than searching out the enemy, which is precisely what happened to the Navy on the Red River. The concept of cotton trading continued to plague the Lincoln administration in 1864. It divided the Cabinet and caused Welles to ultimately label the matter "a disgrace and wickedness."

Despite such schemes, the Union's brown- and blue-water sailors were more than willing to capture and claim cotton for prize money. The South's principal cotton ports were Charleston, Houston, Mobile, New Orleans and Savannah, which made them primary naval targets. Five percent of the southern ships taken as prizes in 1861 included cotton as all or as part of the cargo. The percentage of water-borne cotton-related seizures grew to 11 percent in 1862. It increased to 16 percent in 1863 and rose to 33 percent in 1864. Bales seized by Union riverine forces from plantations or confiscated from wharves and levees also provided exceptional prize money for Union ship crews. While service on larger blockaders might afford greater opportunities to share in prize money, service on smaller ships had advantages too. Unlike larger ships, where service could be ho-hum, sailors on smaller ships often enjoyed a variety of different assignments that made their service-time exciting. When called upon, the sailors aboard USS *Cowslip*, a 123-foot side-wheeler, as example, worked her as a tug, dispatch ship, rescue and salvage ship, mail ship, picket boat, gunboat, and ammunition runner. She also conducted salt work raids, wrecking four off the Mississippi and Florida coasts. *Cowslip's* only prize during the war was the seizure of 75 bales of cotton. An especially large brown-water seizure occurred as part of the joint Army-Navy expedition at Steele's Bayou between 14 and 27 March 1863, in conjunction with a plan to capture Vicksburg, when the Navy discovered a mother lode near Rolling Fork, Mississippi—an estimated 20,000 bales. To impede Rear Admiral David Dixon Porter's progress, and thwart the cotton seizures, Rebels began felling trees in front of his flotilla's path in the narrow creeks and waterways. They also began felling trees behind his position too, prompting a well-advised withdrawal. The waterways were so narrow that the ships had to glide out backwards with the current. While much of this prize had to be destroyed, Porter reported that enough cotton was saved "to pay for the building of a good gunboat." Such seizures enabled some naval officers and their sailors to amass sizeable fortunes in prize money.

Black Sailors in the Civil War

Some seizures created problems for Welles, especially whenever Secretary of State William Seward was involved. *Emma* was a case in point. Capable of making 12-knots, the British screw steamer was attempting to blend in with her blockaders, falling in line in front of USS *Arago*, a side-wheel coastal survey ship under the command of the Navy, off Wilmington on 24 July 1863. *Arago* was loaded with Union wounded. *Emma* was loaded with cotton. Oddly, *Emma's* crew began dumping cotton bales overboard for no apparent reason, which made *Arago's* crew suspicious. Realizing something wasn't right *Arago* gave chase as *Emma* began pulling away. Capable of making 12-knots, *Arago* was twice *Emma's* size. During the seven-hour run-down *Emma's* crew jettisoned additional cotton bales and put on as much steam as possible in attempting to outrun her Army pursuer. None of these efforts worked and when seized, *Emma's* captain admitted his guilt. The British ship was adjudicated in prize court in New York City on 30 September 1863, and the 156-foot-long vessel was sold. The Navy purchased the ship for naval use. *Emma* was sent to the Brooklyn Navy Yard for hasty conversion into a warship. There she was armed with six 24-pound howitzers and a pair of 12-pound rifles. Unbeknownst to anyone, Secretary Seward had given assurances to the British government in May 1863 that nothing would happen to any captured British vessels until they were consulted on the validity of the seizures. By the time Welles learned of Seward's pledge, *Emma* was well on her way to entering naval service. Lincoln ultimately had to intercede. The President was visibly annoyed with Seward's haste and impudence in making such a promise, especially with respect to *Emma*, which was clearly operating in violation of the blockade, but his decision was that Seward's pledge needed to be considered and redeemed, if possible. Welles was furious. His opinion of Seward's persistent meddling was that it was the cause of constant difficulty and embarrassment. With Seward, Welles believed "Our rights he almost invariably surrendered to foreign demands during the war."[22] Welles had the satisfaction of knowing that Seward's promise wouldn't apply to *Emma*. USS *Emma* put to sea on 4 November 1863, with orders to join the North Atlantic Blockading Squadron, where she served as a picket and dispatch ship. There she participated in the blockade and shared in the grounding of the 404-ton paddle steamer blockade-runner *Ella* off Wilmington on 6 December 1864.

Ella was owned by Fraser, Trenholm and Company, a prominent cotton brokerage that amassed a fortune running cotton to Europe and returning with overpriced essentials for the South. The company owned or had a stake in over 60 blockade-runners, including sleek and swift

15. Prizes and Problems Along the Red River

steamers like *Fox, Badger, Alliance,* and *Gibraltar. Fox* slipped in and out of southern ports so often that she earned her own Union nickname—"an old and successful sinner." Fraser, Trenholm and Company's Liverpool office was the base of operations for Confederate purchasing agents. The firm's wartime profits amounted to about $9 million. George Alfred Trenholm was the firm's director. Trenholm was the Confederacy's Secretary of the Treasury from July 1864 to April 1865 and one of the wealthiest men in the South. *Emma* also participated in the attacks on Fort Fisher. *Emma's* most crucial role in the war came in April 1865, when she conveyed an urgent massage to Rear Admiral John Dahlgren, commanding the South Atlantic Blockading Squadron, to be on the lookout for Jefferson Davis and other Confederate officials attempting to flee to Cuba. USS *Emma* ended her naval career on 30 August 1865. She was sold on 1 November 1865.

Arago had her share of distinctions too, including the honor of transporting Major General Robert Anderson and the American flag that had flown over the unfinished Fort Sumter with its 137 defenders in April 1861 back to the fort, where the flag was ceremonially hoisted again four years to the day after it was lowered by then–Major Anderson, marking the surrender of the fort and the start of the Civil War.

All in all, the Red River campaign strategy was ill-conceived and neither the Army nor the Navy cooperated as planned. The expedition had questionable strategic value and no clear overall operational control. Major General Nathaniel P. Banks, commanding the Army's portion of the mission, and Rear Admiral Porter, commanding the river forces, each had independent commands, and each distrusted the other. In addition, Banks was accompanied by an army of cotton buyers, revealing where his true motives lay in the outcome of the operation. Logistically, the campaign was iffy from the start. The whole enterprise began later than originally planned. And it commenced at a time when the water levels on the Red River were already far too low for a viable naval campaign, hindering Porter's attempts to get all his vessels above the rapids at Alexandria, Louisiana, which was occupied on 16 March 1864. The deficient water levels at the start should have forewarned Porter of the potential doom and foolhardiness of the undertaking, but the lure of all that cotton may well have clouded his better judgment. The joint Army-Navy Red River Expedition between 10 March and 22 May 1864 was the largest such joint riverine operation of the war, involving a combined Army-Navy fleet of 90 vessels ... and it was an absolute fiasco from start to finish. In addition to possibly taking Texas out of the war, a further underlying aim of the Red River campaign was to get at the estimated 100,000 bales of cotton reportedly held along the Red River.

Porter's Navy moved faster than Banks's Army. Arriving first, between Fort DeRussy and Alexandria, Louisiana, Union bluejackets fanned out like ants in search of cotton. Alexandria's warehouses offered up about 300 bales, and at one plantation sailors discovered a cache of unginned cotton, which they promptly ginned and baled themselves. Cotton bales were seen rolling end-over-end towards the river from every possible direction. Black sailors had an easier time getting slaves to tell them where cotton was hidden. This confiscated cotton hoard was stashed in every naval nook and cranny, including the empty coal bunkers of Porter's ships, for immediate shipment to Cairo, Illinois. When Banks and his cotton buyers arrived at Alexandria's wharf, they were appalled to see that the Navy had already cornered the cotton market. If cotton was easy pickings, Confederates weren't. From the start, Confederate forces along the Red River confounded Porter's Navy. At Springfield Landing, Louisiana, about 20-miles below Shreveport, for example, Rebels did something that Major General William T. Sherman admitted even made him laugh. "It was the smartest thing I ever knew the Rebels to do," he said. "They had gotten that huge steamer, *New Falls City*, across Red River, one-mile above Loggy Bayou, 15 feet of her on shore on each side, the boat broken down the middle, and a sand bar making below her." Porter's flotilla could get no closer to Shreveport than the hulk of the *New Falls City*. By the time the bisected boat could be cleared away, Union forces under Major General Banks had already been handily defeated in a series of battles, leaving the whole campaign in doubt and Porter without Army protection along the river's edge.

In late April 1864, Porter sent Secretary Welles a confidential communiqué outlining the Army's failed actions, including defeats at Carroll's Mills, Louisiana (7 April); Sabine Crossroads, Louisiana (8 April, 4:00 p.m.); Pleasant Grove, Louisiana (8 April, 6:00 p.m.); Pleasant Hill, Louisiana (9 April); and Blair's Landing, Louisiana (12 April), all of which showed Porter that Banks had no military capacity. After reading Porter's dispatch, Welles noted in his diary, "The whole affair is unfortunate." Porter had committed an exceedingly large naval force to this expedition. The sheer size of his naval force prompted some to believe that Porter, like Banks, was perhaps more interested in the potential prize money or sales that might be gained from seizing Louisiana's cotton. That was more important, some argued, than the credit gained by taking control over Confederate waters or by capturing Shreveport. This, some claimed, was why the expedition needed so many ships. Porter and Banks needed

15. Prizes and Problems Along the Red River

them to carry off their anticipated cotton hauls, some believed. Porter ultimately came away with roughly 3,000 bales.

For Porter's sailors, finding cotton now wasn't the primary concern. Avoiding Rebel forces was more of an issue. Confederate forces took every opportunity to harass the Union's ships, peppering them along the river with near constant musket and light artillery fire. The frequency and accuracy of these attacks caused one naval commander to use a periscope to sight potential targets just to keep from getting shot himself, a first in Civil War naval annals. The Rebels also began sending fire ships down river at Union ships, and they mined sections of the waterway. And any Union ship that attempted to "choke a tree" at night ran the risk of being boarded by a southern raiding party.

Mother Nature conspired with the enemy too. Having gotten above the rapids at Alexandria, the continually falling water levels threatened to trap all of Porter's ships there. Further compounding Porter's plight, the gradually declining levels exposed sand bars that repeatedly grounded many of his vessels, leaving them vulnerable to the Confederate's hit-and-run attacks, which were constant. At low water the river was also thick with deadheads and sawyers that threatened to damage hulls. Rebel forces also helped Mother Nature along by diverting water into other outlets, further lowering the water levels on the Red River. By the end of April, the Navy's position was becoming precarious, forcing Porter to admit to Secretary Welles that his entire force was in jeopardy. By 27 April, Porter had what was left of his fleet assemble above Alexandria where he was struggling with how best to get them all safely past the rapids, which by then were running at a depth of only about three feet, far too low for boat traffic. Porter's boats typically required roughly seven feet to safely clear the rapids. Porter advised Secretary Welles that, as painful as it might be to contemplate, because of what he called, "this fatal campaign,"[23] he might have to destroy his entire squadron to keep it from falling into enemy hands.

Only a miracle was going to save Porter's flotilla. Lieutenant Colonel Joseph Bailey, an engineer with the Fourth Wisconsin Cavalry, delivered that miracle, proposing to build a coffer dam just above the first of two stretches of rapids forcing water levels to rise behind the blockage. Between the rapids, which were roughly a mile apart, the water fell about 13 feet. In theory, if all went well, the dam's sluiceway effect would allow Porter's ships to surf through the cascading water over both rapids to safety. Bailey initially raised his scheme on 9 April, but his "plan was looked upon by the most as wild and chimerical," he recalled. Reluctant at first, Porter ultimately had no other viable options for saving his ships. On 30 April, Bailey was given the go-ahead. Using soldiers from Maine and New York, as well as two regiments of colored troops, Bailey started building his dam. Bailey picked a spot where the river was about 760-feet wide and had at that time an average depth of five-feet. Bailey began by sinking two 170-foot by 24-foot coal barges on the right side of the falls. These were filled with stones, bricks and iron scrap taken from foundries and sugar mills in the area. Sailors fanned out in search of lumber. Barns, shed and gins, as well as houses were pulled down or stripped of lumber for use in constructing the dams. Between the barges, construction crews created a series of 22-foot by 14-foot log-framed stone cribs that were packed with thousands of rocks, bricks, and other debris. On the left bank of the falls, crews constructed tree dams, as well as bracket dams to hold back the river. By the time Bailey's workers were nearly done, the dam stretched nearly 1,000 feet across the Red River and had a water depth of about six-and-a-half-feet. In a matter of days this massive undertaking was almost accomplished, when early on 9 May, a portion of the dam broke under the sheer weight of the water it was holding back. Without a moment's hesitation, Porter ordered those ships with the shallowest drafts to immediately shoot the unexpected spillway. *Lexington*, the oldest ship in the flotilla and therefore the most expendable, went first. *Neosho, Hindman* and *Osage* quickly followed. All four ships made it safely over the rapids. This success lifted the spirits of Porters sailor's and encouraged Bailey's troops to redouble their efforts to rebuild the dam so that the process could be repeated. On the eleventh, *Mound City, Carondelet* and *Pittsburgh*, Porter's *City*-class gunboats, ran the river.

    The following morning, *Louisville, Chillicothe*, and *Ozark*, along with a pair of tugs, successfully made the run. Once all his ships were safely over the rapids, Porter, who realized how close he had come to dodging a potentially lethal professional bullet, collapsed from exhaustion. But Porter's ships weren't safe yet. Confederate forces harassed the flotilla every chance they got over the course of the next 150-mile gauntlet back to the Mississippi River. On 16 May, Porter's riverine force entered the Mississippi, ending their agonizing ordeal on the Red River.

    Back in Washington, D.C., as the days dragged on, Secretary Welles waited to hear the worst. He had mentally prepared himself to face the news of the destruction of the entire Red River naval force. Finally, on 21 May, he received a late dispatch from Cairo, Illinois, informing him of the dam's construction at Alexandria and its success in saving the Union's Red River fleet. "The news of the passage of the whole fleet is since confirmed.

15. Prizes and Problems Along the Red River

The makeshift Red River Dam at Alexandria, Louisiana, was constructed largely by African-Americans. Their efforts saved the Union's Red River Expedition from utter disaster. (Library of Congress)

It is most gratifying intelligence," he recorded in his diary two days later.[24] What soon troubled Welles was that some in the North began spinning the Army's Red River operation as a success. "There is an attempt to convert this reverse into a victory, but the truth will disclose itself," he noted in his diary.[25] The truth did out ... the campaign was one of the North's greatest naval fiascos. Other than capturing cotton, it accomplished little, while risking a lot. While militarily the Red River campaign was a disaster for the North, it was also the last clear military victory of the war for the South. The experiences on the Red River deeply affected Rear Admiral Porter, who for medical and personal reasons never sought a river command again. Assistant Secretary Fox congratulated Porter for his miraculous escape on 25 May, and suggested, "After you get your feathers smoothed and oiled, I don't see why you should not come east, if you desire it."[26] Porter visited with Welles in July and then went on extended leave, joining his family on vacation in New Jersey.

Brown-water, coastal and high seas cotton captures continued throughout the war. Most were typical of *Lynx*, a steamer that was run down, shelled and run aground in flames off Wilmington on 25 September 1864, by USS *Howquah*, *Niphon* and *Governor Buckingham*; or USS *Mobile's* capture of the British schooner *Annie Verden* off Velasco, Texas, on 5 October 1864, with a cotton cargo (the amount of distributed prize money adjudicated for this seizure amounted to $22,847.30), and USS *Fort Jackson's* seizure of the British steamer *Wando* in the ocean off South Carolina on 21 October 1864, hauling southern cotton. (The amount of distributed prize money adjudicated for this seizure amounted to $409,486.89, which is one of the highest rewards paid out in the war.) The goal was to take a blockade-runner intact, not to destroy her, as with *Lynx*, which was fired upon when she attacked her attackers and was destroyed in the process. Other Union sailors were a bit more adventurous. The lure of prize money compelled some bluejackets to attempt daring exploits to make a

Union river monitor USS *Ozark* on a western waterway. Twenty African American sailors served aboard *Ozark*, including several who may well have opted the change their names after emancipation. Among the crewmembers with interesting names are George Washington and Horace Greeley. Both men signed aboard *Ozark* on 1 July 1864, along with several others. *Ozark's* crew shared in the distribution of prize money on the capture of 2,158 bales of cotton during the war. (Naval History and Heritage Command)

15. Prizes and Problems Along the Red River

seizure. On 26 December 1864, sailors of the Western Gulf Blockading Squadron from USS *Virginia* captured the schooner *Belle* with a load of cotton in a nighttime raid inside Galveston Bay, right under the noses of Confederate gunners at Fort Point. A little over a month later, the feat was repeated when the schooners *Annie Sophia* and *Pet* were seized in nighttime raids inside Galveston Bay, this time by 22 sailors from USS *Princess Royal* and USS *Bienville*. Both hijacked vessels contained a total of 476 bales of cotton. In submitting his report on these latter two audacious seizures, the commander of the Second Division of the Western Gulf Blockading Squadron, Captain George Emmons, made it a point to say that he expected the sailors involved would all receive a fair share of the prize money from the sale of the cotton and disposal of the schooners. Emmons was a real entrepreneur. In September 1862, he was found to be issuing safe conduct passes to merchant ships importing and exporting merchandise at ports under blockade. This practice prompted Secretary Welles to remind his Western Gulf Blockading Squadron commander, David Farragut, that New Orleans was the only port open to southern general traffic and that such "permits" could only come from the Secretaries of Treasury, War or Navy. Any vessels caught evading this order were to be immediately seized.

16

Coffee

If prize money were new to Black sailors, so was real coffee. Most runaways were unaccustomed to it. It was too costly to give to slaves prior to the war, and largely unavailable after the naval blockade of the south was implemented. Confederate coffee was brewed largely from parched wheat, peanuts, peas, or corn. A slave of North Carolina planter, George Herndon, remembered how "[w]e used ground parched corn for coffee and cane molasses for sweetening. That wasn't so bad with a heap of thick cream." Other slave families used dried parched potatoes.

Coffee was a mainstay for military men in the North and South. It was one of the great advantages of the Union. In the North, real coffee was plentiful. In the South it was costly and scarce. By 1863, in some parts of the South, a pound of real coffee went for $1.50.[1] Merchants were called "extortioners" for charging such prices. Other than drinking the Confederate substitutes for coffee, southern raiders tried to steal as much of the real thing as possible during northern food raids, while blockade runners tried to slip into southern ports with as much of it as cargo for sale to anyone with the gold to buy it, and Rebel soldiers tried trading anything for it across the lines. The South's coffee deprivation took on an ironic twist when Rebel soldiers realized they were being forced to brew their "coffee" from the same meager ingredients as their slaves.

Union soldiers received a ration of 36 pounds of unground beans a year. Each soldier ground and brewed his own or pooled his beans if his company had a cook. The best contraband cooks were the ones who could get the unfiltered grinds to settle to the bottom of the buckets used for brewing.

In the United States Navy, coffee was an essential commodity. The steam lines of gunboats were the ideal temperature for brewing hot coffee and keeping it so. Warships had cooks, messmen and stewards, most of whom were Black, so coffee was constantly available. Cooks were often judged most on the drinkability of their coffee, with soldiers and sailors

16. Coffee

USS *Monitor* mess being cooked on deck, July 1862, on the James River. Cooks were predominantly Black. (Library of Congress)

rating cooks in the diaries. According to Spencer Bonsall, who was in the military's Hospital Service, cook Joe Song was "entirely too fastidious in his cleanliness, invariably licking the spoons and knives with his tongue before handing them to us, for fear they might contain a little dust or something else."[2] Bonsall's favorite cook was Jose Webb, who he said made great bean soup and hotcakes. According to Bonsall, "he is the greatest slapjackist of the age and ought to wear the belt."[3]

17

The Safest Service

Even though masters had economic incentives to keep their slaves alive, as property, slaves knew they could be killed by a vengeful or drunken master. Beatings often went too far and forced onlookers witnessed firsthand the deadly consequences. Murder was also a distinct possibility. Lewis Brown knew that firsthand. He belonged to Doctor Jordan, said to be the largest slave holder in Arkansas and a notorious slave killer. "If the overseer couldn't make a slave behave, the old doctor went out with a gun and shot him. When the slaves on other plantations couldn't be ruled, they was sold to Dr. Jordan and he ruled 'em or killed 'em," Brown told an interviewer with the Slave Narrative project.

Analiza Foster, held in bondage by Harriet Cash in Raleigh, witnessed a worker beaten to death. The field hand fainted at the plow and was whipped until she'd get up. Passed out, she couldn't get up but regardless, the beatings continued. Finally, her motionless bloody body was washed with vinegar, salt, and red peppers. Miss Foster recalled decades later, "In a few minutes she am stone dead."

As a result of such abuses, mortality had a different meaning for slaves. Deaths by accidents, diseases, suicide, or brutality were equally possible.

Slaves dreaded the idea of drowning. Aside from the fact that most freed slaves couldn't swim and feared drowning, the truth was that most White sailors, including many senior naval officers, couldn't swim either. That was perhaps of little comfort to Black recruits, but the truth was that the Navy was the safest service.

In some cases, it was more dangerous escaping from bondage then fighting to destroy it. Brevet Brigadier General Willoughby Babcock told the story of "Bony," who escaped in a skiff. As he paddled away from shore a Rebel sentry challenged him with the standard "Who goes there?"

Bony laid flat in the skiff hoping he wouldn't be spotted, but the guard persisted. Shots were fired, but Bony did nothing except pray. "I prayed

17. The Safest Service

to God that if I get shot, I fall in the bay and the sharks eat me up, so they don't think I didn't get away." He made it to freedom.[1]

During the entire war, the United States Navy reportedly lost only 4,523 sailors killed in action or from accidents or disease. More seamen died of disease than in combat (2,411 versus 2,112).

The casualty rate within the Navy was roughly 2.7 percent. Comparatively, Union Army losses during the war due to combat, accidents or disease have been estimated at 325,000, or roughly 27 percent, although this number is now thought to be under-estimated.[2] Whether accurate or not, clearly sailors were far more likely to survive the war than the typical soldier.

Regarding the number of casualties, the clash at Hampton Roads between USS *Monitor* and CSS *Virginia* was hard on the United States Navy. In those two days in March 1862, the Navy suffered the loss of roughly 13 percent of all sailors killed in action during the war. USS *Cumberland* lost nearly one-third of her entire crew and USS *Congress* lost over one-quarter of hers. *Cumberland's* losses, including 121 sailors killed, was the worst loss endured by the Navy during the war.

One of the greatest tragedies involving Black sailors was the loss of USS *Tulip*. *Tulip* was built as a steam tug in New York in 1862 for the

Rendering of the sloop-of-war USS *Cumberland* as a lithograph by Currier and Ives depicting her great loss during the Battle of Hampton Roads on 8 March 1862. (Naval History and Heritage Command)

Black Sailors in the Civil War

Chinese Navy, but was purchased instead by the United States Navy for use as a gunboat in July 1863. She was assigned to the Potomac River Flotilla in August 1863.

While she was limping back to the Washington Navy Yard for repairs to *Tulip's* faulty starboard boiler, it exploded on 11 November 1864. Despite being advised not to use the starboard boiler, the crew ignored those instructions and the faulty boiler exploded, sinking the vessel, and killing all but eight of her 57-man crew. Most of the 49 dead were Black crewmembers. Records for *Tulip* show that 21 Black sailors were serving aboard *Tulip* on 1 October 1864 but there is no further record of their service after that. Most of their bodies were never recovered.

Not following simple instructions could also prove fatal in other ways, as in being told to duck for incoming ordnance. Unfortunately, not all of Captain Henry Walke's sailors aboard USS *Carondelet* listened and learned that simple lesson, as he explained, "So I repeated the instructions and warned the men at the guns and the crew generally to bow or stand off from the ports when a shot was seen coming. But some of the young men, from a spirit of bravado or from a belief in the doctrine of fatalism, disregarded the instructions, saying it was useless to attempt to dodge a cannon-ball, and they would trust to luck. The warning words, 'Look out!' 'Down!' were again soon heard; down went the gunner and his men, as the whizzing shot glanced on the gun, taking off the gunner's cap and the heads of two of the young men who trusted to luck, and in defiance of the order were standing up or passing behind him. This shot killed another man also, who was at the last gun of the starboard side, and disabled the gun. It came in with a hissing sound; three sharp spats and a heavy band told the sad fate

Sextant recovered from *Tulip's* wreckage near the Piney Point lighthouse on the Potomac River. (Naval History and Heritage Command)

17. The Safest Service

of three brave comrades. Before the decks were well sanded, there was so much blood on them that our men could not work the guns without slipping."[3]

Freak accidents also took a toll. When the gunboat USS *Colonel Kinsman* struck a "Sawyer" (a bobbing snag that hid just below the surface that often harpooned a hull) while operating at night in Berwick Bay in 1863, the Sawyer pierced the *Kinsman's* hull and impaled her starboard wheel. *Kinsman* immediately began taking on water. Her captain promptly ordered her bilge pumps turned on and the greatest amount of steam raised to operate the pumps at their maximum output. The ship's carpenter and damage control team quickly went to work to stem the leak, but they couldn't. Her crew all began bailing and pumping, but to no avail. Several nearby steamers were summoned to help take off *Kinsman's* sailors. Isaac Deer and William Parker remained at their posts—heaving coal to keep the bilge pumps working until the last. Both Black coal heavers and their two White counterparts died at their posts when the ship sank. The bodies of the four were never found. The ship's commander considered the four to have been saviors. He was particularly impressed with their endurance as coal-heavers and their coolness under fire. Others held the same opinion. In July 1864, an engineering officer claimed, "A negro is worth two, if not three, white men [with a coal shovel]."

Regarding disease, yellow fever was the major killer of White and Black sailors alike. Yellow fever was also a major hindrance to naval operations. In June 1864, just before attacking Mobile Bay, when he'd need every able-bodied sailor he could get, Rear Admiral Farragut advised Commodore James Palmer, commanding his Squadron's first division, that he couldn't use many of the 436 Black and White sailors he had just received for the West Gulf Squadron due to their "stopping at Key West, together with the filthy condition of the men, the fever has broken out, and we will now have to take great care to prevent its spreading."[4]

Within days, Farragut converted USS *Elk*, which was completely broken down and utterly worthless as a tin-clad, into an improvised summer hospital ship for his new arrivals and other sick people.

Farragut's brother officer, Rear Admiral John Dahlgren, commanding the South Atlantic Blockading Squadron, also feared the summer. He called it the "sickly season." The summers of 1863 and 1864 were indeed unwell times. Dahlgren's fleet faced coal shortages in August 1863 because the bark *Faith* ran aground and bilged, washing away her 500-tons of coal. This left many of Dahlgren's steamers low on or out of coal that month, resulting in few operations and opportunities for rejuvenating breezes

USS *Elk*, a tin-clad, was transformed into a makeshift hospital ship to accommodate Black and White sailors stricken with yellow fever and other ailments. Fourteen of *Elk's* sailors were Black seaman. The majority of these mustered aboard in 1864. These were largely young sailors serving as medical assistants. There was a suspicion that Blacks had an inherited immunity to yellow fever. This led to their use as aides in fever wards. The notion of immunity was untrue. *Elk's* young aides included second-class boy John Washington who was 12 years old. Moses Harris, also rated as a second-class boy, served at 14. Henry Parker was 15 when he mustered aboard as a second-class boy. James Johnson was 16. James Henry was also 16. Louis Joseph was 17. He enlisted as a first-class boy. Jacob Jones was also 17. He was rated as a second-class boy. And Manuel Smith was a 17-year-old aide. (Library of Congress)

17. The Safest Service

while cruising. Besides the usual yellow fever fears, many of his men came down with scurvy that summer. USS *Marblehead* had to be sent North because her entire crew had scurvy or were showing signs of soon getting it. Black sailors on *Marblehead* at that time included John M. Roberts, Nat Blake, Sylvester Slaughter, and Robert Boyan. Dahlgren justified this action by telling Navy Secretary Welles on 9 August 1863 it was necessary, "because to remain here would break down the whole of the crew." Lemons and other fruits were hastily furnished to the South Atlantic Blockading Squadron to stem the 1863 scurvy outbreak. Health-wise the summer of 1864 was worse. Not only was yellow fever severe, but cases of smallpox, typhus and cholera broke out. In July 1864, USS *New Hampshire* was afflicted with 24 cases of smallpox. Four crew members died. *New Hampshire's* sick were transferred to what Dahlgren referred to as a "Lazaretto ship," a reference to Lazarus. In *New Hampshire's* case, Dahlgren took the remaining crew off the ship and quarantined them on Bay Point so they could spread out to avoid contaminating each other. Dahlgren also established strict quarantine protocols for his fleet. A quarantine anchorage off Tybee Island was also established and vessels with sick on board anchoring there were to hoist the yellow flag on their fore masts. Contaminated vessels were to remain there until the contagion passed, plus 30 days. In cases of yellow fever, Dahlgren ordered that those ships "shall not enter the port until after the autumn frosts."

At sea, Black sailors suffered the same fates as White seamen. Ships were lost, battles took place and accidents happened.

Some ships foundered at sea with great loss of life. USS *Bainbridge*, for example, capsized in a storm off Cape Hatteras on 21 August 1863. All but one of her 100-man crew drowned, including five Black sailors who had mustered aboard *Bainbridge* only four days earlier. The five missing seamen were Henry Fisher, James R. Gardner, Thomas Goven, William Grant and Gustavus White. *Bainbridge* was a bark that was totally at the mercy of the winds and waves.

Sea battles took a toll too. USS *Hatteras* was chasing an unknown vessel off the coast of Texas on 26 January 1863. As *Hatteras* began overtaking the dark craft, the Union ship's commander called out for the strange vessel to identify itself. Almost as soon as the words "HMS *Vixen*" were heard, the unknown runner admitted its identity—CSS *Alabama*.

Within seconds of that admission, cannon fire began. *Hatteras* was repeatedly struck, and sank in a matter of minutes. Of the eleven Black crew members aboard, four died. The dead included Edward Mathes, David Symmes, Paul Herald and Richard Hatton. The Black survivors

Black Sailors in the Civil War

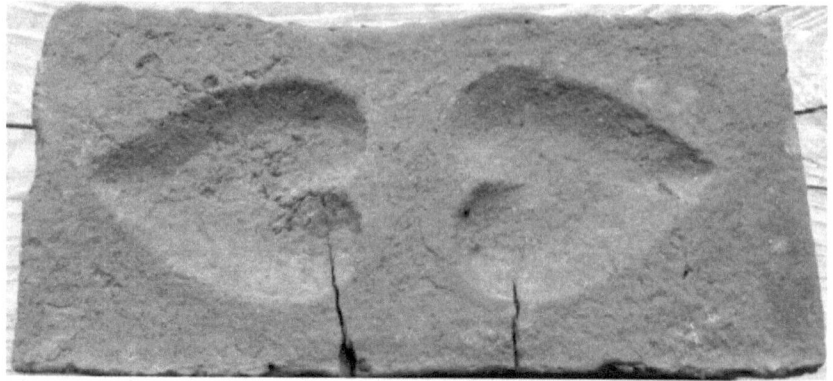

This was found in the bricks made at a small plantation in Jackson, Mississippi, and is believed to be an example of a brick used to mark slave burial. The marking consists of a finely shaped pair of hearts pointing in opposing directions. At least two other examples of this type of marking have reportedly been unearthed at the same former plantation site in digging done roughly two decades ago. One has a single heart imprint, another has a pair of hearts facing each other, and the third, shown above, has the hearts facing in opposite directions. The plantation house and outbuildings were destroyed during or after the Civil War. (Author's collections)

from *Hatteras* were scattered around the fleet. Francis Wood and William Tennant were reassigned to USS *Roanoke*; John H. Cornish was sent to USS *Connecticut*; William H. Moseley was mustered aboard USS *Gertrude*; Fortune A. Jones was reassigned to USS *Circassian* and Samuel Lewis was reassigned to USS *New Berne*. Theophilus Johnson was another of the lucky ones. The 24-year-old ordinary seaman from Norfolk survived the sinking of *Hatteras* and was reassigned to USS *Eutaw*. Johnson was aboard *Eutaw* when she towed the monitor *Tecumseh* to join the attacking force being assembled to capture Mobile Bay. On 5 August 1864, *Tecumseh* struck a mine during the attack and capsized in seconds. Ninety-four of *Tecumseh's* 100 crewmembers died. No Black sailors are recorded as having been aboard *Tecumseh* at the time.

Freak accidents also occasionally occurred. Black landsman James Bromley, for example, was killed in an ordnance accident on 7 February 1863 aboard the storeship *Brandywine*. Oddly, Bromley's service record is not listed for *Brandywine* or any other vessels. Such ordnance accidents were among the greatest causes of accidental deaths aboard ship.

18

Marked Passing

In most cases, identifiable Black soldiers killed in action while fighting for the Union received a headstone. These were like White headstones used at National Cemeteries, except for the added notation "U.S.C.T." (United States Colored Troops) or "U.S.CLD. INF." (United States Colored Infantry) or similar abbreviations for the artillery or cavalry. This was something new to emancipated soldiers. Permanent headstones and memorial markers were seldom used in slave burials. In fact, a permanent headstone was a previously unthinkable legacy for any slave turned soldier. Unfortunately, that was not the case for blue-water sailors, whether White or Black. Blue-water seamen received no headstones to mark their passing. Instead, in keeping with naval tradition, they were committed to the deep. Burials at sea were formal affairs. The ship's company would be piped to assembly at the stern of the vessel. A temporary gangplank was rigged on the starboard side of the ship to accommodate the body, which was stitched into the sailor's hammock and weighted with a cannon ball to assure that the body would sink. That side of the ship was traditionally used in such ceremonies. At the designated time, the flag would be lowered, and the ship's company would be led in a service by the chaplain or captain. After that the crew was ordered to "uncover" and in silence the body was committed to the ocean. Following a period of brief reflection, the captain would give the command to "Carry on." Brown-water sailors had the advantage of being close to land where they might reasonably envision receiving a traditional burial at a national cemetery. Having a permanent grave marker became a very special tribute because, for the first time, it signified that a Black life mattered and needed to be remembered beyond the cherished memories held by a smaller community of a plantation's slaves for a friend or loved one buried in an unmarked or undermarked grave.

Josephine Bacchus was only a child when her mother passed. Eighty year later she recalled the experience, saying, "My Jesus, my brother tell about when they had my mother layin out on the coolin board, I went in the room were she was and asked her for something to eat and pushed her head that way. You know, wouldn't touch my hand to do nothing like that, but I never know. That it, the coolin board, that's what they used to have to lay all the dead people on, but this day and time, the undertaker takes them an fixes them up right nice, I say."[1] Such treatment was uncommon. Most slaves were simply buried in a blanket without graveside services.

James V. Deane never recalled seeing any services, although he attended many burials. His plantation in Charles County, Maryland, had a slave plot, but only wooden posts were used to mark resting places, and those rotted away overtime.

If used at all, among the most common burial markers were slave-made bricks. These have been found in archeological digs in many locations throughout the South. Slave families made bricks in their after-hours as part of their daily chores. The children and mothers prepared the clay during the day, the fathers molded the bricks and the children turned out the bricks from the molds. In taking the damp clay out of the molds, many slave children left their fingerprints impressed in the soft clay, which have been discovered in many plantation houses and structures throughout the

Integrated ship's company attending a worship service aboard USS *Passaic*. (Naval History and Heritage Command)

18. Marked Passing

South. Firing the bricks was typically done under the supervision of a slave brickmaster who created the kiln and watched over the night-long process. Each family had a quota of bricks that had to be cast before they could eat their nightly meal. To ensure that they met their quota, each family had some sort of symbol to mark their bricks, so that a proper tally could be kept at the end of each firing. Marks included rabbit paws and chicken feet impressed in the soft unfired clay, or some other common symbols. These fired bricks were used to build or expand the plantation house, slave quarters or outbuildings, or were sold by the masters as an added income stream for the plantation. Broken or open pots were also used to mark a slave's resting place; and, like the bricks, most have been removed over the years.

Some pristine bricks have been found at southern plantation sites away from the main houses and out structures. They are impressed with hearts, and believed to have been burial markers for slaves. Unfortunately, over the years they've been picked up in fields, plowed under or taken away as odd finds that have later been sold or discarded, leaving no trace of the burial sites they were meant to mark. More often as not, Civil War sailors received no such similar treatment as their Army brethren. If killed in action, or more commonly, from disease, they were buried according to naval tradition ... interred at sea. The only record of their passing was maintained by the Navy's Muster Roll Department. (During World War I this office was led by an African American chief who insisted upon having 14 Black Yeoman [F] as his assistants. This was the first all-Black office in the Navy.)

The Navy's version of the Medal of Honor. (Naval History and Heritage Command)

19

Black Bluejacket Valor

Established at the request of Navy Secretary Gideon Welles, the Navy's Medal of Honor was the first to be authorized. Congress approved the issuance of the Navy's Medal of Honor on 21 December 1861. The design was the handiwork of Christian Schuller, a craftsman with the firm of William Wilson & Sons of Philadelphia in 1862. This was to be awarded to enlistees as the nation's highest honor for valor. Officers during the Civil War were excluded from receiving this medal.

The naval award was first bestowed upon sailor John Davis for his exceptional courage during the capture of Roanoke Island and Elizabeth City on 10 February 1862. When his ship, USS *Valley City*, caught fire, Davis, a White seaman, literally covered an open keg of gunpowder with his body to keep sparks from igniting the barrel and blowing the vessel apart until the fire could be extinguished, all while still passing powder to gun crews. Davis received his medal on 3 April 1863.

Black sailors were honored too. Robert Blake was a runaway who enlisted as a sailor aboard USS *Marblehead*. While his ship was off Johns Island, South Carolina, Blake ensured that his ship's main gun was kept in constant action, forcing the Rebel forces to abandon their position on 25 December 1863. For his steadfast bravery he was awarded the Medal of Honor. The commander of the gunboat *Marblehead* was one of those who praised his Black sailors for their conduct during a naval engagement with a Rebel shore battery off Legareville, South Carolina, on Christmas Day 1863. "Robert Blake, a contraband, excited my admiration by the cool and brave manner in which he served the rifle gun," reported Lieutenant-Commander Richard Meade, Jr., to his superior, Rear Admiral John Dahlgren. In the same action, Meade also reported the serious injury of Alexander Henderson, a 22-year-old Black sailor from Evansville, Indiana, in that same engagement. Dahlgren's Black sailors, like those elsewhere, repeatedly proved themselves, sometimes at the cost of their lives. On 17 December Benjamin Brown, a sailor assigned to USS *Oleander*, was

19. Black Bluejacket Valor

dispatched as part of a boat crew to rescue sailors from USS *Clover* and *Mangham* treading water when their small boats capsized in heavy surf off Morris Island. Unfortunately, Brown's whaleboat faired no better. It too capsized and the young landman from Beaufort, South Carolina, who only had enlisted two months earlier, was lost in the surf. His body was never recovered.

Many other acts of sacrifice and bravery went unhonored. *Weehawken* was lost off Morris Island at 2:40 p.m. on 6 December 1863, when her forward anchor hoister hatch was inadvertently left open. When she got underway, this mistake allowed seawater into the forward compartment, weighing the vessel down by the head. It was estimated that the inrushing water amounted to at least 100,000 pounds. Fifty of her sailors perished, among them, John Rutledge and William H. Williamson. Both were Black bluejackets. Williamson's enlistment was to end in 32 days.

USS *Water Witch*, a side-wheel steamer, was one of Dahlgren's blockading vessels. Dahlgren considered *Water Witch* to be "probably the most efficient vessel of the eight stationed south of Wassaw, viz, Ossabaw...." At the time she was 17 men short. When *Water Witch* was boarded on 3 June 1864 by 132 Rebels at about midnight off Ossabaw Sound on the coast of Georgia, not all her crew fought to retain control of their ship. According to the ship's surgeon, Jeremiah Sills was among those who did, at the cost of his life. He reportedly "fought most desperately, and this while men who despised him were cowering near with idle cutlasses in the racks jogging their

John H. Lawson wearing his Medal of Honor after the war. (Library of Congress)

elbows." Seventy-seven of *Water Witch's* crew were captured. The ship's commander, Lieutenant-Commander Austin Pendergrast, was court martialed and found guilty of culpable inefficiency in the discharge of his duty.

Of the 311 Medals of Honor issued by the Navy during the Civil War, Black sailors received eight. This represents 2.5 percent of the total recipients at a time when Blacks constituted roughly 25 percent of the total enlisted warfighters. This doesn't mean that Black bluejackets weren't heroic. What it does mean is that they were under-recognized for their valor by many of the captains and flag officers of that era. Flag Officer David Farragut was one of the better skippers when it came to recognizing such heroism. He was far better than most of his other brother officers in this regard.

More Black sailors were recommended for the Medal of Honor than received it. Commander William G. Temple, in command of USS *Pontoosuc*, recommended several men for the honor. His recommendation stated: "After mature consideration and careful consultation with the officers of this vessel, I would recommend that medals of honor be awarded to the following men under my command for gallantry, skill, and coolness in action during the operations in and about Cape Fear River, which extended from December 24, 1864, to February 22, 1865, and which resulted in the capture of Fort Fisher and Wilmington." Clement Dees was one of those Temple recommended. Dees was a Black sailor who possessed previous skill as a mariner before enlisting at Eastport, Tennessee, in 1864. Unfortunately, Dees's medal was forfeited because of claims he deserted.

John H. Lawson was another of those recipients. He was recognized for his valor during the capture of Mobile Bay. Admiral David Farragut wanted to capture Mobile in the worst way. He had held this hope since 1862, but in August of that year was advised by Secretary Welles that it was beyond his reach. By mid-1864, Mobile, Alabama, was one of three remaining major ports for Confederate blockade-runners. Now, Farragut was ready to eliminate that thorn. Farragut's instincts were correct; 1862 was an ideal time to attack. At the time, Alabama's Governor, John Gill Shorter, described the roughly 3,000 Confederate defenders near Mobile as "mostly fresh raw troops and poorly armed." Farragut's sailors hoped for the same, but as Second Assistant Engineer Hiram Parker wrote to his father while off Mobile Bay aboard USS *Kanawha*, with Farragut's squadron, things would have to wait. "Our fleet are nearly all up the [Mississippi] river storming Vicksburg which offers a stout resistance. As soon as he is done there, we expect he will attack this place." That wait would prove

19. Black Bluejacket Valor

to be a long one. The loss of Vicksburg in July of the following year forecast the loss of Port Hudson and the entire Mississippi River. While this would split the Confederacy, it would also release the Union Army and Navy to concentrate on attacking the Gulf. On 16 July 1863 Major General Dabney Maury, commanding the Confederate Department of the Gulf, advised the Inspector General of the Confederate Army, Samuel Cooper, that "after the fall of Port Hudson, the [Union Army and Navy] may be available for an attack on Mobile." Maury insisted that it might be best to relocate the civilian population of Mobile. That suggestion meant moving an estimated 15,000 people, including slaves. Maury also wanted 20,000 men to defend Mobile. At this point Jefferson Davis weighed in, ordering that "the removal of non-combatants may well be postponed until an attack is proximate." Davis also wished to wait on increasing Mobile's troop strengths until "the intent of the enemy is better developed."

From Maury's perspective there was indeed evidence that someplace was in the Union's crosshairs. That year Union troop movements in the Gulf of Mexico convinced him that an attack somewhere in the Gulf of Mexico was imminent ... but where? Most of the Confederate military leaders in the deep South, like Maury, bet on an attack on Mobile in 1863. As a result, mines were laid in the access to Mobile Bay, the fortification in the channel to the Bay was strengthened, and supplies were amassed to meet the much-anticipated attack. But the assault on Mobile that year didn't happen either. Maury was off by a year.

By mid–1864, Mobile, Alabama, was one of three remaining major ports for Confederate blockade-runners. Again, Farragut was ready to eliminate that thorn. Others agreed the time had come. On 6 June 1864, Lieutenant General Grant suggested that forces should be pulled from other fronts for a move against Mobile. General Sherman concurred, as did Rear Admiral David Dixon Porter. On 6 June Porter wrote Sherman expressing his view that "I think now is the time to go to Mobile, as you say there is no one there." There were Rebel troops there, roughly 3,000 of them.

By 18 June 1864, Union army forces were being gathered at Memphis for a demonstration against Mobile. Simultaneously, Admiral Farragut was quietly also preparing for the naval move on Mobile. By the end of June Farragut was distracted briefly by an outbreak of yellow fever at his base in Pensacola.

During the Battle of Mobile Bay on 5 August 1864, landman John Lawson was serving on Admiral David Farragut's Flag Ship USS *Hartford*. During the battle he was seriously wounded while serving as a member of the ship's berth deck ammunition party. Despite his wounds, he remained at his post, continuing to pass ammunition to one of *Hartford's* 11-inch Dahlgren guns. For his heroism in this action, he was awarded the Medal of Honor. Other Black bluejackets distinguished themselves at Mobile Bay by receiving Medals of Honor, including William H. Brown, a Landsman aboard USS *Brooklyn*; Wilson Brown, a landman aboard USS *Hartford*; and James Mifflin, a cook aboard USS *Brooklyn*.[1]

William Brown's award was made in recognition of how he "remained steadfast at his post and performed his duties in the powder division throughout the furious action which resulted in the surrender of the prize rebel ram *Tennessee* and in the damaging and destruction of batteries at Fort Morgan."

Obverse of William H. Brown's Medal of Honor. (Naval History and Heritage Command)

Wilson Brown was a shell boy/landsman who was honored after being "[k]nocked unconscious into the hold of the ship when an enemy shell burst fatally wounded a man on the ladder above him, Brown, upon regaining consciousness, promptly returned to the shell whip on the berth deck and zealously continued to perform his duties although 4 of the 6 men at this station had been either killed or wounded by the enemy's terrific fire." Brown was a runaway from the Carthage Plantation on the Mississippi River when he enlisted aboard a passing warship in March 1863.

James Mifflin's award was for remaining "steadfast at his post and perform[ing] his duties in the powder division throughout the furious action which resulted in the surrender of the prize rebel ram *Tennessee* and in the damaging and destruction of batteries at Fort Morgan."

19. Black Bluejacket Valor

For gallantry under fire as a loader of USS *Kearsarge's* Number Two 11-inch Dahlgren gun, ordinary seaman Joachim Pease was awarded a Medal of Honor for his conduct during the sinking of CSS *Alabama* off the coast off Cherbourg, France, on 9 June 1864. As an ordinary seaman, Pease had previous maritime service. Pease never actually received his medal. When it came time to present it, he couldn't be located. Whether he shipped out on a merchantman following his discharge, relocated overseas, or moved somewhere within the country is unknown.

Signal Quartermaster Thomas English received his Medal of Honor for extraordinary heroism aboard USS *New Ironsides* during December 1864 and January 1865 in the bombardment of Fort Fisher, North Carolina. During the shelling *New Ironside* silenced nearly every Confederate cannon within its section of fire. Like Joachim Pease, Thomas English, a free Black man, never received his Medal of Honor. It remains unclaimed and in the possession of the Navy.

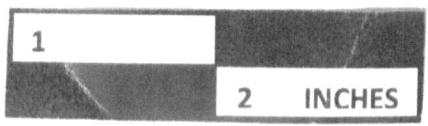

The obverse of Joachim Peases' Medal of Honor reads: "Personal Valor / Joachim Pease / (Colored Seaman) / U.S.S. Kearsarge / Destruction of the Alabama / June 9, 1864." (Naval History and Heritage Command)

Aaron Anderson received his Medal of Honor while serving aboard USS *Wyandank* on 17 March 1865 for saving crewmembers from several Potomac Flotilla ships that were participating in the clearing of Mattox Creek, Virginia. The landing force included about 70 sailors. Landsman Anderson was in one of the landing boats. When the boats came under attack from the shore Anderson carried out his duties courageously in the face of a devastating fire, which cut away half of the oars and pierced the launch in multiple places. Under constant fire, he singlehandedly loaded and fired the boat's small landing party howitzer, scattering the attackers on the shore. For his bravery under heavy fire, he was awarded a Medal of Honor. Unfortunately, the last name on his medal was inscribed "Sanderson" by mistake because the "A" was misread from the ship's log as "SA."

20

The Union Navy's War on Salt

Salt was one of the Confederate States of America's three crucial white commodities. Cotton and sugar were the others. For cotton, the Confederacy depended upon the crop for both hard currency to finance the war and as diplomatic leverage in its goal to be recognized by foreign governments. Salt, on the other hand, was a staple of everyday life. It was vital to basic nutritional needs of every family. Salt also had important industrial application in the manufacturing of leather goods, as tanners used the mineral to cure animal hides and as a preservative. The pre-war South consumed roughly 450 million pounds of salt annually for personal and industrial consumption, mostly imported from foreign or northern sources. The average southerner before the war annually consumed an estimated 50 pounds of salt. For southern states, availability of salt and cotton was vastly different. Southern states grew a vast portion of the world's cotton. Salt, unlike cotton, was not an abundant commodity in the South. There were a few large salt deposits in the South, such as extractive operations at New Iberia, Louisiana, and Saltville, Virginia.

Manpower shortages crippled the output at New Iberia, limiting production to a point where in September 1862 Mississippi's Governor, John J. Pettus, suggested nationalizing the works, taking them away from their private owner, Daniel Dudley Avery, who reportedly was barely able to produce one bushel of the rock salt per day per worker. Pettus wished to put 1,000 hands to work digging out salt at Avery's Island in Iberia Perish, presumably using impressed slaves. "If promptly done, salt can be procured from there sufficient for Mississippi and Louisiana," Pettus told Jefferson Davis on 23 September 1862. Jefferson Davis agreed with Pettus, provided Judge Avery would accept the southern government's terms. As an alternative, the governor was advised by Augustus Chew, the agent assigned to evaluate the possibilities of maximizing the outputs of Louisiana's salt bed, to sink the state's own salt mines 200 yards from Avery's, digging into the same salt dome, which was no more than 30 feet below the surface. Instead, President Davis appointed a lieutenant-colonel to oversee the expansion of output from Avery's mines, telling Pettus on 25 October 1862, "I am deeply conscious of the necessity existing for a vigorous prosecution of this work, and am endeavoring to secure to the country the full benefit to be derived from it." The South's exploitation of New Iberia's salt was short lived. In the summer of 1863 Union forces occupied the area.

Salt became a scarce commodity in the South. "The salt famine in our land is most lamentable," wrote Alabama's governor in October 1862. His state had $40,000 worth of contracts on Saltville salt, but the state's shipments always were diverted elsewhere. "What is shipped is taken by the State of Virginia, and other states," he complained to the Confederacy's Secretary of War. Alabama wasn't alone in suffering from salt deprivation. "Large amount of pork is lost to our army and people in North Mississippi for want of salt," wrote Mississippi's governor, John J. Pettus, to President Davis in November 1862.

At a time when the Union Navy was heavily reliant upon runaways as warfighters, the Army used them merely as laborers and teamsters believing them to be too timid to fight. Only one General at the time thought otherwise. He was an officer the fugitives called "General Peg-leg"[1] because of his limping gate. In the late summer of 1862 Major General Benjamin Franklin Butler proposed creating a special brigade to capture the salt works at New Iberia. The Army denied his request to mount this attack using White soldiers, so Butler decided to "call on Africa for assistance,—i.e., I would enlist all the colored troops I could from the free Negroes."[2] The troops would come from men of all Black "National Guards, Colored," from Louisiana, a group organized by the Rebels but never used. Butler met with the top 20 leaders of the group and told them that he required 2,000 men to form two regiments, and he wanted them formed up within a fortnight. At the appointed time Butler went to see what men he might have for the enterprise. "On that morning I went there and saw such a sight as I never saw before: two thousand men ready to enlist as recruits, and not a man of them who had not a white 'biled shirt' on,"[3] Butler recalled. Butler had his two regiments.

Butler had been a trailblazer when it came to utilizing Black troops. When Richard Slaughter was saved by the Union Navy on the riverbanks as a young boy, but decided to join Butler's Army instead, he recounted late in life why General Butler was so keen to rely on Colored troops. When interviewed at age 91, Slaughter said it was because of his horses. "Wouldn't no General but one take the colored boys. General Peg-leg

20. The Union Navy's War on Salt

Butler, he say 'I'll take 'em.' And you know why? Cause his cavalry didn't have nothin' but black horses, an' them white men didn't look right on black horses."[4] That wasn't the real reason, but it was sufficient in Slaughter's mind to explain Butler's willingness to enlist Black troops.

Saltville was one of the South's largest suppliers, until it was destroyed by Union forces during a two-day rampage of destruction in December 1864. Almost immediately salt became scarce. The loss of Saltville caused much of the Confederacy to rely largely on locally produced salt from small-scale salt works where outputs were limited. States offered bounties for finding salt deposits and inducements for setting up salt works.

Alabama began rationing salt for its civilians if any could afford to buy it. Mississippi's governor suggested trading Confederate cotton for Union salt, but Jefferson Davis vetoed that idea. North Carolina appointed a Salt Commissioner to coordinate salt production and distribution within the state. It also established state-operated salt works along its coast. These salt works gave North Carolina a great deal of barter power. At Salisbury, North Carolina, in 1863 the Confederacy's first quartermaster general, Abraham Myers, advertised in the local newspaper that he was willing to trade three pounds of government salt for one pound of bacon. His notice in the *Carolina Watchman* was certain to attract attention, appearing under the banner heading—"SALT! SALT!! SALT!!!"—but many North Carolinians weren't so keen on barter considering how much salt it took to cure bacon and uncured pork quickly spoiled. Salt riots broke out around the state. Women in some areas raided railroad depots looking for salt. The salt famine merged into the general food shortage throughout the South, forcing many local mill owners to declare that they could not be responsible for any grain deposited with them for milling that might be stolen by mobs. Other southern states faced similar conditions as North Carolina and responded in the same way.

Salt had become in short supply throughout the South as early as October 1862. That month the governor of Mississippi, John J. Pettus, told Jefferson Davis that "Many families of volunteers have no salt." Pettus' advice was "I hope you may favor (the) suggestion to exchange cotton for salt with the French. I know of no reason weighty enough against it to counterbalance the great utility and necessity of a present supply of salt." Alabama's governor, John Gill Shorter, agreed, calling the South's scarcity of salt a calamity, saying: "there is scarcely any misfortune which can befall us which will produce such wide-spread complaint and dissatisfaction." Davis immediately accepted Pettus' suggestion, confessing that "the necessity of salt weighed much with me." That October the Confederacy's

Black Sailors in the Civil War

President authorized the importation of 50,000 sacks of French salt. He also ordered the South's salt mines in Louisiana to increase the extraction of salt. That salt was to be shipped throughout the South in private boats so that no southern naval resources were withdrawn from combat for such purposes. Davis' actions amounted to a drop in the bucket.

Slaves weren't typically given salt, but they were allowed to dig salt and sand from the smokehouse floor and pour water over it to get the salt drippings for seasoning.

Such scarcity was a far cry from the way things were before the war. Prior to the war most of the South's salt came from the North, particularly from deposits and brine wells in New York, Pennsylvania, and Ohio. As a result, much of the salt consumed on southern tables was imported either from the Northern suppliers or from suppliers overseas, such as Great Britain, which reportedly shipped hundreds of tons of salt each day to southern ports as ballast aboard vessels destined to carry cotton back to Europe. The North experienced no such salt deprivation. The giant Onondaga salt works, located in Syracuse, New York, alone produced over 9 million bushels of salt in 1862. At the same time, by comparison, all the salt producing facilities in the South combined are thought to have only been capable of producing about one-third of Onondaga's output. As both the cotton and salt trade depended upon ships to take cotton outbound and salt in-bound, both trades were vulnerable to distribution by the United States Navy's blockade of southern ports.

A major impediment in the South was that by November 1862 few southern farmers, merchants, and suppliers were accepting Confederate currency. This situation prompted Captain John Cavanaugh, commanding the Eighth Battalion of Louisiana's artillery, to complain to his superior, Lieutenant-General John C. Pemberton, that "Gold, silver, or U.S. Treasury notes seem to be the only money they want." Cavanaugh's command—and most southern civilians—had nothing but Confederate cash.

Blockade-runners attempted to slip past the Federal blockaders carrying cotton, tobacco, turpentine, lumber and other commodities out of the South and bringing essential war material and civilian luxuries back. Iron, tin, and lead pigs were commonly run into southern ports to support the war effort, as was salt. At first, few blockade-runners were caught but as the war progressed more and more were captured or destroyed, with salt as a frequent cargo. Because of its importance in curing pork and beef, a staple for the Confederate Army in the field, General Sherman classified salt as "eminently contraband." The first salt cargo captured by blockaders happened off Wilmington, North Carolina, when the schooner *Alert* was

20. The Union Navy's War on Salt

taken by USS *Roanoke* and *Flag* on 8 October 1861. By then salt was selling for $7 a bushel in southern cities. Twelve days later USS *Gemsbok* captured the brig *Ariel* when it tried to run into Wilmington with a salt cargo. A third and final salt bearing blockade-runner captured in 1861 was the *Admiral*, taken on 12 December off Tybee, South Carolina, by USS *Alabama*. In 1862, six salt haulers were captured, followed by three in 1863. After 1863, other commodities became more critical than salt, such as arms and munitions. As the blockade tightened, and imported salt supplies dwindled, attention turned to coastal Texas, and along tidal waterways. Finding these salt works became an even more daunting task than blockading the coastline because such facilities could be established anywhere along the South's tidal shorelines or tributaries. But the Union Navy had allies. Slaves knew where all the salt works were! They supplied an abundance of accurate information that directed dozens of salt raiders to their targets. In December 1863, a ten-day naval expedition by three gunboats operating along Saint Andrew's Bay in Florida, reported the destruction of 290 small salt works, including the confiscation of 4,000 bushels of salt and 529 iron kettles, each capable of holding 150 gallons of saltwater, plus 105 iron boilers for boiling brine. The salt workers saw the Navy coming and destroyed much of their equipment in advance of the landing party.

With the scarcity, salt prices skyrocketed from $7 a bushel to $50. In addition to the profitability, southern salt workers, which numbered in the thousands, were exempt from the draft. Finding and destroying these salt factories became a blue-water priority. These frequent naval search parties were a great way of breaking up the boredom of blockade duty later in the war and the subsequent discovery of a salt work was a great way to blow off steam. Raiding parties immediately set to work smashing up everything they could find, including boilers, cast iron caldrons and evaporation pans. Sledgehammers and axes were typically used to break things up, but in cases where there were larger structures, the sailors used them for gunnery practice for their Dahlgren howitzers. Any salt that could be consumed by the Navy was carried off. Abandoned salt was mixed with sand or otherwise contaminated, or it was dumped back into the water. Before leaving the salt site, the sailors would put any timbers to the torch. Some of these salt works were operated on an industrial scale. The Union's largest naval salt raid occurred on 8 September 1864 on Mobile Bay. This expedition was ordered by David Farragut and involved three of his ships, plus an Army transport and two tow-barges in what ended up being a two-day operation at a facility known as the Memphis Salt Works located at the mouth of the Bon Secours River. The specific target was called "Salt House

Black Sailors in the Civil War

Point." The salt works there were substantial. It included over 20 structures that housed 55 furnaces capable of producing 2,000 bushels of salt a day.[5] The facility involved pumping saltwater collected in brine wells into the facility's 990 evaporation pots. The Union raiding party destroyed the facility's pumps and demolished the timber structures, placing much of the reusable lumber on the two barges. Two substantial structures were blown up and all remaining building materials were burned. Navy after-action reports to Secretary Welles include details of such salt raids along the southern coastline, particularly in tidal South Carolina, Georgia, and especially Florida. Particularly hard-hit Florida raid sites were on the Gulf coast between Choctawhatchee Bay and Tampa and along the Atlantic coast. Union naval reports described a steady stream of destructive raids, reports such as:

> "I have the honor to report the following, since relieving the United States bark *Restless* on this station ... on the 30th of November last, I dispatched an expedition, with twenty-four men ... up [St. Andrew's Bay, Florida] to destroy salt-works and salt, which they did effectually. They captured and brought away with them the sixteen salt-makers, whom I have since paroled." (Acting Master J.C. Wells, USS *Midnight* 4 December 1864[6])

> "I have the honor to report an expedition from the bark *Midnight* left the vessel on the 12th of February, to destroy salt-works on [St. Andrew's Bay, Florida] and returned to the vessel ... having destroyed salt-works of 13,615 gallons of boiling power, besides 70 bushels of salt and 125 pounds of Epsom salt." (Acting Rear-Admiral C.K. Stribling, Key West, Florida 23 February 1865[7])

> "I have the honor to report an expedition from this vessel on the 23rd [of February], to Palmetto Point [South Carolina], on the main land [*sic*], in charge of Acting Master William L. Bowers, and destroyed and rendered useless for further operation three extensive salt-works. The result of the expedition was the destruction of 100 pans and boilers, a large quantity of salt, brine-vats, two wind-mill pumps, and numerous sheds and out-buildings." (Acting Master William Walton, USS *James S. Chambers* 25 February 1865[8])

Within a matter of months of these last two reports, the necessity for the United States Navy's war on salt would evaporate, gone with the end of the war.

21

Mobile Bay

Admiral Farragut wanted to capture Mobile in the worst way. He had held this hope since 1862, but in August of that year was advised by Secretary Welles that it was beyond his reach. On 19 August 1862, Welles told Farragut, "The unsettled state of affairs on the Mississippi, the want of a sufficient military force to make all secure, and the present condition of your vessels, do not seem to admit of the expediency of attempting the concentration of an adequate force at Mobile for the reduction of that place." By mid–1864, Mobile, Alabama, was one of three remaining major ports for Confederate blockade-runners. In entering Mobile Bay, Rear Admiral Farragut knew that his ships would have to contend with his old friend, Admiral Franklin Buchanan, commanding CSS *Tennessee*, and the Confederate naval forces. Confiding to his son, Loyall, on 22 May 1864, Farragut said that he was looking forward to a battle at Mobile Bay. "I am lying off here, looking at Buchanan and waiting his coming out. He has a force of four iron-clads and three wooden vessels. I have eight or nine wooden vessels. We'll try to amuse him if he comes.... I have a fine set of vessels here just now and am anxious for my friend Buchanan to come out."[1] Buchanan had his share of difficulties up to that point, not the least of which was getting *Tennessee* over the Dog River Bar, which he accomplished on 18 May, so that he and Farragut could face off.[2] Both sides took their time preparing. On 26 May, Farragut wrote to a colleague saying, "I can see [Buchanan's] boats very industriously laying down torpedoes, so I judge that he is quite as much afraid of our going in as we are of his coming out; but, I have come to the conclusion to fight the devil with fire, and therefore shall attach a torpedo to the bow of each ship, and see how it will work on the rebels—if they can stand blowing up any better than we can."[3]

Farragut feared that Buchanan would simply keep to shallower waters and stand off to fight, which gave Buchanan the advantage, because the deeper draft of the Union's steam-sloops could not get close in to fight. "But," Farragut advised Secretary Welles in a letter, "if he takes the offensive and comes out of port, I hope to be able to contend with him."⁴ Farragut hoped that Buchanan would come out, because it might enable him to use spar torpedoes, although the thought left him with a bad taste in his mouth. In that same letter Farragut said, "Torpedoes are not so agreeable when used [by] both sides,—therefore I have reluctantly brought myself to it. I have always deemed it unworthy of a chivalrous nation,—but it does not do to give your enemy such a decided superiority over you."⁵ Farragut issued his plan of attack on the iron-clad on 14 June 1864, telling his commanders that he was conveying his battle orders with them then because it might not be possible once they encountered *Tennessee*. His plan was to overwhelm *Tennessee* with as much firepower as possible, attacking from all sides, with *Richmond* leading the way on the starboard and *Brooklyn* on the port. "The heavy ships should keep as close to each other as possible, run at the ram *Tennessee* and strike her, if practicable, just abaft the casemate, firing only when within a few yards, and then concentrating at the water line and ports. If the broadside guns will bear, direct one or two to throw grape into the ports when they are opened," Farragut ordered.⁶

Rear Admiral Farragut was concerned that several of his ships were proving to be coal hogs. He advised Secretary Welles on 20 June 1864 that he was greatly concerned about the inadequate coal supplies at Pensacola and that USS *Circassian* was burning as much as 40 tons a day in steaming from Key West to Pensacola. The following month Farragut complained to Secretary Welles that he was desperate for coal, telling him, "I have been writing to Commodore [Henry Allen] Adams for some time, urging a supply, and to-day I received a letter informing me that there are only two or three hundred tons at Pensacola." Farragut wanted as much of this coal as possible, reminding Welles, "I am getting ready for coming events." Despite the lessons learned in the clash of iron-clads at Hampton Roads a few years earlier, Farragut saw the up-coming battle as a case of "New versus Old"—wood against armor—and he hoped that it would vindicate the value of wooden ships. "This question has to be settled, iron versus wood; and there never was a better chance to settle the question of the sea-going qualities of iron-clad ships," he wrote on 21 June.⁷ That conclusion wasn't a fair assumption. It wasn't going to be simply a battle of "wood versus iron," and Farragut knew it. He was going to use his monitors in the fray too. And he expected to gang up against *Tennessee* with as many ships as possible. Thanks to an informant, by 7 July 1864, Farragut had amassed a reliable report on *Tennessee's* construction and capabilities. The intelligence came from an informant who spoke with those who worked on her construction and who, upon wished to ingratiate himself with the Federal authorities,

21. Mobile Bay

anticipating the ultimate capture of the city. From this information, Farragut realized that *Tennessee's* weaknesses were precisely what he thought; she was slow and somewhat hard to steer, her four-inch-thick scissoring gun port shutters, which were operated by tackle and could be rendered inoperable if accurately targeted, and she was vulnerable to ramming. Farragut was also led to believe that *Tennessee's* crew was "disaffected." In addition to learning everything he could about Admiral Buchanan's ship, he also watched the weather for the most auspicious time for Buchanan to act. On 16 July, Farragut advised Rear Admiral Theodorus Bailey, commander of the East Gulf Squadron, "Now is his time; the sea is as calm as possible and everything propitious for his iron-clads to attack us; still he remains behind the fort, and I suppose it will be the old story over again. If he won't visit me, I will have to visit him."[8] Mobile was expecting Farragut's "visit" at any time. For weeks the city's newspapers reported that the Union Navy would certainly do something very soon.

The readers wouldn't have long to wait. Farragut's plan of attack would mirror his attack at Port Hudson on the Mississippi River. This time his ships were to go in side-by-side, with his iron-clads on the eastern side facing Fort Morgan. Once clear of the forts, the iron-clads and several of his wooden warships were to break away to attack the *Tennessee* and the Rebel gunboats. Because the channel required Farragut's ships to pass close by Fort Morgan, any smaller wooden ship was to be lashed to the port side of a larger wooden screw steamer for protection. To make this approach abundantly clear, a drawing was distributed showing the arrangement of his ships.

Prior to going into action, every commander was told to strip his vessel, taking down all superfluous spars and rigging. Crews were to put up splinter nets on the starboard sides and barricade the wheel and steersmen with sails and hammocks. They also were to lay chains and sandbags on the deck over the machinery to resist plunging fire, and to hang chains over the sides for chain-cladding. On 5 August 1864, Admiral David G. Farragut, on board his flagship USS *Hartford*, commanded a Union squadron comprised of four monitors and 14 wooden ships. The iron-clads included *Tecumseh, Manhattan, Winnebago,* and *Chickasaw.* Farragut specifically requested that *Tecumseh* be sent to him on 3 August, from Pensacola, Florida, to add to his force, telling the senior officer at Pensacola, "I must go in day after to-morrow [sic] morning at daylight or a little later. It is a bad time, but when you do not take fortune at her offer you must take her as you find her." Acting like Civil War era Navy Seals, that night a small party of Union sailors led by Lieutenant John C. Watson in a small boat entered Mobile's shipping channel under the guns of the southern forts and began disabling Confederate mines. This work party slipped away before dawn undetected.

The secret work party of sailors could do nothing about the Confederate iron-clad CSS *Tennessee*, three gunboats, and three strategically placed forts that defended the bay. As Farragut's fleet sailed north into the bay at about 6:00 a.m., it encountered heavy fire from Fort Morgan on the right and Fort Gaines to the left. In addition, shoals, obstructions, and underwater mines protected the entrance to the bay. Despite the loss of *Tecumseh* to a mine that Lieutenant Watson failed to neutralize, which culminated in the deaths of over three-quarters of her crew, these hindrances failed to stop Farragut's fleet. Once past the forts, the ensuing battle between the opposing warships ended with Farragut winning control of the bay and capturing the iron-clad CSS *Tennessee*, which surrendered on 5 August 1864, at about 10:00 a.m. *Tennessee* was hastily patched up by Union mechanics, including receiving a new smokestack, and by 13 August, was turned against Fort Morgan, a massive, masonry star-fort completed in 1834. At one point David Farragut boastfully thought that with one iron-clad he could destroy all the Rebel forces in the Mobile Bay. That proved to be far from the case. In the battle with *Tennessee*, the pair of 15-inch Dahlgren guns in USS *Manhattan* came closest to supporting his claim. That monitor was a deciding factor, doing deadly duty. One of *Tennessee's* officers reported the event, noting: "a hideous-looking monster came creeping up on our Port side, whose slowly revolving turret revealed the cavernous depths of a mammoth gun. 'Stand clear of the Port side!,' I shouted. A moment after a thunderous report shook us all, while a blast of dense, sulpherous smoke covered our portholes, and 440 pounds of iron, impelled by 60-pounds of powder, admitted daylight through our side, where, before it struck us, there had been over two feet of solid wood, covered with five inches of solid iron. This was the only 15-inch shot that hit us fair."[9] Meanwhile, all of Farragut's available ships surrounded *Tennessee* and pounded her mercilessly with their 11-inch and nine-inch guns, most firing only feet way. The blizzard of shells crippled *Tennessee's* steering and wounded Admiral Buchanan. Of the contest, Farragut reported that he lost more sailors in fighting *Tennessee* than he did in assailing the batteries of Fort Morgan. Despite Farragut's presence in Mobile Bay, the forts had not yet surrendered. To force surrender, Farragut's fleet kept up a constant day and night bombardment, slowly battering down the defensive walls. Besieged, Fort Gaines surrendered on August 7, followed by Fort Morgan on 23 August. In surrendering Fort Morgan, Confederate Brigadier

21. Mobile Bay

General Richard L. Page reported the sorry situation he faced in deciding to capitulate. Surrounded by bluecoats under the command of Major General Gordon Granger on land and confronted by Farragut's sailors offshore, Page concluded, "My guns and powder had all been destroyed, my means of defense gone, the citadel [a ten-sided barracks], nearly the entire quartermaster stores, and a portion of the commissariat burned by the enemy's shells." Under the circumstances, surrender was the only reasonable solution.

President Lincoln was thrilled with Farragut's initiatives, ordering a 100-gun cannonade fired at noon on 5 September 1864, from the Washington Navy Yard and all other naval installations in honor of "the recent brilliant achievements of the fleet and land forces of the United States in the harbor of Mobile and in the reduction of Fort Powell, Fort Gaines, and Fort Morgan...."

The combined Army-Navy operation effectively sealed off Mobile. Mobile itself remained in southern hands and by September 1864, it had three iron-clads—CSS *Nashville*, CSS *Tuscaloosa* and CSS *Huntsville*— at its disposal to potentially threaten the Union fleet. Of the three, *Nashville* was the greatest threat, mounting six of the South's heaviest rifles. She was also heavily armored and capable of greater speeds than the other two Rebel ships. September 15, Farragut advised Secretary Welles that he was having the Confederate iron-clad trio watched by USS *Winnebago* and *Chickasaw*, as well as four gunboats.

Mobile Bay remained a deadly black hole for Union vessels, with naval communications from Henry K. Thatcher, the Acting Rear Admiral in command of the West Gulf Squadron who took over that command on 23 February 1865, two months after David Farragut's departure, to Secretary Welles, reporting a steady stream of losses due to southern torpedoes, especially off the Blakeley River, even beyond the end of the war. Previously, Thatcher had commanded USS *Constellation*, the nation's oldest warship in service, which was assigned to the Mediterranean. That was a safe place for the old sailing warship, as Thatcher was all too aware when in June 1863, he wrote to Welles saying, "At this season of prevailing calms the *Constellation*, though an efficient vessel in her class [as a sailing ship], could not successfully pursue a steamer."

USS *Pampero* was another of Farragut's wooden sailing ships. She had been built in Mystic, Connecticut, in 1853 and purchased by the Navy at the start of the war for service as a supply ship. She was assigned to the Gulf Blockading Squadron and arrived off Florida in September 1861. When that Squadron was sub-divided, *Pampero* was given to Flag Officer

Black Sailors in the Civil War

Farragut for his West Gulf Blockading Squadron. David Farragut always strived to be fair with all his men and he tried hard to maintain happy ships, but this is not to say that there weren't occasionally problems. Some sailors had a tough time getting along. This seemed to be exacerbated by the competitive nature of different gun crews. Fist fights between Black and White sailors were commonly the result of insults over lineage or seamanship, but the worst seem to have been over gunnery or guns. One of the worst incidents was between an Irish and a Black sailor, where the White seaman, James Conlan, was killed when his head struck an object on the deck of USS *Pampero*. The fight between the two started when the Irish seaman put his hands on one of the ship's four 32-pound guns that was manned by Black sailors. That insult led to a verbal exchange over pride of ownership of the gun which quickly escalated into an exchange of insults over parentage which led to a fist fight. The Black sailor, James Dixon, was court-martialed but was exonerated because the sitting judges ruled that both men were mutual combatants and the "death was not premeditated by the accused" therefore both got what they got. Dixon remained aboard *Pampero* until the war ended. Gun crews were highly protective of their cannons. It often became a naval turf war when one gun crew disrespected another crew's cannon.

On 28 March 1865, the Union lost the monitor USS *Milwaukee*, followed by USS *Osage*, another monitor, on 29 March. On 1 April, the tinclad USS *Rodolph* struck a torpedo and sank while attempting to raise *Milwaukee*. Eleven days after that, USS *Althea* was sunk when it ran afoul of a torpedo. The following day the Union tug *Ida* also was sunk by a torpedo, followed on 14 April, with the reported loss of the steamer *Sciota* when it ran against a torpedo. Mobile finally surrendered on 12 April 1865.

The capture of Mobile Bay showcased Farragut's capabilities as a leader, including his consummate skills as a planner, his thoughtful ability to assemble a powerful force necessary to ensure victory, his ability to build a cooperative relationship with the Army, his decisiveness under fire, and his selection of the best officers to have around him. He tried to impress the importance of this latter quality upon his son, Loyall, bestowing on him the fatherly advice that a significant part of his education as a potential naval officer was to possess an understanding of the qualities of the men around him. "Where your analytical geometry will serve you once, a knowledge of men will serve you daily. As a commander, to get the right men in the right place is one of the questions of success or defeat," he told his son on 13 October 1864.[10]

The first Union monitor to pass in front of Fort Morgan, *Tecumseh*,

21. Mobile Bay

maneuvered too far to the west, striking a mine, and sinking in a matter of minutes. Fearing a similar fate, the captain of the next ship in line ordered his vessel to pause. Realizing the danger of remaining under the guns of the Confederate fort, Farragut ordered his fleet to follow his lead into Mobile Bay, ordering *Hartford* to advance at full speed. When a sailor reminded Farragut that additional mines might be just beneath the surface ahead, legend records that Farragut brushed off the warning shouting, "Damn the torpedoes." Because no one recorded Farragut's exact words during this incident, many subsequent versions added "Full steam ahead" or "Full speed ahead." In retrospect, John Crittendon Watson, Farragut's trusted flag lieutenant, recalled that Admiral's command was "Full speed ahead." Regardless of what he said that day, these additions to Farragut's known order have lent a legendary quality to his courage and leadership. What amazed Union sailors was the sounds of mines bumping against the hulls of their ships without exploding as they advanced into Mobile Bay. All of *Hartford's* 146 Black crewmembers who served on her during the war signed aboard during or after 1863 and were shuffled between the other ships in his command as necessary. This enlistment pattern was common throughout the Navy.

The paired Union warships entered Mobile Bay's main shipping channel on 5 August 1864 with *Brooklyn* and *Octorara* in the lead, followed by *Hartford* and *Metacomet*, *Richmond* and *Port Royal*, *Lackawanna* and *Seminole*, *Monongahela*, and *Kennebec*, *Ossipee* and *Itasca*, and finally *Oneida* and *Galena*. The attack plan called for Farragut's four Union ironclads to be to the right of the wooden warships and to the left of Fort Morgan. The first of these iron-clads, *Tecumseh*, struck a mine and quickly sank. The Confederate iron-clad *Tennessee* and her four gunboats were waiting. A crewmember of the screw sloop USS *Oneida* recorded the ship's operations in July 1864 outside Mobile Bay. His rendering of events, however, is not exact because the sketch describes the attacks of two different days. After all that Farragut had already been through, Welles wasn't done with him. Welles wanted him to lead the attack on Wilmington, North Carolina, the South's last remaining major seaport on the Atlantic coast open to blockade running. But by then Farragut was worn out. In September 1864, he told Welles that his health was failing owing to the strains of leading the Gulf Squadron. He requested shore duty and rest. This caught Welles off guard because Farragut was his principal choice to lead the North Atlantic Blockading Squadron and carry out the orders to capture Wilmington. Now, Welles had to find a suitable replacement, which wasn't going to be easy.

Black Sailors in the Civil War

In September 1864, Welles ran through all the merits and failings of all the most likely candidates in his mind recording his assessments in his diary. Du Pont was a favorite among the news media and some political leadership, but Welles judged Du Pont against Farragut, and he couldn't measure up in the overall comparison, noting in his diary: "The contrast between Farragut and Du Pont is marked. No one can now hesitate to say which is the real hero; yet three years ago it would have been different. Farragut is earnest, unselfish, devoted to the country and the service. He sees to every movement, forms his line of battle with care and skill, puts himself at the head, carries out his plan, if there is difficulty leads the way, regards no danger to himself, dashes by forts and overcomes obstructions. Du Pont, as we saw at [Charleston], puts himself in the most formidable vessel, has no order of battle, leads the way only until he gets within cannon-shot range, then stops, says his ship would not steer well, declines, however, to go in any other, but signals to them to go forward without order or and plan of battle, does not enjoin upon them to dash by the forts; they are stopped under the guns of [Fort] Sumter and [Fort] Moultrie, and are battered for an hour, a sufficient length of time to have gone to Charleston wharves, and then they are signaled to turn about and come back to the Admiral out of harm's way."[11] Du Pont was written off because he was blamed for the failure to penetrate the harbor defenses and take Charleston in April 1863. He countered criticisms by in turn blaming the failure on the poor performance of his monitors, which he claimed was due to Welles and the Navy Department placing far too much faith in their capabilities. Du Pont claimed they were sorry ships, incapable of living up to their unreasonable expectations, especially when it came to fighting hard packed batteries and fortification at close range. He justified his belief by saying, "I had hoped that the endurance of the iron-clads would have enabled them to have borne any weight of fire to which they might have been exposed; but when I found that so large a portion of them were wholly or one-half disabled, by less than an hour's engagement, before attempting to remove the obstructions, or testing the power of the torpedoes, I was convinced that persistence in the attack would only result in the loss of the greater portion of the iron-clad fleet...."[12]

Back in March 1863, Du Pont told Assistant Secretary Fox, "I think these monitors are wonderful conceptions, but, oh, the errors of details, which would have been corrected if these men of genius could be induced to pay attention to the people who use their tools and invention."[13] Du Pont also claimed that he was being made the scapegoat by Welles and others for their overly optimistic faith in the monitors, and their poor judgments.

21. Mobile Bay

Du Pont claimed Welles was biased, and in many respects he was. Welles wanted to use the monitors to create a fear factor in France and Great Britain, and that strategy appeared to have worked. European newspapers were one of Gideon Welles's best barometers for gauging foreign opinion.

In September 1863, Secretary Welles was struck by a change in tone and tenor resounding in the British press, and, he assumed, equally in French papers as well, because of his heavily armed monitor forces. "I think our monitors and heavy ordnance have a peaceful tendency, a tranquillizing effect," he wrote in his diary on 28 September, adding, "The guns of the *Weehawken* have knocked the breath out of British statesmen...." And, as unrealistic as this mental image might have been at the time, visions of Uncle Sam sending the *Monitor* up the River Thames to shell London nevertheless further chilled British imaginations when it came to siding with the South. Du Pont backed his assertions with a litany of evidence he said illustrated the iron-clad's faults under fire, claiming that five of his monitors were seriously disabled after firing only a few rounds, including: USS *Nahant*, which had her turret jam, preventing it from turning, and many of the rivets and bolts heads in her pilothouse become shrapnel when they popped under impact; USS *Passaic*, which also had her turret jam after she took only four shots at the enemy (her crew was ultimately able to free the turret after a significant delay); and USS *Patapsco*, which became disabled after only five shots. These were typically armed with at least one 15-inch Dahlgren gun, firing the Navy's largest projectile. And USS *Keokuk* was only able to get off three shots before she took a hit that sank her the following day off Morris Island. During the engagement, *Keokuk*, which had seriously weak experimental armor, was riddled by nearly 100 hits. The ship ended up looking like metallic Swiss cheese. *Keokuk's* crew was taken off by USS *Dandelion*, a 90-foot tug that was purchased by the Navy for blockade support in November 1862. The loss of *Keokuk* was a serious disappointment to Secretary Welles. He had done everything humanly possible to get *Keokuk* to Charleston, including repeatedly bullying Rear Admiral Paulding with letters and telegrams, like the one he sent on 8 March 1863, telling his Navy Yard commander to "[h]ire a steam-tug to take her to Hampton Roads where the *Sacramento* will take her in tow." At the same time Welles ordered Hiram Paulding, the head of the Brooklyn Navy Yard, to send USS *Florida* and *Nantucket* too. This telegram was followed by another that same day telling Paulding to ignore any complaints from the harbor pilots, demanding "[i]f they can go to sea send them." The loss of *Keokuk* was also a serious blow because she was thought of as a state-of-the-art iron-clad.

Black Sailors in the Civil War

In truth, Du Pont was correct. *Passaic*-class monitors, which included *Nahant*, *Patapsco*, and *Passaic*, had problems. They were slow, capable of roughly four knots in strong current, the turret had a propensity to jam when it was hit close to the turning ring on the deck, and the pilothouse wasn't well protected. These latter two issues were addressed in what amounted to a Civil War era "product recall." Additionally, loading a 15-inch gun with a 440-pound shell was a time-consuming process. What Du Pont didn't know was that the naval gun fire on Fort Wagner in particular was doing very little good. The fortification's sand walls were absorbing the incoming fire so that the greater part of the 165 cubic yards of sand was displaced by the roughly 55-tons of projectiles fired. This meant that the sand walls were simply falling back into place. After Fort Wagner was taken, engineers calculated that this amounted to discharging one-pound of metal to shift roughly three-pounds of sand. This demonstrated the effectiveness of "sand armor."[14] Du Pont believed that he was being made the victim of character assassination, writing to Welles: "Having indulged the hope that my command covering a period of 21 month afloat, had not been without results, I was not prepared for a continuance of the censure from the Department which has characterized its letter to me since monitors failed to take Charleston...," but he concluded, "these censures of the Navy Department would be keenly felt if I did not know they were wholly undeserved."

The odd thing is that Navy's *letterbooks* show that Du Pont had cold feet well before the attack and that Welles gave Du Pont the option of making the attack or not. The evidence of that is a 24 January 1863 confidential communiqué sent by Du Pont where he advised Welles that he didn't believe he had enough monitors to do the job, and Welles confidentially responded by telling his officer that if that was indeed the case, he should abandon the attempt as he could expect no others for at least six weeks, if then. As Acting Rear Admiral Lee had done a short time earlier before Wilmington, Du Pont simply could have done a wave-off at Charleston, but *he* chose not to do so. Regardless of what Du Pont thought, in Welles' mind the criticism of his leadership was indeed well founded, and he wasn't serious about considering Du Pont for command of the North Atlantic Blockading Squadron, especially after he had been allowed to retire after failing in operations against Charleston in 1863 and blaming his failure on the Union's precious monitors. To Secretary Welles that was unforgivable. Du Pont, however, still had powerful friends who were willing to make a case for his come-back.

22

The Union's Starships

For Gideon Welles, the Navy's turreted monitors were the technological hallmark of his administration. They were his wonder-weapons, his starships and he was prepared to build an armada of them to suppress the South. They represented a whole new category of warships. There actually was an array of different classes of Union monitors and the classification system can seem a bit confusing. To simplify things, broadly speaking, monitors during the Civil War can be divided into three basic categories: River monitors, Coastal monitors, and Ocean monitors. Welles wanted some of every type to overwhelm any areas of opposition to Union control of southern waterways. River monitors had shallow drafts. Of the river monitors there were five different classes, including the *Casco*-class, with a six-foot draft; *Neosho*-class, with a four-and-a-half-foot draft; *Ozark*-class, five-foot draft; *Marietta*-class, also with a five-foot draft; and *Milwaukee*-class, with a six-foot draft. The draft wasn't the only difference with these classes, but it is useful to show that they were meant to work in marginal waterways such as minor bays and sounds and western rivers.

All monitors had the common characteristic of being hot, cramped, and flat bottomed which tended to make sailors seasick. With 20 light-draft vessels of this type envisioned, Secretary Welles expected the *Casco*-class to be the workhorse of his shallow coastal and riverine monitor fleet. They were to be capable of defeating any iron-clad the Confederacy might put against them on any inland or coastal waterway. The 20 monitors of this class included *Casco, Chimo, Coohoes, Etlah, Klamath, Koka, Modoc, Napa, Naubuc, Nausett, Shawnee, Shiloh, Squando, Suncook, Tunxis, Umpqua, Wassuc, Waxsaw, Yazoo,* and *Yuma*.[1] Ordered in 1863, the first 13 *Casco*-class single-turret monitors were to be delivered in just six months. To watch over this massive project, which involved several shipyards, Welles' assistant secretary, Gustavus Fox, selected Alban C. Stimers. While that might have been enough time under normal circumstances, the design called for several new features, including floodable ballast tanks that would enable the vessels to become partially submerged in combat.

These outer tanks also were seen as ideal protection against torpedoes. A steady stream of additional design changes followed, impacting timelines. While the design changes were being submitted to John Ericsson for review, he and Stimers were not on speaking terms. Ericsson was also immersed in the process of designing and building USS *Dictator*, his latest pet project which was among the largest turreted vessel constructed to that time, he wasn't paying much attention to what Stimers was doing in modifying the basic monitor design. To make matters worse, contractors were using green timber and poorly rolled iron in the construction of the first of the *Casco*-class monitors, the *Chimo*. In coming off the ways *Chimo's* stern settled in with 5 inches below water, even before taking on coal and ammunition, Stimers had miscalculated the ship's displacement. Instead of having a 15-inch freeboard, *Chimo* ended up having a mere three-inches even before her turret and ordnance was added.[2]

By June 1864, Welles, who had been kept in the dark on all of the design modifications being made by both Stimers and Fox, was alerted to the extent of the problems, recording in his diary: "There have been mistakes and miscalculations in this class of vessel of a serious character."[3] Fox assured his boss that all of the problems were resolvable and that any concerns were groundless. Welles recorded that Fox told him that the *Chimo* was indeed a little deep, "but this would be obviated in all the others, and [the problem was] not very bad in her case."[4] That wasn't true! By July the newspapers were aware of the problems and questions led to recriminations. There were published attacks on the Navy and Welles. In July famed naval architect Donald McKay, builder of many of America's record setting clippers such as *Sovereign of the Sea*, *Stag Hound* and *Flying Cloud*, came to the Navy's defense assuring the public in a masterful letter that appeared in the *New York Times* and the *Evening Post* that when developing innovative ships, such as a light draft iron-clad, which had never before been attempted, unforeseen problems occasionally crop up.

In October McKay also sent a letter to the *Boston Daily Advertiser* entitled "Our Navy" saying: "Nothing is easier than to find fault, and I can state, from my own experience, that with all my care, I never yet built a vessel that came up to my own ideal; I saw something in each ship which I desired to improve. But I should have felt unfairly dealt with if my ships had been judged by their blemishes rather than their merits. The same rule I propose to apply to a review of our naval affairs, that those interested may see what has been done, and is still doing, by the Navy Department."[5] Welles was

22. The Union's Starships

thankful for the support of the Boston shipbuilder in July, briefly noting in his diary that McKay's letter was "very well done and unexpected." At the same time, he seems to have anticipated that the ever-critical *New York Tribune*, which also received a copy, would be slow to print McKay's July letter, if it ran it at all. Welles believed there were reasons for that reluctance. "Greeley of the *Tribune* is secretly hostile to the President and assails him indirectly in this way," Welles reasoned on 26 July 1864. As Welles expected there were others who also wished to continue to rub the Navy's nose in the monitor matter. McKay's letter that summer appeared to placate the public, but it didn't quell the quest for answers when it came to the Committee on the Conduct of the War. The Committee demanded a full accounting of the monitor mess. Fox furnished much of the facts, telling the Committee that in June the Navy had put together a panel to determine what to do with the faulty monitors. The panel reported back the following month recommending that the first five light draft vessels should be converted into torpedo boats. The remaining 15 should have their drafts extensively modified to make them meaningful monitors.

In December 1864, Fox went on record as saying that while the Department of the Navy had the idea for creating the light draft monitors, the "mechanical details belong to those permanent officers whose specialty it is to put into practical operation." In other words, the Navy Department wasn't responsible for anything other than having the original idea. Fox didn't mention that he was one of those who was deeply involved with the mechanical and technical details for the ships, but he did say, "The whole subject has given the Secretary much anxiety."[6] That was an understatement. Welles was deeply peeved that his department was bearing the brunt of the blame for Fox's and Stimers' failures. Regardless of his upset, in a way, Welles was guilty of trusting the two men with such an important project without ensuring that they were getting adequate supervision from John Ericsson.

Welles had wrongly assumed that Ericsson was constantly looking over Stimers' shoulder. He hadn't been. In his 15 December statement to the committee, Fox also reported that Stimers had been removed from his position. That was only half true. Stimers hadn't been fired as might be inferred. As an alternative, the ever-kind-hearted Secretary had offered Stimers command of USS *Powhatan* instead, but the beleaguered officer opted to simply resign. As for Fox, in addition to weathering his boss's ire, in submitting his December statement to the committee, he realized just how much hot water he was also in politically. Mindful of the mess he had made, Fox began thinking about other employment opportunities. That December, he told Welles that he had been offered a job as the head of a Pennsylvania coal company, but that he couldn't accept that position unless they offered a great deal more money.[7] A month later he informed Welles that he had been offered the presidency of a new steamship line that was about to establish a route between New York and San Francisco.[8] Nothing came of either offer. Given his compassionate nature, Welles privately expressed regrets over potentially losing Fox, in his diary, noting on 17 January 1866, that he still considered Fox to be "of almost invaluable service." This had been the case back in May 1861 when Fox was under consideration of the job as Welles' clerk. Back then Fox's appointment hadn't come without opposition, but Lincoln was firmly in his corner and instructed Welles to stick by his choice. "My wish, and advice is, that you do not allow any ordinary obstacle prevent his appointment," said Lincoln, adding "He is a live man, whose services we cannot well dispense with."[9] While that was still true, at the same time the Secretary also realized that the embarrassment was simply too great, and that Fox had to go.

That opportunity finally came when *Miantonomah* went on its European tour in the summer of 1866. Fox was told he could go with her with the expectation that he might be hired as the agent of some foreign governments wishing to build turreted vessels of their own; but, regardless of the outcome of the voyage, the understanding was that when she returned, he'd be expected to resign, if not before. Prior to Fox's departure Welles was advised by his trusted chief clerk, William Faxon, that he didn't believe Fox really intended to resign. "That cannot be, and I am unwilling to believe he would, if he could, be guilty of the bad faith and duplicity that would be involved in such a procedure," wrote Welles in his diary in May on the eve of Fox's planned departure aboard *Miantonomah*. Fox resigned on 26 November 1866. This had been a low point for Welles. Two trusted subordinates that he relied upon had monumentally failed him. "I look upon the whole transaction as the most unfortunate that has taken place during my administration of the Navy Department," he wrote.[10]

Fixing the problem required extensive modifications to the overall design of this class of monitor and the make-over was made at great expense. Unusable as it was, *Chimo* was converted into a turret-less "torpedo boat." In its new form, *Chimo* was equipped with a bow-mounted device for launching spar torpedoes and a single deck gun mounted on greatly reduced deck plating. Unfortunately, *Chimo* didn't work well in this configuration either. Torpedo boats needed to be fast, and her service speed was a mere four-knots. None of the *Casco*-class monitors that were completed amounted to much. Additionally, of the roughly 140 vessels used by the Union Navy on the Mississippi River system, nine were monitors. Ideal

22. The Union's Starships

for riverine warfare, the *Osage* and *Neosho*, both part of the *Neosho*-class, were shallow-draft river monitors designed by James Eads. These monitors featured a "turtleback" design to protect their sternwheel. *Osage* was also fitted with a periscope late in the war for protected fire control.

Another Eads innovation was the four *Milwaukee*-class river monitors, which included *Milwaukee, Chickasaw, Kickapoo* and *Winnebago*. These were the most sophisticated river monitors of the war. The dual-turreted *Milwaukee*-class was a hybrid, one turret was an Ericsson type, while the other was of Eads' design.[11] The Eads forward gun turret platform was capable of being lowered into the hull of the ship for loading. The *Milwaukee* also featured watertight compartments, which slowed its sinking when it struck a torpedo in March 1865. No sailors were lost.

The Coastal monitors included *Monitor, Passaic, Onondaga*, and *Canonicus*-classes. These were dominated by John Ericsson's genius, all basically variations of his original USS *Monitor* design. The draft of these monitors tended to be 10-foot or more. The *Passaic*-class consisted of 10 monitors (*Passaic, Camanche, Catskill, Lehigh, Montauk, Nahant, Nantucket, Patapsco, Sangamon* and *Weehawken*). The *Canonicus*-class included nine monitors (*Canonicus, Catawba, Mahopac, Manayunk, Manhattan, Oncota, Saugus, Tecumsch*, and *Tippecanoe*). These were single-turreted vessels. If USS *Passaic* is any example, perhaps to reduce racial tensions aboard the cramped quarters of a monitor, many of the Black crewmembers assigned to these classes of ships appear to have been mulatto. Three-quarters of *Passaic's* 12 Black sailors during the war were identified as mulatto. One-third of *Montauk's* crewmembers during the war were listed as mulatto.

The Ocean monitors included the *Dictator, Kalamazoo, Miantonomoh* and *Roanoke*-classes. Compared to the original *Monitor*, which was 172-feet long with eight-inch turret armor, the overall length of *Dictator* was 314-feet. The beam of the larger ship was 50-feet, and she boasted a pair of 15-inch Dahlgren gun in a turret plated with 15-inches of iron. She was driven by 100-inch diameter cylinders that produced a 16-knot service speed, compared to *Monitor's* nine-knots. *Dictator* was commissioned on 11 November 1864, but not in time to see combat. Her sister ship, USS *Puritan*, which also was not completed before the end of the war, was to be even larger. *Puritan* was to be 340-feet long and mount a pair of massive 20-inch Dahlgren guns. Constantly striving for bigger and bigger warships, at one point, the Navy wanted *Puritan* to have dual turrets, but John Ericsson objected claiming that the vessel's displacement would be totally wrong. The *Miantonomoh*-class, which included four

Black Sailors in the Civil War

monitors (*Miantonomoh*, *Agamenticus*, *Monadnock* and *Tonawanda*), were double-turreted. Although they were slow, with an average service speed of seven-knots, naval officers considered this class of monitors to be among the finest Union iron-clads ever built. Only *Monadnock* was completed in time to see service during the war. Following the war *Monadnock* was assigned to the Pacific Squadron, transiting Cape Horn to San Francisco. *Miantonomoh* was sent to Europe to demonstrate the ability of American naval weaponry to reach foreign shores.

During her foreign port visits *Miantonomoh* was mobbed with visitors. The four monitors of the *Kalamazoo*-class (*Kalamazoo*, *Passaconaway*, *Quinsigamond*, and *Shackamaxon*) were the largest armored ocean-going warships conceived during the Civil War. With an overall length of 345 feet and a 56-foot beam, these were considered the Navy's new "big guns" of that era. In terms of lethality, however, *Roanoke* was the Union's most powerful "monitor," but in reality, she was anything but. Although USS *Roanoke* featured three Ericsson-type turrets, each mounting two cannons, she was not strictly speaking a monitor. She really was more of a surface ship, built on the hull of a steam frigate. As a monitor *Roanoke* never really worked. Her hull, which had been given four-and-a-half-inches of armor plating, was simply too weak to support the trio of 23-foot diameter gun turrets, plus her massive array of ordnance, which included two 15-inch Dahlgren guns, two 11-inch Dahlgren guns and a pair of 150-pound Parrott rifles. The gun turrets alone weighed 125 tons each. With all this weight, she was also simply too top heavy to function as a gun platform. She ended up serving as port security.[12] Although many of the monitors built during the war, or still under construction at the end of it, had serious flaws, these defects would have been rectified and improved upon if the war had progressed.

In this way, Welles' execution of the war was a stellar success in that he had amassed, and was amassing, an overwhelming force to dominate his enemy and control the water-borne war front. Additionally, while many of these ships were commissioned late in the war, or were not completed by mid–1865, their creation signaled the extinction of the Navy's old Ships-of-the-line. From this point forward the lineage of the evolution of the modern surface Navy had a new common ancestor—the turreted iron-clad. Welles wrote his own verdict of his leadership of the Navy's war on the water on 21 February 1865. "Others could have done better, perhaps, than I have done, and yet, reviewing hastily the past, I see very little to regret in my administration of the Navy."[13]

23

The Aftermath

The great reward for Black Union warfighters came on 3 March 1865 when Congress passed an act that declared that the wives and children of slaves enlisted in the U.S. Services were free. Secretary Stanton informed his generals of this on 11 March, saying a copy of the law would follow. Other than that, towards the end of the war, Black and White sailors were expected to either go home when their terms of service expired and begin life anew or to reenlist in the Navy. Up until 1864 no thought had been made for the care of disabled or infirmed sailors. While there had been numerous "Soldiers' Fairs" conducted by United States Sanitary Commission, and other similar groups, to care for soldiers but nothing had been done for sailors until the creation of the Grand National Sailors' Fair, held in Boston from 9 to 22 November 1864.[1] Such fairs were like mini-World's Fairs. Army fairs were held in Philadelphia, Brooklyn, St. Louis and Albany. Only one Navy fair was conducted.

A gimmick of the Navy event was to sell ten-cent "Cinderella" Fair stamps that would be affixed to letters as a show of support and as a way of raising money for a sailors' home. The home was to accommodate sailors in need of care, provided space was available. President Lincoln was highly supportive of the Navy Fair, sending a telegram to the Fair's organizers saying: "Allow me to wish you a great success. With the old fame of the Navy, made brighter in the present war, you can not [sic] fail. I name none, lest I wrong others by omission. To all, from Rear Admiral, to honest Jack [a common seaman] I tender the Nation's Admiration and gratitude."

Lincoln contributed $3,500 to the Navy Fair's fundraising campaign, and the free Black community of Boston contributed greatly to the success of this patriotic effort.

At war's end, few Blacks opted to remain in the Navy. Ordinary seaman William Thompson was one of those who did. He continued to serve aboard USS *Don* until mid–1868. Most others were honorably discharged. For them, the agonizing search for family members began. Such searches usually began at the loved one's last known place of bondage. Painfully, often by then, many family members had been sold elsewhere, moved by their masters to keep them from being emancipated, such as to Texas, had escaped to places unknown, or had changed their names

President Lincoln's acknowledgment letter for his $3,500 in financial support for the National Sailors' Fair from Mrs. S.T. Hooper, the Fair's Secretary, dated 2 December 1864. (Library of Congress)

23. The Aftermath

following emancipation and moved on. With all the name changing taking place, one enlistee switched his last name to "Freeborn" to leave no doubt as to his status. Starkey Nereus was among the Black sailors who took the name of his ship. The New Inlet, North Carolina, native was a 3rd class boy aboard USS *Nereus* in 1864–1865. With new first and/or last names, many slave families were never reunited. The government's slave narratives are full of heart-wrenching tales of shattered families and broken hearts.

James V. Deane only witnessed one such loss, his aunt. She was slapped by her mistress, and she slapped her owner back. "She was sold and taken south," Deane told an interviewer with the slave narratives project. "We never saw or heard of her afterwards."

Black ordinary seaman John Frank from Watertown, New York, enlisted at Boston for a one-year term. He initially mustered aboard USS *Sassacus* on 30 October 1863. He re-enlisted and continued to serve as one of *Sassacus* 145-man crewmembers until his discharge in 1864. A double-ended side-wheeler, *Sassacus* was commissioned at Boston on 5 October 1863. Frank was aboard *Sassacus* during her three-hour battle with the iron-clad ram CSS *Albemarle*. The fight was a lopsided contest. *Sassacus* and the other ships accompanying her were greatly outgunned by the iron-clad, which had already sunk USS *Southfield*, on 5 May 1864 in the Albemarle Sound. To gain a possible advantage *Sassacus* rammed *Albemarle*, literally running up over *Albemarle*'s deck, while all the time her integrated gun crews continued to fire at the iron-covered beast. *Sassacus*'

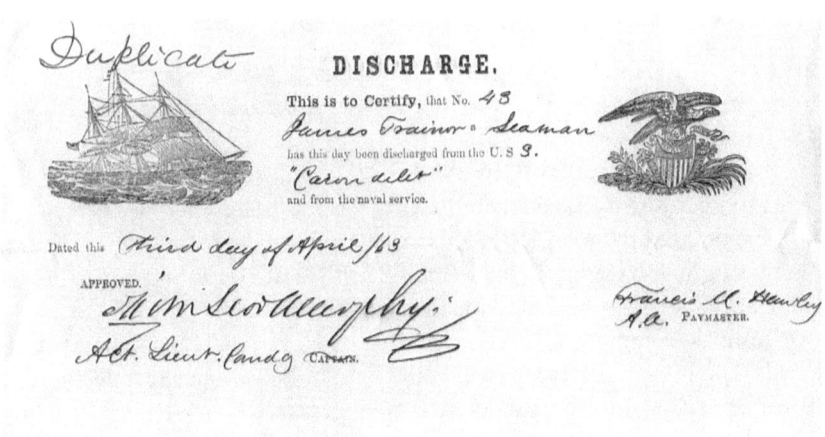

Discharge paper for James Trainor, honorably discharged on 3 April 1863. (Library of Congress)

Black Sailors in the Civil War

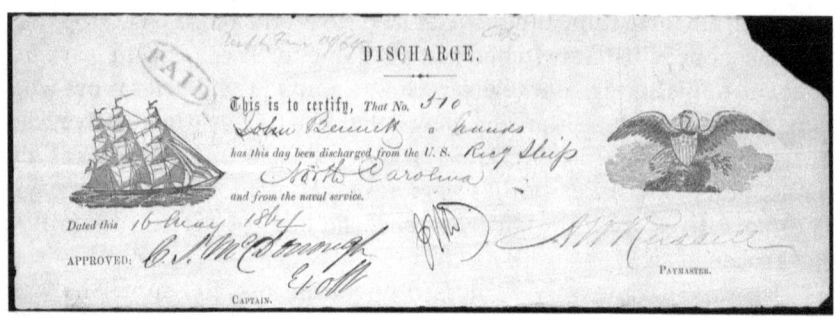

Top and above: Black landsman John Bennett's discharge order. Bennett enlisted at New York on 7 March 1861 for a three-year term. His entire service was aboard USS *Charles Phelps*, a coal supply ship assigned to the North Atlantic Blockading Squadron. At any given time, she had a complement of 23 men. In all 53 Black sailors served on the *Charles Phelps* throughout the war. (Library of Congress)

sailors even started throwing hand-grenades at *Albemarle's* gun ports in the hopes of successfully lobbing one inside. *Albemarle* subsequently fled. David had beaten Goliath.

For Henrietta Ralls: "Our White folks took some of us clear out in Texas to keep the Yankees from getting 'em.... The owners was tryin' to hide the colored people." Ralls' mistress told her before the trek to Texas, "You thought you was goin' to be free!" Senia Rassberry was taken to Texas too. Her master kept her there for three years.[2]

June 19 became a special day for many slaves in Texas. It was when they learned they were truly free. Will Glass talked about that special day. "Both of my grandfathers said their masters used to give picnics. They would have a certain day and they would give them all a good time and let them enjoy themselves. They would kill a cow or some kids and hogs and have a barbeque. They kept that up after freedom. Every nineteenth of June

23. The Aftermath

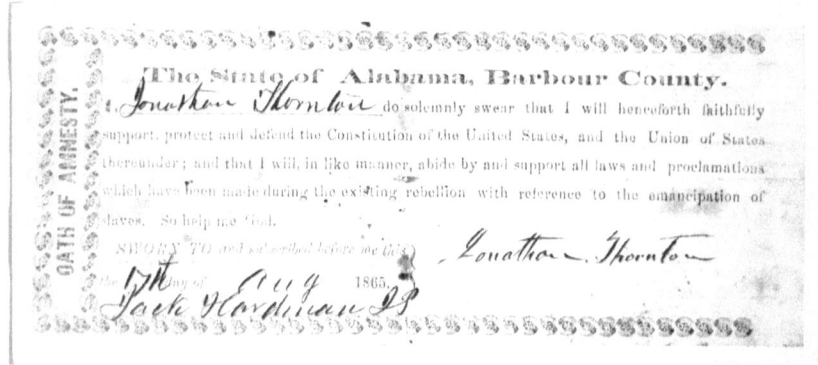

To become part of the United States again, southerners had to take an oath of allegiance. Some also had to take an oath of amnesty which required them to accept formally the emancipation of the slaves. This is the signed oath for Jonathon Thornton from Barbour County, Alabama. (Library of Congress)

After the Civil War, Black sailors assumed greater leadership roles aboard ships, including USS *Galena*, shown here in the 1880s. (Naval History and Heritage Command)

they would throw a big picnic until I got big enough to see and know for myself."[3]

There was a significant benefit of military service. Judging from the stories recorded as part of the slave narrative projects, old age was hard for many who did not serve. For those who did, the ability to receive a military pension went a long way towards improving their quality of life in their later years.

Chapter Notes

Chapter 1

1. Letter to Joshua Speed, 24 August 1855, *Lincoln's Writings: The Multi-Media*. n.p.
2. Lincoln's First Inaugural Address, 4 March 1861., n.p.
3. *Official Records of the Union and Confederate Navies in the War of the Rebellion* (Washington, D.C.: Government Printing Office, 1897), 53.
4. Charles B. Boyton, *The History of the Navy During the Rebellion*, Volume I (New York: D. Appleton and Company, 1867), 85.
5. Letter from Secretary of State William Seward to Lord Lyons, 16 October 1861 (Washington, DC: Office of the Historian, United States State Department, 1861).
6. Howard K. Beale, ed., *Welles Diary*, Vol. I (New York: W.W. Norton & Co., 1960), 71.
7. *Ibid.*, p. 407.
8. Letter to Horace Greeley, 22 August 1862.
9. James McPherson, *Battle Cry of Freedom* (New York: Oxford University Press, 1988), 504.
10. William Howard Russell, *My Diary North and South*, Volume I (New York: T.O.H.P. Burnam, 1863), 273.
11. *Ibid.*, 394.
12. Letter from Flag Officer Goldsborough to Navy Assistant Secretary V. Fox, 9 November 1861.
13. Howard K. Beale, ed., *Welles Diary*, Vol. II, 53.
14. B.A. Botkin, ed., *A Civil War Treasury of Tales, Legends and Folklore* (Secaucus, NJ: The Blue and Grey Press, 1960), 234.
15. *Ibid.*, 234.

Chapter 2

1. *Former Slave Narratives*, Writers Project, Works Progress Administration, 1936–1937 (Washington, D.C.: National Archives), n.p.
2. *The Liberator*, 27 June 1862 (Boston) p. 3.
3. Gideon Welles Papers, *Letterbooks*, 1862–1869 (Washington, DC: Library of Congress).
4. *Former Slave Narratives*, Writers Project, Works Progress Administration, 1936–1937 (Washington, DC: National Archives), n.p.
5. *Ibid.*
6. *Ibid.*
7. *Ibid.*
8. *Ibid.*
9. *Ibid.*
10. *Ibid.*
11. *Ibid.*
12. *Ibid.*
13. *Ibid.*
14. *Ibid.*
15. *Ibid.*
16. *Ibid.*
17. *Ibid.*
18. *Ibid.*
19. *Ibid.*
20. *Ibid.*
21. *Ibid.*
22. *Ibid.*
23. *Ibid.*
24. *Ibid.*
25. *Ibid.*
26. *Ibid.*
27. *Ibid.*
28. *Ibid.*
29. *Ibid.*
30. *Ibid.*

Notes—Chapters 3, 4, 5, 6 and 7

31. *Ibid.*
32. *Ibid.*
33. *Ibid.*
34. *Ibid.*

Chapter 3

1. *Civil War Naval Chronology, 1861-1865*, section II (Washington, D.C.: Naval History Division, Navy Department, 1971), n.p.
2. Naval History and Heritage Command, Washington, D.C.

Chapter 4

1. Frederick Douglass, *Life and Times of Frederick Douglass* (Hartford, Connecticut: Park Publishing Company, 1881), 198.

Chapter 5

1. *Civil War Naval Chronology, 1861-1865*, section I.

Chapter 6

1. Gideon Welles Papers, *Letterbooks*, 1862-1869 (Washington, DC: Library of Congress).
2. *Ibid.*
3. Howard K. Beale, ed., *Welles Diary*, Vol. II (New York: W.W. Norton & Co., 1960).
4. *Former Slave Narratives*, Writers Project, Works Progress Administration, 1936-1937 (Washington, DC: National Archives).
5. *Ibid.*
6. *Ibid.*
7. B.A. Botkin, ed., *A Civil War Treasury of Tales, Legends and Folklore* (Secaucus, NJ: The Blue and Grey Press, 1960), 242.
8. Joseph P. Reidy, "Black Men in Navy Blue," *Prologue Magazine* (Washington, DC: National Archives), Parts 1, 2 and 3.
9. Lester B. Tucker, *Pull Together* "History of the Petty Officer Grade," Spring-Summer 1993 (Naval Historical Foundation: Washington, DC) as referenced by Joseph P. Reidy, *Prologue Magazine*, "Black Men in Navy Blue," Parts 1, 2 and 3. Not discussed are the Petty Officer grades at the staff rating, which include master-at-arms, yeoman, surgeon's steward, paymaster's steward, master of the band, schoolmaster, ship's corporal, armorer, painter, carpenter's mate, sailmaker's mate, fireman first class, cooper, armorer's mate, steward and cook.
10. Howard K. Beale, ed., *Welles Diary*, Vol. I, 407.

Chapter 7

1. Gideon Welles Papers, *Letterbooks*, 1862-1869.
2. *Ibid.*
3. *Ibid.*
4. *Ibid.*
5. Howard K. Beale, ed., *Welles Diary*, Vol. I.
6. Gideon Welles Papers, *Letterbooks*, 1862-1869.
7. *Ibid.*
8. Howard K. Beale, ed., *Welles Diary*, Vol. II, 121.
9. *Civil War Naval Chronology, 1861-1865*, section II (Washington, DC: Naval History Division, *Navy* Department, 1971), 41.
10. The Joseph Smith letter to Foote, July 11, 1862, is in the collections of the Gilder Lehrman Institute of American History (GLC05060).
11. Lot 137, Stan V. Henkels auction sales catalogue, Philadelphia, January 4, 1924.
12. *Ibid.*, Lot 139.
13. Joel T. Headley, *Farragut and Our Naval Commanders* (New York: E.B. Treat, 1880), 209-223. Headley allowed each of the living officers highlighted in his book to submit their own write-ups for inclusion in this work. This was done he said to ensure accuracy, but it afforded each officer the opportunity to tell their particular side of their story of service.
14. Howard K. Beale, ed., *Welles Diary*, Vol. 1.
15. Gideon Welles Papers, *Letterbooks*, 1862-1869.

Notes—Chapters 8, 9, 10, 11, 12 and 13

Chapter 8

1. *Official Records of the Union and Confederate Navies in the War of the Rebellion*, Series I, Volume 14 (Washington, DC: Government Printing Office 1902), 69.
2. Song sheet from Library of Congress sheet music collection.

Chapter 9

1. *Former Slave Narratives*, Writers Project, Works Progress Administration, 1936–1937 (Washington, DC: National Archives).
2. *Ibid.*
3. *Ibid.*

Chapter 10

1. David Dixon Porter, *Incidents and Anecdotes of the Civil War: Volume I* (New York: Appleton and Company, 1886), 146.
2. *Former Slave Narratives*, Writer's Project, Works Progress Administration.

Chapter 11

1. Katharine Prescott Wormeley, *The Other Side of War on the Hospital Transports with the Army of the Potomac*, Introduction.
2. Brig. Gen. F.C. Ainsworth and Joseph W. Kirkley, eds., *The War of the Rebellion*, Series III, Volume II (Washington, DC: Government Printing Office, 1899), 807.
3. *Ibid.*, 807.
4. *Ibid.*, 807.
5. *Ibid.*, 809.
6. Katharine Prescott Wormeley, *The Other Side of War on the Hospital Transports with the Army of the Potomac*, 175.
7. *Ibid.*, 107.
8. *Ibid.*, 69.
9. *Ibid.*, 69–70.
10. *Ibid.*, 70.
11. *Ibid.*, 61.
12. B.A. Botkin, ed., *A Civil War Treasury of Tales, Legends and Folklore*, 82–83.
13. Katharine Prescott Wormeley, *The Other Side of War on the Hospital Transports with the Army of the Potomac*, 163.
14. *Ibid.*, 182.

15. Howard K. Beale, ed., *Welles Diary*, Vol. I, 213.
16. *Ibid.*, 213.
17. Katharine Prescott Wormeley, *The Other Side of War on the Hospital Transports with the Army of the* Potomac, 172.
18. B.A. Botkin, ed.., *A Civil War Treasury of Tales, Legends and Folklore*, 149–151.

Chapter 12

1. Letter from Mayor John T. Monroe to Flag Officer David Farragut, April 26, 1862.
2. Letter from Mayor John T. Monroe to Flag Officer David Farragut, April 28, 1862.
3. *Ibid.*
4. *Ibid.*
5. Howard K. Beale, ed., *Welles Diary*, Vol.1, 88.
6. *Ibid.*, 88.
7. *Ibid.*, 88.
8. *Ibid.*, 89.
9. *Ibid.*, 145.
10. *General Order 135*: For Passing "Port Hudson," manuscript order from Rear Admiral David Farragut, depicted in *Civil-War Naval Chronology, 1861–1865*, section III (Washington, DC: Naval History Division, Navy Department, 1971), 42–43.
11. Gideon Welles Papers, *Letterbooks*, 1862–1869; 1863, February 2–May 22.
12. *Civil War Naval Chronology, 1861–1865*, Section III, 53.
13. *Ibid.*, p. 70.
14. Howard K. Beale, ed., *Welles Diary*, Vol. II.
15. *Ibid.*, 134.
16. *Ibid.*, Vol. III, 104.
17. *Ibid.*, 104.
18. *Ibid.*, 123.
19. *Ibid.*, Vol. II, 135.
20. *Ibid.*, 177.

Chapter 13

1. Peter C. Luebka, ed., *The Autobiography of Rear Admiral John A. Dahlger* (Washington, DC: Naval History and Heritage Command, 2018), 70.
2. John Mason Hoppin, *Life of Andrew Hull Foote: Rear-Admiral United States*

Notes—Chapters 14 and 15

Navy (New York: Harper & Brothers, 1874), 18.
3. *Civil War Naval Chronology, 1861-1865*, Section II, 6.
4. *Ibid.*, 3.
5. *Ibid.*, 15.
6. *Ibid.*, 7.
7. *Ibid.*, 26.
8. Lot 137, Stan V. Henkels auction sales catalogue, Philadelphia, January 4, 1924.
9. *Civil War Naval Chronology, 1861-1865*, Section II, 26.
10. Gideon Welles Papers, *Letterbooks, 1862-1869*; 1863, February 2–May 22.
11. John Mason Hoppin, *Life of Andrew Hull Foote: Rear-Admiral United States Navy*, 266.
12. Andrew Foote letter to his wife, August 8, 1862, in the collections of the Gilder Lehrman Institute of American History (GLC03910).
13. John Mason Hoppin, *Life of Andrew Hull Foote: Rear-Admiral United States Navy*, 299.
14. *Ibid.*, p. 311.
15. Howard K. Beale, ed., *Welles Diary*, Vol. I, 158.
16. *Ibid.*, 157.
17. *Ibid.*, 158.
18. National Park Service's database of Black sailors during the Civil War.
19. *Report of the Secretary of the Navy*, 1865, 523.
20. National Park Service's database of Black sailors during the Civil War.
21. National Park Service's database of Black sailors during the Civil War.
22. Katherine Prescott Wormeley, *The Other Side of War on the Hospital Transports with the Army of the Potomac*, 29.
23. National Park Service's database of Black sailors during the Civil War.
24. *Report of the Secretary of the Navy*, 1865, 522.
25. *Report of the Secretary of the Navy*, 1865, 529.
26. *Ibid.*, 342.

Chapter 14

1. Howard K. Beale, ed., *Welles Diary*, Vol. 1.
2. *Ibid.*, 295.

3. *Ibid.*, 369.
4. *Ibid.*
5. *Civil War Naval Chronology, 1861-1865*, section IV, (Washington, DC: Naval History Division, Navy Department, 1971), 370.
6. Howard K. Beale, ed., *Welles Diary*, Vol. I, 320.
7. *Ibid.*, Vol. II, 70.
8. *Ibid.*, Vol. I, 384.
9. *Ibid.*, 331.
10. Michael Burlingame and John R. Turner Ettlinger, editors, *Inside Lincoln's White House: The Complete Civil War Diary of John Hay*, 191–192.
11. Gideon Welles Papers, *Letterbooks*, 1862-1869; 1862.
12. Howard K. Beale, ed., *Welles Diary*, Vol. I, 274.
13. *Official Records of the Union and Confederate Navies in the War of the Rebellion*, Series I, Volume 23 (Washington, DC: Government Printing Office, 1910), 227.
14. Gideon Welles Papers, *Letterbooks*, 1862-1869; 1862.
15. *Ibid.*
16. *Ibid.*
17. *Ibid.*
18. Howard K. Beale, ed., *Welles Diary*, Vol. I, 274.
19. *Ibid.*, 285.
20. *Civil War Naval Chronology, 1861-1865*, section III, 91–92.
21. James Russell Soley, *Admiral Porter*, Great Commanders Series (New York: D. Appleton and Company, 1903), 344.
22. *Civil War Naval Chronology, 1861-1865*, section III, 104.
23. Howard K. Beale, ed., *Welles Diary*, Vol. I, 274.

Chapter 15

1. Howard K. Beale, ed., *Welles Diary*, Vol. I, 283.
2. *Ibid.*, 390.
3. Gideon Welles Papers, *Letterbooks*, 1862-1869; 1862-1863, images 184–186.
4. James P. Duffy, *Lincoln's Admiral: The Civil War Campaigns of David Farragut* (New York: John Wiley & Sons, 1997), 220–221.

Notes—Chapters 16, 17, 18, 19, 20 and 21

5. Howard K. Beale, ed., *Welles Diary*, Vol. I, 480.
6. *Punch*, October 24, 1863.
7. *Ibid.*, 445.
8. *Ibid.*, 468.
9. *Ibid.*, 469.
10. *Ibid.*, 453.
11. Gideon Welles Papers, *Letterbooks*, 1862–1869, 1862, June 21–October 4.
12. Howard K. Beale, ed., *Welles Diary*, Vol. I, 267.
13. *Ibid.*, 267.
14. *Ibid.*, 271.
15. *Ibid.*, 274.
16. *Ibid.*, 286.
17. *Ibid.* 304.
18. *Ibid.*, 288–289.
19. *Ibid.*, 140.
20. Gideon Welles Papers, *Letterbooks*, 1862–1869, 1862.
21. Gideon Welles Papers, Speeches and Other Writings, 1822–1878, "The Missouri Compromise," Library of Congress.
22. North American Review and Miscellaneous Journal, Volume 145, 1887, p. 78.
23. Michael J. Forsyth, *The Red River Campaign of 1864 and the Loss by the Confederacy of the Civil War* (Jefferson, NC: McFarland, 2010), p. 118.
24. *Welles Diary*, Howard K. Beale, ed., vol. 2, p. 18.
25. *Ibid.*, p. 37.
26. Richard G. West, Jr., *The Second Admiral: A Life of David Dixon Porter 1819–1891* (Fleetwood, Pennsylvania: Coward-McCann, Inc., 1937), 265.

Chapter 16

1. Milton Meltzer, ed., *Voices from the Civil War* (New York: Harper Trophy, 1992), 109.
2. Michael Flannery and Katherine Odmens, eds., *Well Satisfied with My Position, The Civil War Journal of Spencer Bonsall* (Carbondale: Southern Illinois University Press, 2007), 74.
3. *Ibid.*, 74.

Chapter 17

1. Botkin, ed., *A Civil War Treasury of Tales, Legends and Folklore*, 119.

2. *The DayBook*, Hampton Roads Naval Museum, Civil War Special Edition.
3. Edgar Stanton Maclay, *A History of the United States Navy from 1777 to 1893* (New York: D. Appleton and Company, 1894), p. 344.
4. *Official Records of the Union and Confederate Navies in the War of the Rebellion*, Series I, Volume 23 (Washington, DC: Government Printing Office, 1910), 348.

Chapter 18

1. *Former Slave Narratives*, Writers Project, Works Progress Administration, 1936–1937.

Chapter 19

1. Navy Medal of Honor: Civil War (Washington, DC: Naval History and Heritage Command).

Chapter 20

1. B.A. Botkin, ed., *A Civil War Treasury of Tales, Legends and Folklore*, 155.
2. *Ibid.*, 153.
3. *Ibid.*, 155.
4. *Ibid.*, 155.
5. *Civil War Naval Chronology, 1861–1865*, section IV, 110.
6. Report of the Secretary of the Navy, 1865, 348.
7. *Ibid.*, 351.
8. *Ibid.*, 333.

Chapter 21

1. *Civil War Naval Chronology, 1861–1865* (Washington, DC: Naval History Division, Navy Department, 1971), section IV, p. 61.
2. *Ibid.*, p. 82.
3. *Ibid.*, p. 90.
4. *Official Records of the Union and Confederate Navies in the War of the Rebellion*, Series I, Volume 21 (Washington, DC: Government Printing Office, 1906), p. 298.
5. John Thomas Scharf, *History of the Confederate States Navy from Its Organization*, p. 765.

6. *Official Records of the Union and Confederate Navies in the War of the Rebellion*, Series I, Volume 21 (Washington, DC: Government Printing Office, 1906), p. 336.
7. Loyall Farragut, *The Life of David Glasgow Farragut: First Admiral of the Navy*, p. 402.
8. *Official Records of the Union and Confederate Navies in the War of the Rebellion*, Series I, Volume 21 (Washington, DC: Government Printing Office, 1906), p. 377.
9. John Thomas Scharf, *History of the Confederate States Navy from Its Organization*, p. 568.
10. *Civil War Naval Chronology, 1861–1865* (Washington, DC: Naval History Division, Navy Department, 1971) section IV, page 121.
11. Welles *Diary*, Vol. 2, page 133.
12. *Official Records of the Union and Confederate Navies in the War of the Rebellion*, Series I, Volume 16 (Washington, DC: Government Printing Office, 1906), p. 439.
13. *Official Records of the Union and Confederate Navies in the War of the Rebellion*, Series I, Volume 13 (Washington, DC: Government Printing Office, 1901), p. 766.
14. Alexander L. Holley, *A Treatise on Ordnance and Armor* (New York: D. Van Nostrand, 1865), p. 231.

Chapter 22

1. *Dictionary of American Fighting Ships*, Volume III (Washington, D.C.: Naval History Division, 1977), pp. 757–786.
2. *Ibid.*, p. 771.
3. Howard K. Beale, ed., *Welles Diary*, Vol. II, 52.
4. *Ibid.*, p. 52.
5. *Report of the Secretary of the Navy*, 1864, pp. 715–718.
6. *Reports of Committees of the House of Representatives for the Second Session of the Fifty-Second Congress, 1892–1893* (Washington, D.C.: Government Printing Office, 1893), p. 30.
7. Howard K. Beale, ed., *Welles Diary*, Vol. II, 350.
8. *Ibid.*, 395.
9. Lot 15, Stan V. Henkels auction sales catalogue, Philadelphia, January 4, 1924.
10. *Ibid.*, p. 418.
11. *Dictionary of American Fighting Ships*, Volume III (Washington, D.C.: Naval History Division, 1977), 781–785.
12. Howard K. Beale, ed., *Welles Diary*, Vol. II, 761.
13. *Ibid.*, p. 241.

Chapter 23

1. Robert and Marjorie Kantor, *Sanitary Fairs* (Sidney, Ohio: Amos Philatelics / Scott Publishing Company, 1992), 158–161.
2. *Former Slave Narratives*, Writers Project, Works Progress Administration.
3. *Ibid.*

Bibliography

Botkin, B.A., ed. *A Civil War Treasury of Tales, Legends, and Folklore.* 1960. Secaucus, New Jersey: The Blue and Grey Press.

Boyton, Charles B. *The History of the Navy During the Rebellion,* Volume I. 1867. New York: D. Appleton and Company.

Douglass, Frederick. *Life and Times of Frederick Douglass.* 1881. Hartford, Connecticut: Park Publishing Company.

Hoppin, John Mason. *Life of Andrew Hull Foote: Rear-Admiral United States Navy.* 1874. New York: Harper & Brothers.

McPherson, James M. *Battle Cry of Freedom.* 1988. New York: Oxford University Press.

———. *War on the Waters: The Union and Confederate Navies, 1861–1865.* 2012. Chapel Hill: University of North Carolina Press.

Meltzer, Milton, ed. *Voices from the Civil War.* 1992. New York: HarperTrophy.

Porter, David Dixon. *Incidents and Anecdotes of the Civil War.* 1886. New York: D. Appleton and Company.

Russell, William Howard. *My Diary North and South.* 1954. New York: Harper & Brothers.

Welles, Gideon. *Welles Diary.* Howard K. Beale, ed. 1960. New York: W.W. Norton & Co.

Wormeley, Katharine Prescott. *The Other Side of War on the Hospital Transports with the Army of the Potomac.* 1998. Gansevoort, New York: Corner House Historical Publications.

Index

Numbers in **_bold italics_** indicate pages with illustrations

abandon ship 82, 98, 113
abolition 10, 12, 58, 118–19; *see also* Emancipation Proclamation
Admiral (blockade-runner) 197
USS *Adolph Hugel* **_32_**, **_83_**
CSS *Alabama* 181, 191
USS *Alabama* 150, 197
Alabama 195; *see also place names*
USS *Albatross* 112–14
CSS *Albemarle* 217–18
Albert, John 112
alcohol consumption 67, 76–78
Alert (blockade-runner) 196–97
Alexander Nevsky (Russian frigate) 152
Alexandria, Louisiana 167–68, **_171_**
Alexandria, Virginia 84
Allen Collier (merchant ship) 164
Alliance (blockade-runner) 167
Almy, James 9
USS *Althea* 204
Anderson, Aaron 191–92
Anderson, Confederate Brig. Gen. James Patton 70
Anderson, Maj. Gen. Robert 167
Andrews, Gov. John (Massachusetts) 52
Annie Sophia (blockade-runner) 173
Annie Verden (British schooner) 172
Antietam, battle of 13
USS *Arago* 166–67
Ariel (blockade-runner) 197
Army transfers 67–70
Ashton, Beverly 112
Avery, Daniel Dudley 193

Babcock, Bvt. Brig. Gen. Willoughby 176–77
Bache, George 143
Badger (blockade-runner) 167
Bailey, Joseph 169–70
Bailey, Rear Adm. Theodorus 114, 201
USS *Bainbridge* 181
Baltimore, Maryland 85
Bankhead, John P. 97–98

Banks, Maj. Gen. Nathaniel P. 112, 167
Barbour County, Alabama **_219_**
barges **_99_**, 100, 114, 137, 142
Barton, Thomas C. 81
Baton Rouge, Louisiana **_29_**, **_127_**
"Batties, Charles" **_64_**
Bayou Teche, Louisiana 38
Beaufort, North Carolina 97
Beaufort, South Carolina **_40_**, 187
Bell, Cornelius 82
bell rack **_25_**
Belle (blockade-runner) 173
Benjamin, Judah P. 141
Bennett, John **_218_**
Benson, Robert 111
USS *Benton* 67, 124, 142
Bettes, James **_64_**
Betts, Judge Samuel Rossiter 159
Biddle, Charles W. **_64_**
USS *Bienville* 173
Big Black River, battle of 143
Black sailors 55, 77–78, **_219_**; as cooks **_175_**; earnings of 14–15; equality aboard ship 9, 13–14; and keepsake photographs **_3_**; as medical assistants **_180_**; and naval service 58–65; northerners 44–46; numbers of 68–69; pre–Civil War 58; and promotion 63; and rank of "boy" 57; unidentified individuals **_64_**, **_71_**, **_74_**; *see also* integration, of naval crews; naval enlistment
Blackwell, Hiram 85
Blackwell, Solomon 85
Blair, Montgomery 12
Blake, Nat 181
Blake, Robert 186
blockade duty 5–9, 48–49, 80
blockade-runners 150–51, 155–59, 166–67, 172–73, 188–89, 196; *see also names of vessels*
bloodhounds 30–31
blue-water warfare *see* ocean warfare

229

Index

Blyden, John Joseph 97
boatswains 76–79
Bon Secours River 197–98
Bonsall, Spencer 175
border states, and slaveholding 10–12
USS *Boston* 19
Boston Daily Advertiser 210
Bowman, John H. *ii*
"boy," rank of 57
Boyan, Robert 181
Braine, Daniel L. 102
Brandywine, storeship 182
Brazil, Proclamation of Neutrality 8
bricks, slave-made *182*, 184–85
Brigham, Samuel W. 82
Brinkley, Levi 112
broadsides *6*, *16*
Bromley, James 182
USS *Brooklyn* 21, 47, 112, 190, 200, 205
Brooklyn Navy Yard 52, 85, 120, 166
Brown, Benjamin 186–87
Brown, Charles 46, 87
Brown, Harvey (slave overseer) 31–32
Brown, Henry 46
Brown, James E. 46
Brown, Jerry 83
Brown, John 46
Brown, Orin H. 59–60
Brown, Robert 46, 87
Brown, Scott 112
Brown, Timothy T. 44
Brown, William H. 190, *190*
Brown, Wilson 190
brown-water warfare *see* inland waters warfare (brown-water)
Brownsville, Texas 48, 148
Brunswick, Georgia 47
Bryson, Andrew 102
Bulloch, James 151
Bull's Bluff, South Carolina 38
Bull's Island, South Carolina 9–10
burial 183–85; at sea 183, 185
burial markers, for slaves *182*
Burton, Isaiah 46
Butler, Gen. Benjamin Franklin *28*, *54*, 105–8, *106*; as military governor 105–8; and use of Black troops 194–95; "Woman Order" 105–6
Butler, Francis 46

Caldwell, Zachariah 44
USS *Cambridge* 97
camouflage, naval use of *84*
Camp Parapet, Louisiana *28*
USS *Canandaigua* 86
Canby, Edward R.S. 115
Cape Fear River 188
Cape Hatteras, North Carolina 98

Carle, William E. 46
USS *Carondelet* 123, 142, 170, 178–79
Carr, Robert 46
USS *Carrabassett* 38
Carter, Charles Hill (slaveholder) 35
Carter, John F. 44
cartes-de-visite 46, *54*, *64*
Casey, Francis 90
Cash, Harriet (slaveholder) 176
casualties 176–82
Cavanaugh, John 196
Cavel, Robert 87
Champion's Hill, battle of 143
Charles County, Maryland 26
USS *Charles Phelps* *218*
Charleston, South Carolina *6*, 47–48, 131, 165, 206
Charlestown Navy Yard 119
Chase, Salmon 157
Chatham County, North Carolina 26
Chew, Augustus 193–94
USS *Chickasaw* 201, 203, 213
children: enslaved, of White fathers 49, *50*; orphaned 52–53
Childress, Green (former slave) 24–25
USS *Chillicothe* 170
USS *Chimo* 210, 212
Chinn, Wilson (former slave) *31*
USS *Chippewa* 102
cholera 181
USS *Cimarron* 67
USS *Cincinnati* 143
USS *Circassian* 200
Clark, Frederick 55–56
Clarksville, Tennessee 122
Clay, Joseph 97
Cleburne, Maj. Gen. Patrick 70
Clyett, Josiah 97
coal supplies 200
coastal monitors 209, 213; *see also* monitors
coffee 174–75
Cole, Alex *94*
Cole's Creek, Mississippi 90, 164
Collins, Levin 87
USS *Colonel Kinsman* 179
Colton, Ephraim 83
USS *Columbia* 34
USS *Columbus* 35
Combahee River Raid 100–102
Committee on the Conduct of the War 211
Commodore, George W. *32*
The Commonwealth 101
Confederacy, and Black exodus 21; *see also* names of key individuals
Confederate currency 148–49, 196
Confiscation *see* seizure of goods
USS *Congress* 85, 177
USS *Constellation* 203

230

Index

contrabands 66–75, 97, **99**, 100, 194; as answer to naval manpower shortage 57–58, 89, 143; cotton 163–65; fugitive slaves as 19, **28**; *see also* runaways
Cook, Isaac 90
cooks 174–75, **175**
Cooler, Nicholas 87
Cooper, Morgan 83
Cooper, Confederate Inspector Gen. Samuel 189
Cornish, John H. 182
"cotton depots" 164–65
cotton, importance of 161–65, **163**, 168, 193
Council, Dr. Kit (slaveholder) 26
courts-martial 22, 61, 63–64, 188
USS *Cowslip* 165
Craven, Capt. Thomas Tingey 21–22
USS *Cricket* **130**
Cruiser, Henderson 85
USS *Cumberland* 71, 85, 118–19, 177, **177**
Cumberland River 121–22
Currier and Ives **177**
USS *Cuyler* 61

Dahlgren, Rear Adm. John A. 39, 48, 102, 118, 120, 125–26, 132, 167, 179–81, 186–87
USS *Dandelion* 207
Daniel Webster (transport) 92
Davis, Charles 125
Davis, Charles Henry 138
Davis, Hamilton 102–3
Davis, Jefferson (Confederate president) 21, 106, 189; and salt supply 193–96
death: and burial 183–85; causes of 177
Deer, Isaac 179
Dees, Clement 188
USS *Delaware* 35
desertion 61, 63–64, 125, 188
"The Devil" device 48
USS *Dictator* 210, 213
disease 177, 179–81, **180**
District of Columbia 90
Dixon, James 204
USS *Dolphin* 34
Douglass, Anna Murray **44**, 44–45
Douglass, Frederick 12, **16**, 44–45, **45**
Downs, Rosina **50**
draft riots 51–56, 68
USS *Dragon* 85–86
drowning 176
Du Pont, Rear Adm. Samuel Francis 42, 57–58, 63, 126, 129–32; on monitors 206–8

East Pascagoula, Mississippi, battle of **28**
USS *Eastport* 164
Eden, Col. Ben (slaveholder) 26
Elizabeth, North Carolina 21, 103
USS *Elk* 179, **180**

Ella (blockade-runner) 166–67
USS *Ella* 90
Ellet, Brig. Gen. Alfred 73
Ellet, Col. Charles 70–75
Ellet, Charles Rivers 72
Ellet, John A. 72–73
USS *Elm City* **129**
emancipation, Lincoln and 5–18
Emancipation Proclamation 39; final 15–17; preliminary 13, 15
Emma (British screw steamer) 166–67
USS *Emma* 166–67
Emmons, George 173
England 150–55, **163**, 196; Proclamation of Neutrality 8; and seizure of *Bermuda* 161; *see also Peterhoff* case
English, Thomas 191
Epps, Dr. Richard (slaveholder) 34–35
Ericsson, John 48, 89, 210, 213
USS *Essex* 108, **127**
USS *Ethan Allen* 37
European newspapers 207
Evansville, Indiana 186

family members, search for 61–62, 215–17
"Farewell to Grog" 76–77
Farragut, Adm. David 13, 49, 73, 104–17, 138–39, 160, 173, 179, 188, 197–205
Farragut, Loyall 204
Farragut, Susan Marchant 110
Farragut, Virginia Loyall 110, 116
Faxon, William 212
Federal Navy *see* US Navy
Federal Writers' Project 1
Fernandina, Florida 47
field hospitals/hospital ships 91–100, **129**, 179–81, **180**
fire ships 169
Fisher, Henry 181
USS *Flag* 197
Flanigan, M.E. 83
flophouses 51
Florida 47
CSS *Florida* 159
food: aboard hospital ships 93; aboard ship 174–75, **175**; shortages 107, 145
Foote, Caroline Augusta Street 119, 128–29, 132
Foote, Caroline Flagg 119
Foote, Rear Adm. Andrew Hull 49, 58, 70, 118–32, 160; *Africa and the American Flag* 119; letters 120, 122–24
USS *Forest Queen* 142
USS *Forest Rose* 35, 90, 164
former slaves, recollections of 1, 19, 22–35, 62; Aarons, Charlie 62; Adams, Ezra 87; Adams, Victoria 26; Adamson, Frank 87; Avery, Celestia 24, 27; Bacchus,

231

Index

Josephine 183–84; Baker, Georgia 26; Bishop, Ank 62; Bolton, James 62; Brown, Lewis 176; Carter, Cato 107; Clinton, Joe 31–32; Cora 27; Cragin, Ellen 22–23; Davis, Virginia 89–90; Deane, James V. 26, 184, 217; Dilliard, Ella 24–25; Dixon, Alice 30; Foster, Analiza 176; Gillam, Cora 49; Glass, Will 27, 218–20; Gordon ("Whipped Peter") **28**; Graves, Wesley 29–30; Gray, Ambus 87; Herndon, George 174; Herndon, Temple 24; Jones, Albert 26; Lassiter, Jane 26; Manson, Jacob 26; Moore, Patsy 26; Moore, William 26; Norcross, Wilson 27–29; Ralls, Henrietta 25, 218; Rassberry, Senia 218; Richard, Dora 27; Richardson, Caroline 33; Rienshaw, Adora 37; Rigger, Charlie 25; Rimm, Walter 31; Robinson, Cornella 24; Slaughter, Richard 34–35, 194–95; Smith, Jordon 29; Sparks, Elizabeth 19; Wilson, Mary Jane 35

Fort Barrancas 47
Fort Donelson 121–22
Fort Fisher 188, 191
Fort Gaines 202
Fort Henry 121
Fort Jackson **83**
USS *Fort Jackson* 172
Fort McRae 47
Fort Monroe 23, 47
Fort Morgan 201–3
Fort Pickens 47
Fort Pillow 125
Fort Point 173
Fort Saint Phillips **83**
Fort Sumter 167
Fort Wagner 208
Fox (blockade-runner) 167
Fox, Asst. Sec. of the Navy Gustavus V. 13, 132, 172, 206, 209–12
France 147–48, 150, 161; Proclamation of Neutrality 8
Francis, Henry 97
Frank, John 217
Frank Leslie's Illustrated Newspaper **36**
USS *Franklin* 116
Fraser, Trenholm and Co. 166–67
Frémont, John C. 11
Fressenden, Sen. William 160
fugitive slaves *see* contrabands; runaways; self-emancipation

USS *Galena* 96, 205, **219**
Galveston, Texas 47, 148
Galveston Bay 173
Gardner, James R. 181
Gardner, Moses S. *ii*
USS *Gemsbok* 197

USS *General Grant* **128**
CSS *General Lovell* 72
General Order Number 3 (Halleck) 11
General Order Number 28 (Butler) 105–6
General Order Number 135 (Farragut) 110
USS *General Price* 142
USS *Genessee* 112–13
USS *George Meade* 161
Georgetown, South Carolina 39, 102
Georgia *see place names*
USS *Germantown* 34
Gettysburg, battle of 52
Gibraltar (blockade-runner) 167
Glisson, Oliver S. 19
Goldsborough, Louis M. 9, 66–67, 86, 102
Gordon, James E. 82
Gosport Navy Yard, Portsmouth, Virginia 34–35
Goven, Thomas 181
USS *Governor Buckingham* 172
Granby, Charles 82
Grand Gulf, Mississippi 48, 114, 131, 143
Grand National Sailors' Fair (Boston, November 1864) 215, **216**
Granger, Samuel **94**
Grant, Gen. Ulysses S. 67, 114, 121–24, 189; and canal project 138; and fall of Vicksburg 133, 141–46
Grant, William 181
Great Britain *see* England
Greeley, Horace 10
"Greeley, Horace" **172**
Greenport, New York 98
Gregory, S.B. 70
Gresham, James (slaveholder) 23
Gross, Thomas 87
guerrillas 35, **36**, 90, **128**, **130**, 164
gun crews, conflict among 204
gunboats *see* river monitors

Halleck, Maj. Gen. Henry 10–12, 115, 122, 135–36, 148
Hammond, Sen. James Henry 162
Hampton Roads, Virginia 85–86, 177, **177**
Harper's Weekly **34**, **38**, **40**, **106**, **144**
Harris, Joel 92
Harris, Matthew 61
Harris, Moses **180**
Harrison's Landing 91–92
Hart, John 112
USS *Hartford* **33**, 49, 62–63, **111**, 112–15, 189–90, 201, 205
USS *Hatteras* 181–82
Hatton, Richard 181
headstones 183–85
Helena, Arkansas 26–27
Henderson, Alexander 186
Henry, James **180**

232

Index

Henry, Thomas 112
USS *Henry Brinker* 80–82, **81**
USS *Henry Clay* 142–43
USS *Henry Janes* **83**
Herald, Paul 181
Hewitt, Edward 102
USS *Hindman* 170
Hodges, Albert G. 17
Hooper, Mrs. S.T. **216**
USS *Hornet* 119
hospital service 91–100
hospital ships *see* field hospitals/hospital ships
Hospital Transport Service 92, 100, **129**
Houston, Texas 165
USS *Howquah* 172
Huger, Rebecca **50**
USS *Hunchback* 81
Hunter, John 19
Hunter, Miles 19
Hunter, Peter 19
Hunter, Samuel 19
CSS *Huntsville* 203

Ida, tug 204
Indianola, Texas 148
inland waters warfare (brown-water) 82–83, 88–90
integration, of naval crews **14**, 58–59, **77**, **83**, **96**, **111**, **184**
intimidation, by slaveholders 32–33
iron-clads, brown-water ("Pook's Turtles") 121; *see also* monitors; *names of vessels;* "wood *vs.* iron"
USS *Isaac Smith* 59
Island Number 10, 122–23, **129**
USS *Itasca* 205
USS *Ivy* 142

Jackson, John 78–79
Jackson, Mississippi 141, 143
James River **23**, 36, **36**, **77**, 92, **175**
USS *James S. Chambers* 198
CSS *Jamestown* 85
Jay, John 52
Jenkins, James 87
USS *John Adams* 119
Johnson, Ben 10
Johnson, Ephraim 83
Johnson, Fortune 10
Johnson, Isaac 89–90
Johnson, James **180**
Johnson, James H. 87
Johnson, Joseph 87
Johnson, Manuel 112
Johnson, Moses 82
Johnson, Theophilus 182
Johnson, William H. 59–60

"Jonahs," aboard ship 63
Jones, Fortune A. 182
Jones, Jacob **180**
Jordan, Dr. (slaveholder) 176–82
Joseph, Louisd **180**
Judd, Cuffee 10

USS *Kanawha* 87, 188
USS *Kearsarge* **191**
USS *Kennebec* 205
Kentucky 10
USS *Keokuk* 207
USS *Kickapoo* 213
Kimball, Judge (slaveholder) 24
USS *Kineo* 112–13
King, Joseph 97
USS *Kingfisher* 38

USS *Lackawanna* 205
USS *Lafayette* 142
Lancaster County, Virginia 85
Langden, Robert 82
Langdon, Francis 55–56
Lee, George (slaveholder) 23
Latimer, John 82
Lawson, John H. **187**, 188–90
Legareville, South Carolina 186
legislation: Compensated Emancipation Act (1862) 15; Confiscation Acts (1861, 1862) 15; Conscription Act (1863) 51, 64–65; Enrollment Act (1863) 68; Indian Removal Act (1830) 162; Kansas-Nebraska Act (1854) 162–63; law of 13 March 1862 on return of runaways 22
USS *Lehigh* **ii**
Leonard, Ezra 38
Lesovski, Rear Adm. Stepan (Russia) 152
Lewis, Henry 97
Lewis, Samuel 182
Lewis, William 90
USS *Lexington* 123, 170
Liberty Party Paper 45
Lincoln, First Lady Mary Ann Todd 54–55
Lincoln, President Pres. Abraham: and battle of Mobile Bay 203; concern with shipboard punishments 62–63; and emancipation 5–18; and fall of Vicksburg 133–35, 145; and integration of naval crews 62–63; letters 17; love of negro spirituals 61; and Navy Fair 215, **216**; and *Peterhoff* case 156–59; and Preble affair 160–61
literacy 3, 26–27, **50**, **71**
Louisiana *see place names*
Louisiana Native Guards **28**
USS *Louisville* 142, 170
Lowndes, Bob 10
Lynx (steamer) 172
Lyons, Lord Richard 8, 151, 153, 158

233

Index

USS *Macedonia* 47
mail, seizure of 149-51, 155-59
Mallory, Stephen 60
USS *Manhattan* 201-2
USS *Maratanza* 96
USS *Marblehead* 181, 186
Mare Island Navy Yard, California 110
Marshall, Moses 85
Martha (slaver) 119-20
martial law, imposed in Missouri 11-12
Maryland 82, 90; *see also place names*
Matamoros, Mexico 147-51, 159
Mathes, Edward 181
Mattie Stephens, steamer 90, 164
Maury, Confederate Maj. Gen. Dabney 189
Maxmore, John *ii*
McClellan, Gen. George 91
McCulloch, Confederate Brig. Gen. Henry 148
McElroy, Thomas 82-83
McKay, Donald 210-11
McKee, Henry (slaveholder) *40*
McKenney, B.B. (slaveholder) 23
Meade, Richard, Jr. 186
Meigs, QM Gen. Montgomery 91-92
memorial markers 183-85
Memphis, Tennessee 48, 125
Memphis Salt Works 197-98
USS *Mendota* **77**
USS *Mercedita* 161
Mercer, J.W. **28**
meritorious conduct, recognition/reward of 63
USS *Merrimack*/CSS *Virginia* 35
Merrill, Henry 119-20
USS *Metacomet* 205
Mexico 147-51, 161
USS *Miantonomah* 212, 214
USS *Midnight* 37, 198
Mifflin, James 190
Miller, Joseph 112
Milne, Adm. Sir Archibald Berkeley 153-54
USS *Milwaukee* 204, 213
mines, Confederate 101, 169, 189, 202, 205
USS *Minnesota* 63, 84-86
Mississippi *see place names*
USS *Mississippi* 112-13
Mississippi River 7, 35, 48, 70, **126**, **144**, 189, 201; canal project 138-39; lower Mississippi 104-17; upper Mississippi 118-32
Missouri 10-12
Mitchell, Albert 90
USS *Mobile* 172
Mobile, Alabama 24-25, 47, 165, 188-90, 199-208
Mobile Bay 189-90, 197-208
USS *Monadnock* 214

USS *Monitor* 86, 96-99, **175**, 177
monitors: classification system 209; Du Pont on 206-8; Welles and 209-14
USS *Monongahela* 112-13, 205
Monroe, John 104-5
Montell, F.M. 38-39
Montgomery, Col. James 100-101
USS *Monticello* 102, 159
Moore, Joseph (slaveholder) 19
Morehead, Randal 83
Morse, Richard R. 112
mortar vessels **83-84**, **144**, 144-45
Moseley, Joseph 82
Moseley, William H. 182
Mosque, Philip 10
USS *Mound City* 142, 170
Mound City, Illinois **126**
USS *Mount Vernon* 19, 159
mulattos 213
Mumford, William 104-5
music, aboard ship *111*
Myers, Confederate QM Gen. Abraham 195

USS *Nahant* 207
name change 216-17
CSS *Nashville* 203
Nashville, Tennessee 122
naval chaplains 118
naval discharge papers **217**
naval enlistment *ii*, 9-10, 13-15, **16-17**, 19, 21-22, 46, 55-56, 64, 205; "welcome to the Navy" 57-65
Naval Order Number 16 132
naval recruitment 43, 47-56, 63, 69
naval uniforms, embellishment of **32-33**
Navy *see* US Navy
Navy Medal of Honor recipients: Anderson, Aaron 191-92; Brown, William H. 190, *190*; Brown, Wilson 190; Davis, John 186; English, Thomas 191; Lawson, John H. *187*, 188-90; Mifflin, James 190; Pease, Joachim 191, *191*
USS *Neosho* 170, 212-13
USS *Nereus* 217
Nereus, Starkey 217
Netherlands, Proclamation of Neutrality 8
neutrality, issue of 8
New Bern, North Carolina 47, 81
New Falls City, steamer 168
USS *New Hampshire* 181
New Iberia, Louisiana 193-94
New Inlet, North Carolina 159
New Inlet, South Carolina 217
USS *New Ironsides* 66, 191
New Madrid, Missouri 122
New Orleans, Louisiana 47, 49, **54**, 165, 173; fall of 104-8
New Orleans Bee 105

Index

Newton, Dr. (slaveholder) 30
New York City 85; draft riots 52–56, 68
New York Evening Post 210
New York Herald 152–53
New York Times 210
New York Tribune 10, 211
New York World 163
Newton, Kent 102
Nibbe, J.H. 82
USS *Niphon* 172
Norfolk, Virginia 47, 82, 85
North Carolina 195; *see also place names*
The North Star (Douglass) 45

"O! Dear Grog" 77–78
oath of allegiance/amnesty **219**
O'Brien, Patrick **81**
ocean monitors 209, 213–14; *see also* monitors
ocean warfare (blue-water) 80–87
USS *Octorara* 205
USS *Oleander* 186–87
Olmsted, Frederick Law 91–92
USS *Oneida* 205
Onondaga salt works, Syracuse, New York 196
USS *Onward* 42
ordnance accidents 182
orphanage, for Black children 52–53
USS *Osage* **131**, 170, 204, 212–13
USS *Ossipee* 205
USS *Ozark* 35, 170, **172**

Page, Confederate Brig. Gen. Richard L. 203
Palmer, James 179
USS *Pampero* 203–4
Pamunky River 92, 100
Panther Swamp National Wildlife Refuge (Yazoo City, Mississippi) **89**
Parker, Henry **180**
Parker, Hiram 80, 188
Parker, William 97, 179
Parkman, Cyrus 97
USS *Passaic* **184**, 207, 213
USS *Patapsco* 207
Paulding, Hiram 52, 207
USS *Pawnee* 84
Pease, Joachim 191, **191**
Pemberton, Confederate Lt. Gen. John C. 142, 196
Pendergrast, Austin 188
Peninsular Campaign 35, 91
Pennell, J.A. 37
Pennock, A.M. 89
Pensacola, Florida 47, 189
Pensacola Navy Yard 47
USS *Perry* 119
Pet (blockade-runner) 173

USS *Peterhoff* 159
Peterhoff case (English steamer) 150–59
Petrel (British warship) 150
USS *Petrel* 82–83
Pettus, Gov. John J. (Mississippi) 193–95
petty officers, Black sailors as 63
Pettyford, John H. 112
Phelps, Seth Ledyard 127
Philadelphia, Pennsylvania 85
Phillips County, Arkansas 25
photographic portraits, of Black sailors **3**, **42**, **64**, **71**, **74**; *see also names of individuals*
physical appearance, and race **50**
Pierce, Joseph 56
Pile, Spence and Co., and *Peterhoff* case 150–59
Pillow, Confederate Brig. Gen. Gideon Johnson 21
USS *Pink* 79
USS *Pittsburgh* 123, 142, 170
plantations: Blake plantation 100; Carthage 190; Clover Hill 31–32; Heyward 100; Lowndes 100; Middleton 100; Nemours 100; Shirley (Virginia) 35; Singleton (South Carolina) 38–39
Planter (Confederate steamer) 40–43, **41**
USS *Planter* 40–43, **41**
USS *Plymouth* 35
USS *Pocahontas* 86–87
Polk family (slaveholders) 22–23
USS *Pontoosuc* 188
Pook, Samuel 121
Pope, Brig. Gen. John 122–24
Port Gibson, battle of 143
Port Hudson, Louisiana **28**, 48, 110–14, 189, 201
USS *Port Royal* 205
Port Royal, South Carolina **20**, 47
Porter, Capt. David 108
Porter, Rear Adm. David Dixon 21, 58, 63, 67, 83, **83–84**, 88–89, 108–10, 114, 125–27, 133–34, 139–41, **144**, 165, 167, 189; and fall of Vicksburg 142–46; and loss of USS *Indianola* 136–38; and ram fleets 72–75; and Red River Expedition 147–73
Porter, William "Dirty Bill" 108–10, **127**
USS *Portsmouth* 120
Portsmouth, New Hampshire 116
Portsmouth Navy Yard 68
Potomac River **178**
USS *Potomska* 38, 86–87
poverty, in New Orleans 107
powder monkeys 78–79
USS *Powhatan* 66, 102, 211
prayer 27–28
Preble, George H. 159–61
USS *Princess Royal* 173
prisoner exchange 59–60

235

Index

prisoners of war 59–60; murder of, at Jacksonville, Louisiana 61
prize courts 159
prize money 14–15, 56, 86–87, **127**, **130–31**, 165, **172**, 172–73
promotion, for Black sailors 63
Punch 153
punishment: aboard ship 61; of slaves **25**, 26–30, **28**, **30–31**
USS *Puritan* 213

USS *Quaker City* 56
quarantine 181
Queen of the West, Confederate vessel 71–72, 137

racial violence 52–56
railroad track-iron (T-iron) 86
rams and ram fleets 70–75, 88
Rappahannock River 19–20, 23
USS *Raritan* 34
Raymond, battle of 143
Red River 136, 147–73
Red River Dam 169–70, **171**
Red River Expedition 147–73
USS *Red Rover* **129**
USS *Release* 97
USS *Relief* 97
Relyea, C.J. 41
reporting of casualties 59–60
USS *Rescue* 97
USS *Rhode Island* 97
Rhone, Shepherd 25
Richardson, Columbus 83
USS *Richmond* 112–13, 200, 205
river monitors 22–23, **23**, **131**, **172**, 209–13; *see also* monitors
USS *Roanoke* 197, 214
Roberts, John M. 181
USS *Rodolph* 204
Rolling Fork, Mississippi 165
USS *Roman* 19
Rooney, Nicholas 90
Rowan, Commodore S.C. 21
USS *R.R. Cuyler* 87
Ruggles, David 45
runaways 11, **17**, 19–39, **20**, **29**, **34**, **38**, **46**, **55**, 90, 176–77, 194; children *1*; as entrepreneurs 33–34; evacuation of 101; as labor for field hospitals 91–92; to northern cities 51–56; return of 21–22
runaways, names of individuals: Charles 22–23; Gilmore, George 20; Henderson, Crusoe 20; Hudley, Paul 20; James, Wednesday 20; Robinson, Balinar 20; Taylor, Atwell 20; Wester, Newman 20; Wilson, Robert 20
Russell, William, diaries 12

Russia 152–53, 155
Rutledge, John 187

USS *Sabine* 47
Sabine Pass, Texas 148
Sailors Association 118
USS *Sacramento* **78**
USS *Sagamore* 87
Saint Andrew's Bay, Florida 37, 197
USS *St. Lawrence* 85
USS *St. Louis* 47, 121–22
Saint Simon's Sound, Georgia 37
Salisbury, North Carolina 195
salt, importance of 193–98
salt riots 195
salt works 37–38, 193–98
Saltville, Virginia 193, 195
USS *San Jacinto* 87
Sanders, A.M. (slaveholder) 23
USS *Sassacus* 217–18
Savannah, Georgia 47–48, 165
Sawtelle, Charles G. 95–96
Schart, J. Thomas 147
Schuller, Christian 186
Sciota, steamer 204
scurvy 181
USS *Sebago* **94**, 95–96
CSS *Secesh* 86
Seddon, Confederate Secretary of War James 141
seizure of goods 108, **130–31**; cotton 165–69, **172**, 172–73; mail 149–51, 155–59; salt 196–98
seizure, of steamer *Bermuda* 161
self-emancipation 14–15, 59
USS *Seminole* 205
Seven Days Battles 91
Seven Pines, battle of 91
Seward, Secretary of State William 8, 155; and *Emma* affair 166; and Matamoros 148–49; and *Peterhoff* case 155–59
Seymour, Gov. Horatio (New York) 53
Sherman, Gen. William T. 88, 168, 189, 196
Shiloh, battle of 123–25
Ship Island, Mississippi 47
shipboard routines 76–79
ship's pumps 98
shore batteries 68
Shorter, Gov. John Gill (Alabama) 188, 195
Shreveport, Louisiana 147
sickness, aboard ship 129
silence, of slaves 24–25
Sills, Jeremiah 187–88
USS *Silver Wave* 142
Skerrett, R.G. **84**
Slaughter, Sylvester 181
slave families, evacuation of 89; *see also* family members, search for

Index

slave hunters 30
slave market **6, 50**
slave population, US 10
slave trade 118–20
slaveholders 21; *see also names of individuals*
smallpox 181
Smalls, Robert **40**, 40–43, **41**
Smith, Aaron 112
Smith, A.N. 111
Smith, David H. 112
Smith, George 82
Smith, George E. 63–64
Smith, Confederate Gen. E. Kirby 135, 148
Smith, Rear Adm. Joseph 72
Smith, Manuel **180**
Smith, Confederate Gen. Martin 145
Smith, Robert F. 87
soldiers, as sailors 67–70
Song, Joe 175
South Carolina *see place names*
USS *South Carolina* 9–10
South Carolina Volunteers, Second Regiment 101
South Santee, South Carolina 10
Southern planters **4**
Spain, Proclamation of Neutrality 8
spies and spy networks 23, 100–102, 197, 200–201; runaways and 35–38
Springfield Landing, Louisiana 168
Stanley, F. 38
Stanton, Secretary of War Edwin M. 13, 58, 60, 107–8, 133–35, 139; and Conscription Act 64–65; on manpower shortage 68; and ram fleets 71–75
USS *Stars and Stripes* 20
Steele's Bayou Expedition 140
Stephens, Alexander (slaveholder) 26
Stephens, William A. **30**
Stetson, C.A. 132
Stimers, Alban C. 209–11
store boats 93
Stribling, C.K. 198
Strikes, Samuel 87
Stringham, Silas 19
Strong, George Templeton 52–53
sugar, importance of 193
suicide squads 19
Sumner, Sen. Charles 157–59
USS *Supply* 97
supply ships 93, 97
sweat boxes 62–63
Symmes, David 181

USS *T.A. Ward* **83**
Taylor, Charles **50**
Taylor, Henry 112
Taylor, James 87
Taylor, Confederate Lt. Gen. Richard 135

CSS *Teaser* 85
USS *Tecumseh* 201, 204–5
telegraph office, War Department 133–34
temperance movements, aboard ships 118
Temple, William G. 188
Tennant, William 182
Tennessee *see place names*
CSS *Tennessee* 199–203
Tennessee River 121, **128**
Texas 147–51, 218; Juneteenth 218–20
Thatcher, Henry K. 203
Thomas, Daniel 87
Thomas, John H. 55–56
Thompson, William 215
Thornton, Jonathan **219**
Tinsley, Francis Gaines 95
USS *Tioga* 96, **96**
Tiptonville, Tennessee 123
Trainor, James **217**
transports 92
Trenholm, George Alfred 167
Tubman, Harriet **100**, 100–102
USS *Tulip* 177–78, **178**
CSS *Tuscaloosa* 203
USS *Tuscumbia* 142
USS *Tyler* 123
typhus 181

Underground Railroad **44**
underwater obstacles, use of 48
Union Army *see* US Army
Union Navy *see* US Navy
Union, preservation of 8–10
USS *United States* 35
US Army 12–13; and Black enlistment 55–56; and contrabands 66–75; ram fleet 72–75; and segregation 57–59
US Navy: African Squadron 119; age restrictions 64; Anaconda Plan 5–8, 47, 57; ban on shipboard alcohol consumption 76–77; Bureau of Equipment and Recruiting 128; East Gulf Squadron 201; European Squadron 116; Gulf Blockading Squadron 203–4; Gulf Squadron 135; James River Flotilla 66, 85; manpower shortage 9–10, 66–75, 120–21, 143; Medal of Honor **185**, 186–92, **190** (*see also* Navy Medal of Honor recipients); Mediterranean Squadron 119; Mississippi Flotilla 69, 128; Mississippi Squadron 67, 73; Muster Roll Department 185; North Atlantic Blockading Squadron 66, 80–81, 85, 159, 166, **218**; Pacific Squadron 214; Potomac Flotilla 84, 90; Potomac River Flotilla 178; as "safest service" 176–82; and sailors' pay 76–78; South Atlantic Blockading Squadron 57, 126, 131–32, 179, 181; Southern Blockading Squadron 108;

237

Index

and Union Army 12–13, 49; "welcome to the Navy" 57–65; West Gulf Blockading Squadron 204; West Gulf Squadron 203; Western Flotilla 70, 75, 126, 135, 138; Western Gulf Blockading Squadron 173; Western Gunboat Flotilla 118, 125; Western Squadron 75, *126*; *see also* naval enlistment; naval recruitment
US Sanitary Commission 91–97, *129*
US War Department 13

USS *Valley City* 186
USS *Vanderbilt* 150–51
Van Lew, Elizabeth 23
USS *Vermont* 10, *20*
Vicksburg, Mississippi 48–49, *83*, 110–14, 133–46, 189
Vicksburg Whig 137–38
Virginia 82, 90, 134; *see also place names*
CSS *Virginia* 71, 85–86, 177
USS *Virginia* 173

USS *Wabash* 63, 102
Wadsworth, Brig. Gen. James 66
Waites, W. Thomas 83
Walke, Henry 178–79
Walton, William 198
USS *Wanderer* 102
Wando (British steamer) 172
Ward, Anderson 82
Ward, Andrew 82
Ware, Kimble 82
Warren, Tom (slaveholder) 26–27
Warrenton, Mississippi 114
"Washington, George" *172*
Washington, John *180*
USS *Water Witch* 187–88
Watson, John C. 201, 205
Waud, Alfred R. *36*
Weaver, James 82
Webb, Jose 175
Wednesday, James 85
USS *Weehawken* 187
"welcome to the Navy" 57–65
Welles, Secretary of the Navy Gideon 126–27; and Anaconda Plan 7–8; on Anglo-American relations 153–55; and canal project 138–39; and Conscription Act 64–65; on contrabands 70; on "cotton depots" 164–65; diary 2, 12–13, 68–69, 73, 75, 98–99, 114–17, 125, 127, 130–36, 140–41, 146–49, 155–60, 168, 171, 206–7, 210–12; on draft riots 68; and Du Pont 129–32, 206–8; and emancipation 8–9; and fall of Vicksburg 133–37; and Farragut 108–10, 113–17, 139, 199–200, 205; and Foote 120, 122–25; and Halleck 135–36; letters 13, 150; on loss of *Monitor* 98–99; on manpower shortage 57–59, 66, 68–69; and Matamoros 147–51; and monitors 209–14; and naval prisoner exchanges 60; and Navy Medal of Honor 185; and *Peterhoff* case 150–59; and Porter 138–41, 168–69; and Preble affair 160–61; on prisoner exchange 60; and ram fleets 72–75; and Red River Expedition 170–72; on repeal of Missouri Compromise 162–63; on runaways 19, 21–22; and Seward 166; and "trade permits" 163
Wells, J.C. 198
Wells, J.G. 37
West, Harry 83
West, Wesley 83
USS *Western World* 70
Wethers, Alexander *50*
White, Gustavus 181
White, J.N. (slaveholder) 62
White fathers, of slave children 49, *50*
White House, Tennessee 92, *94*, 96, *99*, 100
Whiting, Samuel 82
Whitworth's Landing, Mississippi 164
Wilkes, Charles 66, 150–51, 153, 159
USS *William Bacon* *83*
USS *William G. Putnam* 64
Williams, Griffin (slaveholder) 23
Williams, Joseph 87
Williamson, William H. 187
Wilmington, North Carolina 102, 188; port 47–48
Wilson, William 59–60
USS *Winnebago* 201, 203, 213
USS *Wissahickon* 111–12
women: on hospital service 91–100; of New Orleans 105–6, *106*; treatment of *54*
Wood, Francis 182
Woodhull, M. 67
Woodworth, Selim 21
Wool, Maj. Gen. John Ellis 53
Wormeley, Katharine Prescott 92–93, 95–97, 100
Worthingon, Henry 98
Wright, John 82
USS *Wyandank* 191–92

Yazoo City, Mississippi 49, *89*
Yazoo River 82–83, 140
Yazoo River Expedition 88–89
yellow fever 179–81, *180*, 189
Young, James A. 103
USS *Young Rover* 23

zone defense 80
USS *Zouave* 85

www.ingramcontent.com/pod-product-compliance
Lightning Source LLC
Chambersburg PA
CBHW032038300426
44117CB00009B/1104